# THE RUSSO–JAPANESE CONFLICT
## ITS CAUSES AND ISSUES

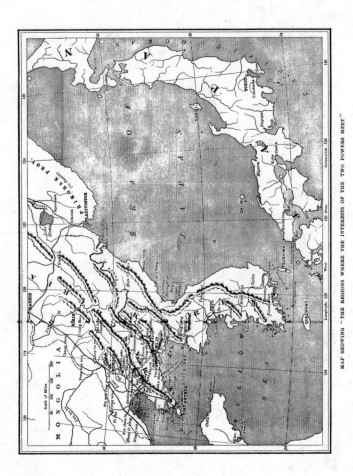

MAP SHOWING "THE REGIONS WHERE THE INTERESTS OF THE TWO POWERS MEET"

# THE RUSSO-JAPANESE CONFLICT

## ITS CAUSES AND ISSUES

BY

K. ASAKAWA, Ph. D.

WITH AN INTRODUCTION BY
FREDERICK WELLS WILLIAMS

*ILLUSTRATED*

KENNIKAT PRESS
Port Washington, N. Y./London

THE RUSSO-JAPANESE CONFLICT

First published in 1904
Reissued in 1970 by Kennikat Press
Library of Congress Catalog Card No: 72-115198
ISBN 0-8046-1091-6

Manufactured by Taylor Publishing Company     Dallas, Texas

# INTRODUCTION

THE issues of the conflict that forms the topic of this little volume are bound inevitably to influence the future of the civilized world for many years. Dr. Asakawa presents them with a logical thoroughness that reminds us of the military operations of his countrymen now in evidence elsewhere, and recalls very pleasantly to my own mind the sane and accurate character of his scholastic work while a student at Yale. It is the sort of presentation which a great subject needs. It is content with a simple statement of fact and inference. It is convincing because of its brevity and restraint.

The generous and almost passionate sympathy of our countrymen for Japan in this crisis of her career has aroused some speculation and surprise even amongst ourselves. The emotion is, doubtless, the outcome of complex causes, but this much is obvious at present: the past half-century has brought both America and Japan through experiences strikingly similar, and their establishment at the same moment as new world Powers has afforded both the same view of their older competitors for first rank among nations. Both have earned their centralized and effective governments after the throes of civil war; both have built navies and expanded their foreign

35248

commerce; both have arrested the belated and rather contemptuous attention of Europe by success in foreign wars. No state of Christendom can appreciate so well as America the vexation of enduring for generations the presumption or the patronage of those European courts who have themselves been free for less than a century from the bonds that Napoleon put upon the entire Continental group; and Japan has suffered under the same observance. With the acknowledgment of the existence of these two Powers of the first class on either shore of the Pacific, the bottom drops out of that system whereon was based the diplomacy of nineteenth-century Europe, and the jealousy with which they are both regarded establishes a certain *rapprochement* between the two newly arrived nations.

The attitude of the American people does not appear to me to be greatly influenced by prejudice against Russia. It is likely, indeed, that we had less to fear directly from the ambition of the Great Colossus than any other state. Yet we have been among the first to discern that Japan is doing the world's work if, by reducing the pressure of Russia's assault upon Eastern Asia, she removes China in the crisis of her awakening from the list of those derelict states whose present decrepitude offers such deplorable temptation to the military nations of the West. There would seem to be fresh need, moreover, of convincing modern statesmen that a policy of conducting diplomatic intercourse by means of tergiversation and lies is unprofitable in the long run, and therefore unjustified by the most cynical school of political ethics. Without debating the righteousness of her pretensions, it is obvious that Russia cannot proceed further in her headway without materially affecting the legitimate ambitions of other peoples of proved vitality, nor can her characteristic diplomacy secure success without debauching the political morality of Christendom. While apprehension of Russian aims need not involve dislike of the Russian people, we have an abiding idea in this country that both alike lie under a necessity of chastisement, and that Japan, as the only nation now really at home on the Pacific, is the hand to hold the rod.

In conclusion — if I may be allowed to extend these reflections a little further — the situation before us suggests the possibility that Asia may at this moment be passing the threshold of a renascence similar to that which awakened Europe at the opening of the sixteenth century from the lethargy of her dark ages. As the able editor of the *North China Herald* has observed, native Asia from Korea to Siam is to-day no more deeply immersed in the mire of poverty, ignorance, and superstition than was Europe in the Middle Ages, nor was the task of relief and enlightenment less hopeless to human agencies then than now. Yet with the Age of Discoveries came not only new worlds and new paths of commerce, but the end of the tyrannies of scholasticism, the church, and the despot. Within a century were laid all the foundations of these political and intellectual institutions that distinguish Europe and her children to-day. A like reconstruction may be effected in Asia during the century just begun. The parallel is not altogether inadmissible, and it may be pushed even further. For as the newly awakened Europe of the sixteenth century developed one monster Power whose aggrandizement threatened the liberties of all the rest, so has the present era brought forth a monster fearful in the same fashion to Asia. It was England, a naval folk and a new Power, that struck at Spain three centuries ago, and by that brave adventure not only won wealth and prestige for herself, but rid Europe of a great menace. It is Japan, also a naval race and a new — so far as Continental history is concerned — that strikes at Russia and hopes by her success both to avert the undoing of the ancient states about her and to establish herself as mistress in her own waters. Confident in their understanding of their great mission, we of America may rightfully bid the dazed Asiatic seek his salvation from the children of the Rising Sun, and declare in the Sibylline utterance of the Psalmist, " The dew of thy birth is of the womb of the morning."

FREDERICK WELLS WILLIAMS.

NEW HAVEN, CONNECTICUT,
  November, 1904.

# PREFACE

THIS is an attempt to present in a verifiable form some of the issues and the historical causes of the war now waged between Russia and Japan. Powerfully as it appeals to me, I would not have discussed a subject so strange to the proper sphere of my investigation, had it not been for the fact that no one else has, so far as I am aware, undertaken the task in the same spirit in which I have endeavored to write these pages. Although I deeply regret that I do not read the Russian language and cannot do full justice to the Russian side of the question, the impartial reader will observe, I trust, that this work is neither a plea for the one side nor a condemnation of the other, but a mere exposition of the subject-matter as I comprehend it. When the author offers what he considers a natural explanation of a question, the reader should not read into it a moral judgment. Indeed, I earnestly wish that the kind reader would thrash out of these pages every grain of real prejudice. Nor can I welcome a greater favor from any person than a more complete and just statement of Russia's case than I have been able to make. After having said so much, it is unnecessary to tell the reader how, when the substance of the introductory chapter to this volume was published last May in the *Yale Review*, some of its critics ascribed to the writer motives utterly foreign to himself. One of those alleged motives was that I had sought to prove that the American trading interest in Manchuria and Korea would be better served by a final victory of Japan than by that of Russia. I neither proved nor disproved such a theme, but I did state that Japan's interest demanded the maintenance in those regions of the principle of the impartial opportunity for all nations. Whether the result of this policy would prove better or worse for the interest of any one nation than the effect of an exclusive policy, did not concern me. It did not and does not belong to me to appeal to the commercial instinct of the reader, or even to his sympathy with, or antipathy to, either of the present belligerents. My only plea is that for truth.

The substance of the introductory chapter, as has been said, and also a brief summary of the body of the volume have been published in the *Yale Review* for May and August of the present year. I am greatly indebted to the editors of the *Review* for allowing me to use the material in the preparation of this work. I also wish to express my sincere thanks to my friends who have encouraged me in the publication of this volume.

ASAKAWA.

HANOVER, NEW HAMPSHIRE,
    August 30, 1904.

# CONTENTS

# LIST OF ILLUSTRATIONS

# THE RUSSO-JAPANESE CONFLICT

## INTRODUCTORY

### SOME OF THE ISSUES OF THE CONFLICT

THE deeper significance of the present dramatic struggle between Russia and Japan over territories belonging to neither of the contestants cannot perhaps be understood, until we examine some of the issues at stake between them. The more fundamental of these issues, however, as in many another international crisis, seem to be oftener understood than expressed, and hence understood only vaguely, although it may fairly be said that they constitute the very forces which have with irresistible certainty brought the belligerents into collision. For Japan, the issues appear to be only partly political, but mainly economical; and perhaps no better clue to the understanding, not only of the present situation, but also, in general, of the activities at home and abroad of the Japanese people, could be found than in the study of these profound material interests.

Among the most remarkable tendencies of Japan's economic life of recent years has been the enormous increase of her population, along with an immense growth of her trade and industries. The

number of her inhabitants increased from 27,200,-
000, as estimated in 1828, to only 34,000,000 in
1875, but since that year it has risen so fast that it is
to-day 46,305,000 [1] — exclusive of the 3,082,404 [1]
in Formosa and the Pescadores — and is increasing
now at the annual rate of nearly 600,000.   At the
same time, the foreign trade of Japan has grown
from 49,742,831 *yen* in 1873 to 606,637,959 *yen*
in 1903.   Up to the end of May, 1904, the total
amount showed 274,012, 437 *yen*, as compared with
the 248,506,103 *yen* of the same period of 1903.[2]
The significance of these figures must be seen in the
light of the important fact that the bulk of the
increase in population and trade has been due
to the decisive change of the economic life of the
nation from an agricultural to an industrial stage.
The new population seems to increase far more
rapidly in the urban than in the rural districts, for
if we consider as urban the inhabitants of communities containing each more than three thousand
people, the ratio of the urban population to the
rural may be estimated as 1 to 3.   If only towns
of more than 10,000 inhabitants each are included
in the urban class, it is seen that their population

---

[1] Official figures for December 31, 1903.  The *Fourth Financial and Economical Annual of Japan*, 1904 (hereafter abbreviated as the *Fourth Annual*), published by the Department of
Finance, Imperial Government of Tokio, p. 5.  The actual numbers may be even higher.

[2] *The Monthly Return of the Foreign Trade of the Empire of
Japan* for May, 1904, published by the Department of Finance,
pp. 91–95.

increases annually 5 or 6 per cent., while the corresponding rate with the rural communities never
rises above 3 per cent. and is usually much lower.[1]
This comparatively rapid growth of the cities also
indicates that the new population must be mainly
supported by commerce and manufacture.

In 1903, 84.6 per cent. of the total export trade
of Japan consisted of either wholly or partly
manufactured articles.[2] On the other hand, agriculture has progressed only slowly,[3] and is no
longer able either to support the increased population or to produce enough raw articles for the
manufactures. The average annual crop of rice
may be put at ~210 million bushels, and that of

[1] *Japan in the Beginning of the 20th Century* (hereafter abbreviated as the *20th Century*), compiled by the Department of
Agriculture and Commerce, Tokio, 1903, pp. 53–58.

[2] Or, 241,891,946 out of 285,971,623 *yen*. As the term manufacture is expansive, the articles herein included should be enumerated. They are: clothing, chemicals and drugs, metal wares,
oil and wax, paper, cotton yarn and fabrics, raw and woven silks,
tobacco, and sundries. Teas, grain, marine products and other
food-stuffs, and furs, as well as reëxported articles, are excluded.
See the *Kwampo* (Official Gazette of Japan), No. 6199 (March
4, 1904), p. 77, table 7.

[3] The crop of rice has increased since 1877 from 26.6 million
to about 42,000,000 *koku ;* that of barley, rye, and wheat from
9.6 million to 19 million *koku*. But the increase has been due
more to an improved cultivation than to an extension of acreage.
Although the wheat, barley, and rye land has grown from 2.35
million in 1877 to 4.43 million acres in 1901, the rice land has increased from 6,517,000 to only 6,982,000 acres. The crops of
hemp and rape are stationary, while those of sugar, cotton, and
indigo have largely fallen off. (These figures have been converted from those in the *20th Century*, pp. 119 ff. One *koku* dry
is equivalent to 4.9629 bushels.)

barley, rye, and wheat, collectively called *mugi*, at
94.3 million bushels, while the average annual consumption of these cereals may safely be estimated,
respectively, at 228.3 and 106.7 million bushels.
In years of poor crops, the importation of rice,
wheat, and flour amounts to large figures; as, for
instance, in 1903, they together were imported to
the value of about 67 million *yen*.[1] Raw material
and food-stuffs, consisting of cotton, wool, rice,
flour and starch, beans and oil-cakes, the importation of all of which was next to nothing twenty
years ago, were in 1903 supplied from abroad to
the value of 169,600,000 *yen*, or 53.5 per cent. of
the total imports of Japan.[2] Japan will not only
always have to rely upon foreign countries for the
supply of these articles, but also have to import
them in ever increasing quantities. Nor does agriculture occupy in the national finances the position
it once did, for in 1875 the land tax, the incidence
of which fell, as it still falls, very largely on the
farmer, supplied 78 per cent. of the total revenue
of the state, while the percentage fell, in the estimated budget for the fiscal year 1902–3, to 16,
the actual amount also decreasing during the in-
terval from 67.7 to 37 million *yen*, and the ex-

[1] These figures have been worked out from the *Kokumin
Shimbun* (National News, hereafter abbreviated as the *Kokumin*) of February 5, 10, and 19, 1904. Also see a table and
comment in the *Tōyō Keizai Shimpō* ("Oriental Economist"),
for May 5, 1903, pp. 17–19.

[2] If sugar is added to the list, the figures will go up to more
than 190 million *yen*, or 60 per cent. of the entire import trade.

penditures of the government, on the other hand, increasing from 73.4 million in 1874, to the enormous figure of 223.18 million *yen* in 1904–5.[1]

No one can say a cheerful word about agriculture in Japan or the life of her farmer. Exclusive of Formosa, the development of which seems to lie in the direction of industry and trade rather than agriculture, less than 13,000,000 acres are under cultivation,[2] or, about 13 per cent. of the extent of the country, while the arable area of the land cannot possibly be increased by more than 10,500,-000 acres,[3] so that the *per capita* share of arable land is less than one half of an acre,[4] which is even below the corresponding rate in England and less

[1] 289.2 million *yen* in 1902–3. The *Fourth Annual*, pp. 4 and 9, and plate 3. Also see the *Tōyō Keizai Shimpō* ("Oriental Economist") for December 5, 1902, pp. 19–21 and chart.

[2] Or, less than 7,000,000 acres of wet fields and less than 6,000,000 of upland fields, the latter including mulberry and tea gardens, besides fields for *mugi*, beans, and vegetables. Based on the *20th Century*, pp. 95 ff.

[3] This figure includes, however, all the land inclined at angles less than 15°, so that, from the practical point of view, it may be considered as highly exaggerated. The actual extent of the reclamation of wild land advances at a slow pace outside of the still largely undeveloped island of Hokkaidō. See *ibid.*, pp. 95–96, 104.

[4] Or, about 23,000,000 acres for nearly 47,000,000 people. If we take only the land under cultivation, on the one hand, and only the farming population, on the other, the ratio still remains the same, for then we have 13,000,000 acres for 28,000,000 people. The aggregate of the capital involved in the agriculture of Japan, including the value of land, buildings, implements, and live stock, is estimated at 7,400,000,000 *yen*, while the annual crops return about 1,000,000,000 *yen*. See the *20th Century*, pp. 105–106.

than one half of that in China. Japan's agricultural life can, however, be no more intensively improved than extensively enlarged. The sedimentary soil so well adapted to the rice cultivation and so abundantly blessed with moisture [1] is too minutely and carefully tilled, the climate conditions are too cleverly made use of,[2] and, above all, the lots of land are too diminutive,[3] to make the importation of new machinery and methods always profitable or desirable.[4] The day-laborers on the farm receive

[1] The annual rainfall of Japan proper averages between 1300 mm. at Awomori and 2040 mm. at Kagoshima. A fairly rich sedimentary formation of soil is found everywhere, owing to the hilly nature of the country and the short and rapid current of the rivers.

[2] Wherever possible, the farmer contrives to raise more than one crop on his land in different seasons during the year. In fact, more than 30 per cent. of rice land yields other crops besides rice, at places mugi, indigo, beans, and rape being cultivated on the same piece of land.

[3] More than half of the wet fields of the country consist of lots smaller than one-eighth acre, and nearly three fourths are each less than one-quarter acre. The average size of the lots outside of Formosa and Hokkaidō is put down as .1 acre for wet fields and .12 acre for upland fields.

[4] Compare the report of the U. S. Consul-General Bellows at Yokohama in the U. S. Consular Reports, advance sheets, No. 1757 (September 24, 1903). In addition to the conditions here enumerated, it must be remembered that there exists little or no pasture land in Japan, and that nearly all the labor is done by hand, there being only 1,500,000 horses and 1,300,000 horned animals in the country. See the 20th Century, chapters on agriculture; the Annual, No. III, tables x-xiii; J. J. Rein's Industries of Japan, English translation, New York, 1889, chapters on agriculture; and H. Dumolard's Le Japon politique, économique et social, Paris, 1903, pp. 109–121.

wages ranging between nine and fifteen cents, though the latter have risen more than 100 per cent. during the last fifteen years.[1] With this meagre income some of the laborers have to support their aged parents, wives, and children. The tenants, whose number bears the ratio of about two to one[2] to that of the proprietors, live literally from hand to mouth, and cannot always afford even the necessary manure, and the proprietor's profit hardly rises above 5 per cent., while the capital he employs pays an interest of 15 to 30 per cent.[3] and his local and central taxes further reduce his income. The farmer would in many cases be unable to subsist, were it not possible for him, as it fortunately is, to try his hand at silk-culture or some other subsidiary occupation.

Japan's agriculture, then, can neither be much extended nor be greatly improved, can neither satisfy the old population nor support the new, and, above all, can only produce smaller and smaller portion of the necessary raw material for her growing in-

[1] The *20th Century*, p. 117; Dumolard, pp. 112–113.

[2] This ratio includes, however, in the tenant class those farmers who are partly lessees and partly proprietors of small lots. In 1888, the ratio between (1) independent farmers, (2) partly lessees, and (3) entirely lessees, was 147:200:95. Since that time the ratio must have grown in favor of the tenants. See the *20th Century*, p. 90.

[3] See the U. S. *Consular Reports*, advance sheets, No. 1529 (December 26, 1902). In 1902 the total debts of the farming classes of Japan were estimated at 400 million *yen*. Mr. S. Nakayama, in the *Tōyō Keizai Shimpō* ("Oriental Economist") for July 15, 1902, p. 14.

dustries. Under these circumstances, it is becoming more evident every year that the time is forever past when the nation could rely solely upon agriculture for subsistence. It is hardly necessary to repeat the well-known law of population — which is at the root of our subject — that every advance in the economic life of a nation creates a situation which is capable of supporting a larger population than in the preceding stage. What agriculture cannot support, industry and trade may. Japan's growing population may only be supported, as it has already begun to be, by an increased importation of raw material and food-stuffs and an increased exportation of manufactures. Trade statistics unmistakably show that such markets for her manufactures and such supply regions of her raw and food articles are found primarily in East Asia, with which the commercial relations of Japan have grown 543 per cent. since 1890, as compared with the 161 per cent.[1] increase of the American and the 190 per cent. increase of the European trade,[2] until the East Asiatic trade amounted in 1903 to 295,940,000 *yen* in value, or 48.7 per cent. of the entire foreign trade of Japan.[3] The

[1] In 1903, Japan's American trade was much below that of 1902. The latter showed an increase of 362 per cent. over 1890.

[2] The actual figures were: —

|  | European | American | Japanese |
|---|---|---|---|
| 1890 | 57,200,000 *yen* | 36,700,000 *yen* | 45,700,000 *yen* |
| 1903 | 166,900,000 *yen* | 95,900,000 *yen* | 295,900,000 *yen* |

[3] In East Asia are included Korea, China, Hong-kong, British India, French Indo-China, Dutch East Indies, the Straits

following table gives a comparison of the importation in the years 1882, 1902, and 1903, of what
may be considered as primarily East Asiatic products : [1] —

| | 1882 | 1902 | 1903 |
|---|---|---|---|
| Cotton | 467,249 *yen* | 79,784,772 *yen* | 69,517,894 *yen* |
| Wool | | 3,397,564 | 4,811,811 |
| Rice | 134,838 | 17,750,817 | 51,960,033 |
| Wheat | | 240,050 | 4,767,832 |
| Flour | | 3,278,324 | 10,324,415 |
| Beans | | 4,956,000 | 7,993,411 |
| Oil-cakes | 44,468 | 10,121,712 | 10,739,359 |

From these eloquent facts, the conclusion would
seem tenable that, should the markets of East Asia
be closed, Japan's national life would be paralyzed,
as her growing population would be largely deprived

Settlements, Siam, the Philippines, and Russian Eastern Asia.
If Hong-kong, an essentially transit-trade port, is excluded, the
East Asiatic trade of Japan amounts to 264,476,239 *yen*, or
43.6 per cent. of the entire foreign trade of Japan.  See the
*Kwampō* (Official Gazette of Japan), No. 6199 (March 4, 1904),
p. 74, table 4.

Of the three great divisions of Japan's markets, Europe sells
her machineries and articles of general consumption, and buys
in return such peculiar products of her soil as silks and teas.
East Asia, including India and the southern islands, takes coal
and manufactured goods in general and furnishes cotton, food-
stuffs, and other articles of more direct need than the European
goods.  America occupies a unique position in regard to Japan,
as it combines to a large extent the peculiarities of both Europe
and East Asia: it exports to Japan cotton and flour, besides
machinery and goods of general consumption, and imports from
her, not only raw silk and tea, but also smaller manufactured
articles.

[1] Oil-cakes are used as manure.  As to rice, wheat, and flour,
it is unnecessary to say that their importation depends largely
upon the conditions of the crop at home.

of its food and occupation. These markets, then, must be left as open as the circumstances permit, if Japan would exist as a growing nation. Observe here the tremendous significance for Japan of the principle of the " open door " as applied to East Asia — the principle, in a more accurate language, of the equal opportunity in East Asia for the economic enterprise of all foreign nations.[1]

In this great problem Manchuria and Korea occupy, perhaps, the most important position, for they together receive a large portion of the cotton yarn and cotton textiles exported from Japan, besides several other manufactured goods and coal, and in return supply Japan with much of the wheat and rice, and practically all of the millet, beans, and oil-cakes, imported into the country. Let us briefly demonstrate these statements by figures. First, consider the exportation of cotton yarns and textiles from Japan to Manchuria and Korea. It is rather difficult from the material on hand to estimate the exact ratio which the import of these articles from Japan into Korea and Manchuria bears to the total import of the same articles from all nations. In the case of Korea, we can make an approximate estimate, as we possess both the export values in Japan and

---

[1] The present author has often met persons who misinterpreted the "open door" to mean the complete throwing open of a country to the ruthless exploitation of the foreigner. The "open door," it is needless to say, merely negatives a differential treatment in favor of one or more foreign nations at the expense of all the others. It does not necessarily imply a wide opening, but an impartial, even if narrow, opening for all nations.

import values in Korea, but with regard to Manchuria, we know only the quantities, but not the values, of the cotton goods imported. By assuming, however, that 40 per cent. of these goods imported by the Chinese Empire from Japan go to North China (of which Manchuria is here considered by far the most important part), it may be said, roughly, that in 1903 about 6 per cent. of the cotton yarn exported from Japan went to Korea and perhaps 40 per cent. to North China. The average import of this article during the past two years was probably 1,200,000 *yen* in Korea and 8,000,000 *yen* in North China, making the total about 36 per cent. of the export value in Japan. On the same basis of calculation, the average importation of cotton textiles from Japan during the past three years was 3,190,-000 *yen* in Korea and 765,000 *yen* in North China, or about 69.5 per cent. of the entire export of these articles from Japan. These figures are only tentative, but may serve to show that Manchuria receives comparatively much yarn and Korea much textiles, and that they together receive at least a large percentage of those articles exported by Japan, where their manufacture occupies an increasingly important place in her economic life.[1] As to the exportation of agricultural products from Manchuria and

[1] Consult the British *Diplomatic and Consular Reports*, Annual Series, Nos. 2995 and 2999; the U. S. *Monthly Summary of Commerce and Finance*, January, 1904, pp. 2410–1; the *Kokumin*, September 19–21, 1901; Minister Kiyoura's address before the Osaka Chamber of Commerce, February, 1904.

Korea, it is seen that wheat is only beginning to be cultivated in Manchuria, while the rice cultivation is there practically unknown except in a few places near the Korean border, where during the campaign of 1894–5 the Japanese troops introduced it. The position which Korea occupies in the importation of wheat into Japan will be seen from the following table : —

Wheat imported into Japan, 1898–1902,[1]   kin = 1.325 lbs. av.
yen = 49.8 cents.

| From | 1898 | 1899 | 1900 | 1901 | 1902 |
|---|---|---|---|---|---|
| Australia... { |  |  | 4,339,845 | 5,554,513 | 18,423 |
|  |  |  | 143,260 | 185,274 | 721 |
| Korea...... { | 2,770,755 | 1,068,207 | 5,182,533 | 1,644,577 | 8,556,813 |
|  | 72,698 | 71,764 | 132,734 | 43,875 | 237,217 |
| Great { |  |  | 457,450 |  |  |
| Britain... { |  |  | 15,502 |  |  |
| The United { | 2,039,371 | 395,009 | 12,370,022 | 1,388,372 | 864 |
| States.... { | 71,173 | 14,697 | 400,829 | 43,720 | 43 |
| Other { | 1,560 | 990 | 547 |  | 77,343 |
| countries . { | 41 | 27 | 14 |  | 2,069 |
| Total....... { | 4,811,686 | 2,064,206 | 22,350,397 | 8,587,462 | 8,653,443 |
|  | 143,913 | 86,489 | 692,341 | 272,869 | 240,050 |

A glance at these figures will show that the import trade of wheat, like that of rice, is dependent on many fluctuating conditions at home and abroad. The poor crop in Japan caused an enormous importation of wheat in 1903 to the value of 4,767,000 *yen*. From the above table, it is seen that Korea supplied during the five years, respectively, 57.5, 80.7, 23.1, 19.1, and 98.8 per cent., in weight, of the wheat imported into Japan. As regards rice, the

[1] The figures were taken from the *Monthly Summary of Commerce and Finance of the United States* for February, 1904, p. 3006.

following table will show that in the five years between 1898 and 1902 Korea supplied, respectively,
5.5, 26.5, 49.4, 46.8, and 19.8 per cent. in weight
of the cereal imported into Japan : —

Rice imported into Japan, 1898–1902,[1] $\begin{cases} picul = 133\frac{1}{3} \text{ lbs. av.} \\ yen = 49.8 \text{ cents.} \end{cases}$

| From | 1898 | 1899 | 1900 | 1901 | 1902 |
|---|---|---|---|---|---|
| British | 2,663,087 | 53,827 | 249,344 | 220,650 | 1,793,362 |
| India .... | 11,642,416 | 174,507 | 973,747 | 876,057 | 7,530,356 |
| China...... | 967,216 | 60,323 | 83,998 | 227,234 | 90,401 |
| | 3,989,422 | 231,625 | 327,673 | 867,272 | 341,689 |
| Korea...... | 649,570 | 436,716 | 1,131,787 | 1,456,661 | 891,186 |
| | 2,704,887 | 1,689,909 | 4,694,166 | 6,009,641 | 3,961,312 |
| Dutch | | | 403 | | |
| Indies ... | | | 1,816 | | |
| French | 6,445,390 | 956,142 | 726,859 | 919,774 | 1,324,789 |
| India .... | 25,762,726 | 3,354,095 | 2,739,752 | 3,199,420 | 4,651,395 |
| Siam ...... | 969,413 | 143,575 | 94,530 | 287,594 | 409,307 |
| | 4,114,065 | 510,007 | 284,178 | 926,486 | 1,265,970 |
| Other | 1,576 | 9 | 58 | 25 | 27 |
| countries | 6,290 | 21 | 200 | 82 | 94 |
| Total ...... | 11,696,252 | 1,650,592 | 2,286,979 | 3,111,938 | 4,509,072 |
| | 48,219,810 | 5,960,166 | 9,021,536 | 11,878,958 | 17,750,817 |

As will be seen in this table, much rice comes also
from Saigon and Bangkok, to which, however, Japan
hardly exports anything. In Korea, on the contrary,
the greater her exportation of rice, the larger her
purchasing power of the goods from the country
to which the rice goes. In the case of beans and
oil-cakes, Manchuria and Korea occupy in the list
of the importation of these articles into Japan an
even more important place than is the case with
wheat or rice, as will be seen in the following
table : —

[1] From *ibid.*, p. 3006. In 1903, rice imported amounted to
51,960,000 *yen* in value. The *Fourth Annual*, p. 77.

Beans and oil-cakes imported into Japan in 1902,[1] $\begin{cases} picul=133\frac{1}{3} \text{ lbs. av.} \\ yen = 49.8 \text{ cents.} \end{cases}$

| From | Beans, pease, and pulse | Oil-cakes |
|---|---|---|
| China............ { | 1,306,103 | 4,064,198 |
|  | 3,524,138 | 8,656,775 |
| Korea ............ { | 777,151 | 5,671 |
|  | 2,254,899 | 12,331 |
| Russian Asia ...... { | 545 | 345,022 |
|  | 1,505 | 1,448,868 |
| French India ...... { | 742 |  |
|  | 2,178 |  |
| The United States.. { | 281 |  |
|  | 2,405 |  |
| Other countries .... { | 545 | 846 |
|  | 1,582 | 3,738 |
| Total............ { | 2,086,367 | 4,415,737 |
|  | 5,786,707 | 10,121,712 |

An explanation is necessary that, to all probability, much of the oil-cakes from Russian Asia was re-exported from Manchuria. In 1903, beans and oil-cakes were imported to the value of, respectively, 7,993,000 and 10,739,000 *yen.* In considering all these facts as a whole, attention is called to a point of immense importance, that Manchuria and Korea supply Japan with necessaries of life, and receive in return, in the main, useful goods, instead of wares of luxury. We shall have occasion further to develop this point.

Let us now take a general survey of the position Japan holds in the trade relations of Korea and Manchuria. In Korea, whence the Chinese merchants withdrew during the China-Japan war of 1894–5 and were replaced by the Japanese traders,[2]

[1] See the U. S. *Monthly Summary*, February, 1904, pp. 3006 and 3013.

[2] At present, Chinese merchants in Korea compete with the

it is Japan alone of all trading nations which enjoys
a large share both in the import and export trade,
as is suggested in the following table : —

| | Japan's export to Korea | Total import of Korea | Japan's import from Korea | Total export of Korea |
|---|---|---|---|---|
| 1902... | 10,554,000 *yen* | (13,823,000 *yen*) | 7,958,000 *yen* | (8,460,000 *yen*) |
| 1903... | 11,764,000 | (18,207,000) | 8,912,000 | (9,472,000) |

while the grains exported from Korea go almost
entirely to Japan. Different ports of Korea present
of course different characteristics in their trade with
Japan : as, for instance, at Chemulpo the Chinese
merchants still enjoy a considerable share in the
import trade ; at Seul nearly all the export consists
of gold bullion, which is almost exclusively bought
by the branch of the First Bank of Japan ; while
at Fusan and Mokpo the Japanese monopoly of
trade is almost complete. With these variations,
however, the Japanese merchants control the major
part of the trade of each port, and consequently of
the entire trade of Korea. They also carry a large
amount of foreign goods to Korea, as seen in the
following table : —

| | Japanese goods | Foreign goods |
|---|---|---|
| 1902 | 9,344,859 *yen* | 1,209,332 *yen* |
| 1901 | 10,410,563 | 961,897 |
| 1900 | 9,423,821 | 529,450 [1] |

The shipping also is largely in the hands of the
Japanese. In 1903, their share in the Korean shipping was as follows : [2] —

Japanese only at the ports on the western coast, principally in
the import trade of silk. The number of the Chinese residents
in Korea is one tenth that of the Japanese, or about 4000.

[1] The *Kokumin*, January 30, 1904.

[2] Based on the figures in the British *Diplomatic and Consular
Report : Trade of Corea for the Year* 1903, pp. 11–13.

|            | Vessels    |           | Tonnage        |
|------------|-----------|-----------|----------------|
| Korean     | 25        | per cent. | 9 + per cent.  |
| Japanese   | 61 +      |           | 78 +           |
| Russian    | 2 +       |           | 9 +            |
| Others     | 11 +      |           | 4 —            |

Turning to Manchuria, it is found that Japan controlled in 1902 more than 44 per cent. of the shipping tonnage,[1] besides 40 per cent. of the direct import trade and over 90 per cent. of the export trade, as is shown below : [2] —

|                          | Exports      | (Japan)        | Imports     | (Japan)       |
|--------------------------|--------------|----------------|-------------|---------------|
| 1901                     | 1,080,345 l. | ( 970,663 l.)  | 635,085 l.  | (247,624 l.)  |
| 1902                     | 1,130,429    | (1,041,395)    | 695,020     | (280,843)     |
| Average five years,<br>1896–99 and 1891 | 965,553 | ( 880,917) | 433,811 | (131,143) |

at Niu-chwang, which was then the only important port in Manchuria open to foreign trade under the ordinary customs rules.[3]

[1] Of the 1430 vessels, aggregating 1,104,000 tons, entered at and cleared from Niu-chwang in 1902, the Japanese had 710 vessels and 491,000 tons, the British, 374 vessels and 350,000 tons, the Germans, 88 vessels and 73,000 tons, and so forth. — The *Kokumin*, April 29, 1904, from the *Tai Shin-Kan Bōyeki Chōsa Hōkoku* (report on the trade with China and Korea), compiled by the Department of Agriculture and Commerce, Tokio, 1904. The Russians could show only 3 vessels and 1,223 tons, which was below their record for 1901 and less than one half of the average of the five years 1886, 1897, 1898, 1899, and 1901. — The British *Diplomatic and Consular Reports*, Annual Series, No. 2999 (on Niu-chwang), p. 9.

[2] *Ibid.*, p. 8.

[3] The direct import trade of any trading nation at Niu-chwang does not represent the actual amount of the articles imported from the country of that nation, for most of the foreign goods come to Niu-chwang through some other distributing centres in China, such as Hong-kong or Shanghai. The Japanese goods, however, are nearly all carried by Japanese vessels. On the contrary, the American imports, besides jeans, drills, sheetings, kero-

In this connection, it should be remembered that both the Korean and Manchurian trade are of recent origin. Niu-chwang was opened as a treaty port in 1858, but its commercial importance may be said to date from 1899. Korea's foreign trade did not begin till 1884, and it exceeded 10,000,000 *yen* for the first time in 1895. The rapid growth of the trade of these places has been largely due to the increasing trade activity of Japan. In the case of Niu-chwang, it is true, the development of its import trade has been as much owing to the energy of the Americans as to that of the Japanese, but its export business would be meagre, and would consequently reduce the imports also, but for Japanese activity. The recent increase in the production of millet in Manchuria, for instance, may be said to be entirely due to Japanese trade at Niu-chwang. Of the three staple products of Western Manchuria, tall millet is consumed by the natives, and beans are partly consumed and partly exported, while millet is cultivated purely for the purpose of exportation.

senes, and flour, are not specified in the customs returns of Niu-chwang, and consequently their nominal figures are insignificant (7396 *l.* in 1901 and 4089 *l.* in 1902), while Hong-kong, through which most of the American goods are imported into Niu-chwang, showed, in 1902, 385,302 *l.*, or 55 per cent. of the entire direct trade. On the other hand, the estimate made by the Bureau of Statistics, Department of Commerce and Labor, Washington, showing 18,000,000 haikwan taels for the *real* import of American goods into Niu-chwang, seems to be pretty liberal. See British *D. and C. Reports*, annual series, No. 2999, p. 8, and the U. S. *Monthly Summary of Commerce and Finance*, January, 1904, p. 2328.

It began to be exported to Korea in August, 1901, and to Japan in 1902. Since the latter year, Japan's demand for millet has steadily increased, and has caused a considerable rise in its price at Niu-chwang. The cultivation of millet, therefore, is a pure gain that has been created by the trade relations of Manchuria with Japan.[1] Far more important than millet as articles for exportation are beans and bean-cakes. The entire trade conditions at Niu-chwang may be said to depend upon the amount of the sale of these articles. The more they are sold, the greater is the importing capacity of the people of Manchuria. The nation which buys beans and bean-cakes in the largest quantities naturally commands the greatest facility in pushing their imports into Niu-chwang. The exportation of these goods doubled during the ten years between 1889 and 1898, while the amount of the bean production in Manchuria for 1900 was estimated at between 1,930,000 and 2,450,000 *koku*. Both the production and the exportation must now be much greater. The increase was due in the main to the growing demand in Japan for beans and bean-cakes, as witness the following ratios of exports to China and Japan from Niu-chwang : —

|  | Beans | | Bean-cakes | |
| --- | --- | --- | --- | --- |
|  | To China | To Japan | To China | To Japan |
| 1889 | 98.0 % | 2.0 % | 95.8 % | 4.2 % |
| 1893 | 67.5 | 32.5 | 68.3 | 31.7 |
| 1897 | 60.7 | 39.3 | 50.2 | 49.8 |

In 1903, the ratios must have been much greater

[1] See the *Tsūshō Isan* for January 22, 1903, pp. 10–11.

for Japan than for China. The increasing demand for these products has induced many Chinese to migrate from Shantung to Southern and Western Manchuria and cultivate beans.[1] As regards the Korean trade, the following table will speak for itself : —

| | Korean trade in merchandise | Korean export of gold | Total | Japan-Korea trade |
|---|---|---|---|---|
| 1897.... | 19,041,000 yen | 2,034,000 yen | 21,075,000 yen | 14,061,000 yen |
| 1898.... | 17,527,000 | 2,375,000 | 19,902,000 | 10,641,000 |
| 1899.... | 15,225,000 | 2,933,000 | 18,158,000 | 11,972,000 |
| 1900.... | 20,380,000 | 3,633,000 | 24,013,000 | 18,759,000 |
| 1901.... | 23,158,000 | 4,993,000 | 28,151,000 | 21,425,000 |
| 1902... | (22,280,000) | 5,064,000 | (27,344,000) | 18,512,000 |
| 1903.... | 27,679,000 | 5,456,000 | 33,135,000 | 20,676,000 |

If we examine the causes of the growth of individual open ports in Korea, nothing can be plainer than that it - has almost entirely resulted from the increasing trade relations between Korea and Japan. It is needless to mention Fusan, for its trade is nearly synonymous with its Japanese trade. Kunsan was opened on May 1, 1899, and its population was only 300 till two years ago, but the great demand by Japan for the rice coming through this port has already tended to enlarge the number of its inhabitants up to 2000 or more.[2] Similar remarks may be made of Mokpo, Chinnampo, and other ports.[3] Most conspicuous, however, is the case of Chemulpo. In 1883, when it was opened as a treaty port, it contained only a few fishers' houses, but now it holds a population of 15,000, and occupies a position in

[1] See the *Tōyō Keizai Shimpō* ("Oriental Economist"), No. 165 (July 15, 1900), and No. 244 (September 25, 1902).

[2] The *Kokumin*, November 26, 1903.

[3] The *Annai*, pp. 58–61.

Korea similar to that of Shanghai in China. Of the inhabitants of the ports, 8000, or more than a half, are Japanese. Streams of Koreans also have flowed hither from inland towns, for there the officials oppress people, while here they are so constantly viewed by the foreigners that undue exactions are impossible.[1] We have already noted the important fact that Korea and Manchuria on the one hand and Japan on the other exchange, not wares of luxury, but useful and necessary articles. We have now come to another equally important fact, that the growth of the Manchurian and Korean trade depends largely upon the commercial activity of Japan. From these considerations, it would seem safe to say that the trade interests of the three countries are largely *common*, for the more Korea and Manchuria export to Japan, the greater will be their purchasing power of Japanese goods, and, also, the larger the exportation from Japan to Manchuria and Korea, the more readily they will dispose of their products to her. On the one hand, Korea and Manchuria encourage the growth of Japan's manufacture, and supply her with food and manure; on the other hand, the economic development and prosperity of Korea and Manchuria must be largely determined by the increasing demand for their products by Japan, and the easy supply of their wants from Japan. The future growth of the three nations, then, must in a large measure depend upon the intimate progress of their trade interests, which, therefore, not only

[1] Mr. Shiga's letter, in the *Kokumin*, July 5, 1904.

are common, but should be increasingly common. If the history of the past suggests the probable development in the future, there is every reason to believe that, with reformed systems of currency and improved and extended cultivation of land and means of transportation, the trade of Manchuria and Korea will show a tremendous increase, and then the community of interest between them and Japan will be most profound.

This theme of the community of interest may further be elaborated. Korea and Manchuria may with profit remain open, not only for the trade, but also for the emigration and industrial enterprise, of the Japanese people. Since 1902 no passports have been required for travelers from Japan to Korea, whither, in spite of the occasional obstacles placed in their way by Korean officials, the emigrants have proceeded, now for years, in increasing numbers, until there resided in 1903 nearly thirty thousand Japanese in the Peninsula.[1] It takes only thirteen hours on sea from Bakan in Japan to Fusan in Korea, and the cost is even less than that of sailing to the Japanese colony of Formosa, the former being

[1] In July, 1903, there were, besides soldiers, 26,705 Japanese in the eight treaty ports and Seul and Pingyang. To these must be added about 4000 who lived on some islands and places outside of the treaty ports. See the *Dōbun-kwai Hōkoku* (Report of the Dōbun Association), No. 41, pp. 95–96, and the *Tsūshō Isan* for October 18, 1903, pp. 29–47; April 8, 1904, pp. 28–52. Mr. Yamamoto places the number of the Japanese residents in Korea at 40,000. See his *Saishin Chōsen Ijū Annai* (latest guide for emigration to Korea; hereafter abbreviated as the *Annai*), Tokio, 1904, p. 14.

fifteen *yen* and the latter twenty.  It seems easier to
go from Bakan to Fusan than it is from Osaka to the
Hokkaidō within Japan proper.[1]  The expense of
living in Korea is also as low as one third the corresponding figure in Japan, a monthly income of ten or
thirteen *yen* being considered sufficient to support a
family of three persons in a rented house.[2]  It is not
strange, under these conditions, that the Japanese
migrate to Korea, not always singly, like the Chinese,
but often in families,[3] so that their settlements
assume there a normal and permanent character
unseen even in Japan's own island of Formosa.  Nor
are all these colonists mere laborers like their
brethren in Manchuria and the Hawaiian Islands,
but many are independent men of business.  They
also naturally manifest a stronger sense of kinship
and coöperation in Korea than the merchants and
capitalists do in Japan.  In several Korean towns
these Japanese settlers have established their own
municipalities, with modern improvements, cham-
bers of commerce, police, and public schools, all of
which compare favorably with those of the larger
cities in Japan, and the advantages of which are

[1] The *Annai*, pp. 8–9, 19–20.

[2] *Ibid.*, p. 81.

[3] In July, 1903, of the 26,645 Japanese in Korea, 15,442 were
men and 11,263 women.  It may be noted, in passing, that, in the
case of Manchuria, a great majority of the Japanese women
residing there are not the wives of the male settlers, and hence
the comparative numbers of men and women there should not
lead us to a similar conclusion as to Korea.  This part of the
problem of Japanese emigration opens up an interesting social
question, which it is hardly necessary for us to discuss here.

enjoyed by native Koreans and resident Chinese.
It is said that in some places the influx of the Japanese and their investments have caused a rise in
the price of land and house rent.[1]  In Fusan, the
port nearest to Japan, the 10,000 Japanese who live
there own large tracts of land and occupy the main
sections of the city.  Here and everywhere else the
Japanese colonists seem to hold a position similar to
that of the foreigners living in the so-called settlements in the larger treaty ports of China.  Tourists
are wont to contrast the clean and well-ordered
streets and the general energetic appearance of the
Japanese quarters in Korean cities with the comparatively filthy and slothful Korean quarters.  The
branches of the First Bank of Japan have been
issuing recently one-, five-, and ten-*yen* banknotes,[2]
which have been of immense value to the foreign
trade in Korea, the native currency of which is in a
deplorable condition.[3]  The coasting and river navigation, so far as it concerns foreign trade, is largely
controlled by the Japanese, who, besides, own the

[1] From the legal standpoint, the Japanese had no right, outside of the treaty settlements, to live or buy land.

[2] On March 31, 1904, there were about 1,234,000 *yen* of
these notes in circulation against a reserve of 944,000 *yen*.  From
the British *C. and D. Reports ; Trade of Korea for the Year* 1903,
pp. 7–8.

The Russians and their sympathizers at Seul have more than
once tried, though unsuccessfully, to induce the Korean Government to suppress the issue of the notes.  See pp. 281–284, below.

[3] The nickel coins of Korea have been so debased and so much
counterfeited that they are at a discount of much more than
100 per cent.

only railway line in operation in Korea, twenty-six miles long, running between the capital, Seul, and its port Chemulpo.[1] They are also building,[2] under the management of substantially the same company, another and longer line — two hundred and eighty-seven miles — between Seul and the port of Fusan, which passes through the richer and economically by far the more important half of the Peninsula.[3]  It is

[1] The right of building this line was originally granted by the Korean Government to Mr. Morse, an American citizen, in March, 1896, who, however, sold it to a Japanese syndicate in November, 1898, and handed the line over to the latter before it was completed. The whole line was in working order in July, 1899. See p. 286 (Article 3), below.

[2] Actual work was begun in August, 1901, but Japan's want of capital was such that by the first of December, 1903, only thirty-one miles from both ends had been built. In view of the immense economic and strategic importance of the line, the Japanese Government, which had for a certain period of time guaranteed 6 per cent. annual interest on 25,000,000 *yen*, which was fixed as the minimum capital of the company, now further promoted its work by liberal measures, so as to make it possible for the company to complete the line before the end of the present year. Both the Korean and Japanese Imperial Houses own shares of the company.

[3] The line passes through the richest and most populous four provinces of Korea, which comprise nearly seven tenths of all the houses in the Empire, and cover more than five sevenths of the cultivated area of the country, with considerable capacity for future cultivation and improvement. The road also connects places to which the Koreans flock from neighboring regions for the periodical fairs held there. These fairs occur six times each month, held alternately in different places, besides great annual fairs in large cities. Among the thirty-nine stations of this railroad, six will be daily seen holding fairs, for which the traffic of passengers and merchandise through the road will be considerable. It is safe to say that five sevenths of the entire Korean

not impossible to suppose that the Japanese people
will succeed in their efforts to secure the right of
extending this line beyond Seul up to Wiju on the
northern border,[1] and thence ultimately connecting
it with the Eastern Chinese and the Peking-Shang-
haikwan-Sinminting Railways, so as to render the
connection by rail between Fusan and China and
Europe complete.[2] The Mitsui Produce Company,
another Japanese concern, monopolized the export
of Korean ginseng, and, in 1903, despite the competition of the Russian Baron Gunzburg,[3] succeeded

foreign trade belong to the sphere controlled by this line, and
also that nearly all of this trade is in reality the fast growing
Japan-Korea trade. The effect of the completion of the line upon
this trade will be tremendous. See Mr. J. Shinobu's *Kan Hantō*
("The Korean Peninsula"), Tokio, 1901.

[1] The French have an agreement with the Korean Government regarding a Seul-Fusan railway. The Seul Government
is to build it with its own money, and the French to furnish
engineers and material. Not a mile of rail has been laid by the
impecunious Government, and the present war is rapidly changing the entire situation. A Japanese railway for strategic purposes has already been started from Seul northward. Another
line, between Seul and Wonsan (Gensan), will also be built by
the Japanese in the near future.

[2] It was one of the first propositions from Japan to Russia
during the long negotiations between them which have ended
in the present war, that Russia should not impede Japan's possible attempt in the future to extend the Fusan-Seul Railway in
the manner above described. See p. 286 (Article 3), below.

[3] A promoter of Russian interests in Korea, and to all intents
and purposes a semi-official diplomat for Russia, living at Seul
and observing the political barometer of the Court at close range.
Another person, perhaps less known to the outside world, but
far more influential at Court, is a woman, Fräulein Sonntag, a
relative of the wife of the ex-Russian Minister Waeber at Seul.
See p. 280, below.

in extending the term of the monopoly for five years. Twenty to forty thousand Japanese fishermen along the Korean coast report an annual catch amounting sometimes to large figures.

No part of Korea's economic life, however, would seem to be of greater importance to her own future, or to depend more closely upon the enterprise of the Japanese settlers, than her agriculture. If it is remembered that nearly all her exports consist of agricultural products, and also that they largely supply the needs of Japan, we can readily comprehend the great community of interest felt by both countries in the agriculture of the Peninsula. It is remarkable to note, to take a single instance, that the production of cereals and beans (respectively about eight and four million *koku*) in Korea has grown to its present dimensions largely owing to the stimulus given to it by the increased demand for these articles in Japan.[1] We shall presently note also that, owing to the peculiar circumstances prevailing in Korea, her purchasing power and general commercial activity are so completely ruled by the conditions of her weather and crops as is seldom the case with other agricultural nations. The Koreans are comparatively happy in good years, while in bad years they are reduced to great miseries and bandits infest all parts of the country. Upon the state of her agriculture, then, must depend the trade conditions of Korea, as well as most of her material strength and much of that of Japan. From this it

[1] The *Kokumin*, January 15, 1904.

is plain that the profound community of interest of
the two nations calls for both the extension and the
improvement of the agriculture of Korea.  It is estimated that the extent of her land under cultivation is hardly more than 3,185,000 acres, or about
6.3 per cent. of the 82,000 square miles known as
the total area of the country,[1] and that there exist
at least 3,500,000 more acres of arable land, which
would be fully capable of sustaining five or six
millions of new population, and of increasing the
annual crops of the land by not less than 150,000,-
000 *yen*.[2]  Unfortunately, however, the Koreans
lack energy to cultivate those three and a half million acres of waste land.  For it is well known that
the irregular but exhaustive exactions of the Korean
officials have bred a conviction in the mind of the
peasant that it is unwise to bestir himself and earn
surplus wealth only to be fleeced by the officials.
His idleness has now for centuries been forced,
until it has become an agreeable habit.  It is in this
state of things that it has often been suggested that
the cultivation of the waste lands may most naturally

[1] From an address by Mr. Suerō Katō, of the Department of
Agriculture and Commerce, who had studied the agriculture of
Korea on the ground three times in succession. — *Ibid.*, May
27, 1904.

[2] Calculated from the data given in the *Kokumin* for January
8, 1904.  The official census of Korea for 1902 gives a population
of 5,782,806, but assuming that there live 145 people per square
mile, which is one half the density of the population in China,
the Korean population cannot be much below 12,000,000.  The
official record of the land under cultivation is also untrustworthy
for institutional reasons not necesary to mention here.

be begun by the superior energy of the Japanese settlers.[1] Not less important than the cultivation of new
land is the improvement of old land in Korea, where
the art of husbandry is far less advanced than in
either China or Japan. Lots are marked out care-
lessly, improvements are crude, and the manure
most universally used is dried grass. The great
rivers with all their numerous ramifications are
hardly utilized for the purpose of irrigation, and the
forests have been mercilessly denuded for fuel and
in order to forestall the requisition. of the government, — which formerly used to order without compensation the cutting and transporting of trees by
their owners, — so that a slight drought or excess
of rain works frightful disasters upon agriculture.
Another serious effect of the absence of a good system of irrigation is the comparative want of rice
land, which always requires a most careful use of
water.[2] These conditions are all the more to be regretted, when it is seen that the soil is generally
fair and the climate favorable. The cultivation of
rice is said to have been first taught by the Japanese
invaders toward the end of the sixteenth century,
and yet, with all their primitive method, the Kore-

[1] The question of cultivating the waste land in Korea by
Japanese enterprise, however, has called forth a very delicate
situation which still awaits the most careful solution. The
progress of this situation will be a matter of great interest, but
it is still too early to discuss it. Cf. the *Korea Review* for July
and August, 1904, and follow its subsequent numbers.

[2] See the *Tsūshō Isan* for August 3, 1903, and the *Kokumin*
for January 7, 15, and 16, 1904.

ans are already exporting rice to the value of four million *yen* or more. Sericulture is still in its infancy, while tea, cotton, hemp, sugar, and various fruits are all declared to be tolerably well suited to the soil. The Japanese farmer finds here, particularly in the south, a climate and general surroundings very similar to his own, and otherwise eminently agreeable to his habits, and, along with the application of his superior methods of cultivation, irrigation, and forestry, the common interests of his country and Korea are bound to develop with great rapidity. The progress of agriculture would also gradually lead the Koreans into the beginnings of an industrial life, while the expanding systems of railways and banking would be at once cause and effect of the industrial growth of the nation. Another inevitable result would be the development of the economic sense and the saving capacity of the Korean, the latter of which has had little opportunity to grow, not so much because of his small wage and high rent and interest, as because of the onerous, irregular local dues and the systematic exactions in various forms by the official.[1] An advanced

---

[1] The rent is of two kinds: either to be decided anew each year after the harvest, or to deliver to the proprietor 50 per cent. of the crop. It should always be remembered that a large majority of actual cultivators are tenants, the proprietors being limited to a small class of rich men, officers, and nobles. The daily wage of the laborer on the farm averages 20 *sen*, but it is usually paid in kind, as are debts and repayments in many cases. The standard of life of the Korean farmer is perhaps lower than that of the Japanese, but apparently not less comfortable. The national land tax is said to be mild and largely discarded, but the house

economic life, itself necessitating a reform of the official organization, would at least make it possible for the peasant to work, earn, and save. Simultaneously and in increasing degree would his wants, as well as his purchasing power, increase. Around the progress of Korea's agriculture, then, must be built all other measures of her growth and power, as, for instance, transportation, industries, trade and commerce, finance, political reform, and military strength. In no other way can we conceive of the possibility of her effective independence, the cause of which has cost Japan, and is now costing her, so dearly. In no other light can we interpret the Korean sovereignty under the assistance of Japan.

In regard to Manchuria, where the chances for development are far vaster, the Japanese people do not possess there as large vested interests, but entertain as great expectations for its future settlement and industry as in Korea. It was estimated before the present war that there resided more than ten thousand Japanese in Manchuria, who were either under the employment of Russian authorities

---

tax, special tax, local tax, and the like, bring up the dues of the farmer sometimes to an unendurable extent. The tenant, after paying his rent and other charges, is obliged to sell what little rice is left to him at the earliest opportunity, so that he henceforth becomes a buyer of rice, and consequently has little to buy other articles with, and still less to save, until his spring harvest of wheat comes in. Woe betide him when both the rice and the wheat crops fail! See the *Kokumin*, January 13 and 14, 1904, and the *Tsūshō Isan* for August 3, 1903, p. 21.

in public works along the railway, or engaged in such small occupations as laundry work, carpentry, restaurant-keeping, photographing, and hair-dressing,[1] while many of the Japanese women, whose numbers in many a town preponderated over those of men, had been allured by unscrupulous parties, who consigned them to disreputable occupations. Merchants and business men of greater capital and resources would be, as they often have been, attracted to Manchuria, were it not for the exclusive, and in the hands of some of their officials, arbitrary, measures of the Russians.[2] Under normal conditions of peace and "open door," the immensely greater resources of Manchuria and the much greater productiveness of its people [3] would seem to promise even a more important economic future than in Korea.

[1] An address by Mr. G. Hirose, a competent eye-witness, in the *Dōbun-kwai Hōkoku*, No. 48, November, 1903, pp. 15 ff. Official census, however, gives only 2806 Japanese in Manchuria (December 30, 1903). See the *Tsūshō Isan* for April 13, 1904, pp. 33-38.

[2] Mr. Hirose, already mentioned, refers to a Japanese capitalist who started a lumber business in Kirin Province and another who discovered coal deposits near Harbin and began to mine them, both of whom, in spite of the permits they had received from the Chinese authorities by regular process, were driven away arbitrarily under threats of the Russian military. The *Dōbun-kwai*, No. 48, pp. 21-22.

[3] The so-called Manchus, the original inhabitants of Manchuria, have migrated to China proper, which they conquered during the seventeenth century. The present inhabitants of Manchuria are immigrant Chinese, whose greater economic capacity has been rapidly developing this immensely rich territory.

In summing up our preceding discussion, it may be stated that the natural growth or unnatural decay of the Japanese nation will greatly depend — ever more greatly than it now does — upon whether Manchuria and Korea remain open or are closed to its trade, colonization, and economic enterprise; and that, in her imperative desire for the open door, Japan's wish largely coincides with that of the European and American countries, except Russia, whose over-production calls for an open market in the East.

Thus far we have discussed only Japan's side of the economic problem in Manchuria and Korea. Passing to Russia's side, it is seen that her vested interests in Manchuria are as enormous as her commercial success there has been small. The building of the Eastern Chinese Railway has cost the incredible sum of 270,000,000 rubles, making the average cost per verst more than 113,000 rubles,[1] or over $87,000 per mile, besides 70,000,000 rubles lost and expended during the Boxer outrages and Man-

---

[1] An official report of the Province of Amur, dated June 22, 1903, denies that the actual cost of construction per verst was, as had been alleged, 150,000 rubles, but 113,183 rubles. The *Tsūshō Isan* for August 8, 1903, p. 46. A ruble is equivalent to about 51.5 cents.

In this connection, it is interesting to note in M. Witte's report to the Czar after the former's tour in the Far East in 1902, that the Siberian Railway had cost 758,955,907 rubles, but, with the Circum-Baikal section, would cost not less than 1,000,000,000 rubles, excluding the salaries of officers, expenses for soldiers, the Pacific fleet, harbor work, and the like. The *Dōbun-kwai Hōkoku*, No. 42, p. 30.

churia campaign of 1900,[1] to say nothing of the
normal annual cost of guarding the railway by
soldiers, estimated at 24,000,000 rubles.[2] The investments in permanent properties alone, besides
the railway, are moderately valued at 500,000,000
rubles.[3] In return for these heavy outlays, the trade
relations between Russia and Manchuria have been
most disappointing. Though it is not possible tò obtain the exact figures of the actual trade between
Manchuria and European Russia, we can establish
approximate estimates in the following manner.
According to official returns, exports from Russia to
her Far Eastern Possessions were as follows : —

    1900 ........................... 56,000,000 rubles
    1901 ........................... 51,000,000
    1902 ...........................; 38,000,000

The decline must be largely due to the decreased
demand for military and railway supplies, for it is
seen that the falling-off has been most conspicuous
in iron and steel wares and machinery.[4] At the
same time there was little or no import trade from
the Russian possessions in the East into Russia,
for the native products sent out from the former
never passed beyond Eastern Siberia. It would be

[1] According to the "Past and Present of the Siberian Railway," compiled in 1903 by the government committee in charge
of the railway, as quoted in the *Dōbun-kwai Hōkoku*, No. 51,
pp. 58–60.

[2] M. Witte's report of September, 1901, quoted in the *Kokumin* for October 1, 1904.

[3] Consul Miller at Niu-chwang, in the U. S. daily *Consular
Reports*, February 15, 1904 (No. 1877), p. 8.

[4] The *Tsūshō Isan*, November 25, 1903, pp. 16–18.

interesting if we could find out how much of these Russian exports went to Manchuria. The figures for the Pacific ports are given as follows :[1] —

| | |
|---|---|
| 1900 ............................ | 51,157,000 rubles |
| 1901 ............................ | 49,827,000 |
| 1902 ............................ | 37,704,000 |

If these figures are reliable, the difference between them and those given above, namely : —

| | |
|---|---|
| 1900 .................... | less than 5,000,000 rubles |
| 1901 .................... | more than 1,000,000 |
| 1902 .................... | less than 300,000 |

might be considered an approximate amount of the export trade from Russia to Manchuria (and Mongolia, which imports very little from Russia),' for, of the Pacific ports, no other port but Vladivostok reëxports Russian goods into Manchuria, which reëxportation seems to be slight enough to be ignored. The approximate correctness of the figures is further seen from the fact that of the total 8,193,000 rubles of the Manchurian trade at Blagovestchensk, Habarovsk, and the South Ussuri region — the three main points of transit trade with Manchuria — only one half showed exports to Manchuria, and again, of this one half, only a portion consisted of reëxported Russian goods. The South Ussuri district, for instance, sent only 130,-800 and 206,000 rubles' worth of Russian and foreign goods to Manchuria, out of the total export trade of 799,500 and 2,221,300 rubles, respectively, in 1898 and 1899.[2] On the other hand, before the

[1] The U. S. daily *Consular Reports*, July 30, 1903.

[2] See the *Shiberiya oyobi Manshū* ("Siberia and Manchuria")

opening of the Manchurian Railway (which took place in February, 1903), the *direct* trade between Russia and the interior of Manchuria must have been so slight as not to materially affect the sumtotal of the Russian-Manchurian trade.

This remarkably unfavorable trade between Manchuria and Russia was probably due to a decreased demand for military supplies since 1900 (for Russia has little to export from Manchuria, and Chinese teas have largely gone through Kiakhta or by the Amur, rather than by the Manchurian Railway), and also to the difficulty of further reducing the freight rates on the railway,[1] and of competing successfully with the American and Japanese traders in certain articles for importation.[2] In spite of all the effort

Tokio, 1904, compiled by T. Kawakami, special agent of the Foreign Office of Japan, who was sent to Siberia and Northern Manchuria to investigate economic and military conditions there, pp. 94, 119–121, 124, 138.

[1] For the relative advantages of the Manchurian Railway and the Amur River, see the U. S. daily *Consular Reports*, August 5 and October 5, 1903, and January 19, 1904.

[2] The Russia-China trade began more than 250 years ago. Before 1860, it was carried wholly on land, and its balance was nearly even. Since 1860, when sea trade from Odessa was opened, the progress of this trade has been slower than the general foreign trade of China, and its balance has been heavily against Russia (6,702,000 against 45,945,000 rubles in 1900). More than half of the Russian imports into China consists of cotton fabrics, and over 80 per cent. of the exports from China to Russia are teas. Russia's share in the entire foreign trade of China has also fallen from 4.6 per cent. in 1899 to 4.4 per cent. in 1900, 2.6 per cent. in 1901, and 2.3 per cent. in 1902, as compared with the growing share of the trade by Japan amounting to 14.2 per cent., 15.9 per cent., 15.7 per cent., and 18.4 per cent.,

made by the late Finance Minister, M. Witte, Russia is not yet primarily a manufacturing country, her exportation of manufactured goods forming in fact only 2.5 per cent. of her entire export trade, and at best remaining stationary during the three years 1900–2, as will be seen below: —

| | 1900 Rubles | 1901 Rubles | 1902 Rubles |
|---|---|---|---|
| Total exports from Russia... | 688,435,000 | 729,815,000 | 825,277,000 |
| Exports of manufacturers ... | 19,553,000 | 21,039,000 | 19,263,000 [1] |

Russia's commercial failure in Manchuria in the past would, however, in no way justify the inference that the future will be as disappointing. All competent observers seem to agree that the undeveloped resources of the 364,000 square miles of Manchuria are enormous.[2] Its unknown mineral wealth, its thousands of square miles of land now

in those respective years. Of the Russian share of 2.6 per cent. in 1901, Russian Manchuria occupied only 0.6 per cent. See the *Tsūshō Isan*, July 8, 1903, pp. 1–4; T. Yoshida's *Shina Bōyeki Jijō* (Trade Conditions in China), Tokio, 1902, pp. 128–129, etc. For the gold values of the figures up to 1903, see the British *D. and C. Reports*, annual series, No. 3280.

[1] From Russian official figures quoted in the *Tsūshō Isan*, November 25, 1903.

[2] The reader is recommended to the reports of the United States Consul Miller at Niu-chwang, particularly those which appeared in the daily *Consular Reports* for January 21 and 24, and February 5, 1904 (Nos. 1856, 1858, and 1869). Reference should also be made to the ex-British Consul at Niu-chwang, Alexander Hosie's *Manchuria*, London, 1901 (new edition, New York, 1904).

The resources of Eastern Manchuria are well described in the *Tsūshō Isan*, October 13, 1903, and those of Northern Manchuria in the *Shiberiya oyobi Manshū*, Tokio, 1904, compiled by the Foreign Office of Japan, pp. 427–485.

under the bean and millet cultivation, but beginning to yield to the wheat culture and producing
wheat at a market price of not more than forty
cents per bushel, and its extensive lumber districts,
as well as its millions of cheap and most reliable
Chinese laborers,[1] would before long enable the
Russians successfully to convert Manchuria into
one of the richest parts of China and one of the
richest countries in the world. A success of such
magnitude must, however, largely depend upon a
systematically protective and exclusive policy on
the part of Russia, or, in other words, upon the
completeness with which Russia transfers the bulk
of the Manchurian trade from the treaty port of
Niu-chwang, and, so far as the Russian import
from China is concerned, even from the once important Russian port of Vladivostok, to the commercial terminus of the Manchurian Railway —
Dalny. Particularly in order to capture the import
trade into Manchuria of cotton goods and kerosene
oil, in the face of the great advantages enjoyed by
American and Japanese competitors, Russia must
at all costs make Dalny overshadow Niu-chwang,

[1] The present population of Manchuria is differently estimated between the limits of 6.5 and 15 millions. Probably there
are more than 10 millions. Immigration was said to have been
progressing rapidly under the Chinese rule.

It is noteworthy that Siberia, with a larger area than Manchuria, contains only about 8,000,000 inhabitants. The productive capacity of the Manchurian population must be measured, however, not only by their larger numbers, but also by
their far superior economic training.

so as to bring the trade under her complete control. Nothing but a highly artificial system could
accomplish such wonders, for, under normal conditions, teas for Russia would go by the less costly
routes through Kiakhta, or up the Amur, or by
sea to Odessa; the native products of Manchuria
for exportation to Japan would be sent to Niu-
chwang by the nearest, cheapest, and most natural
channel, the Liao River, and, when the latter freezes
between the end of November and March, by the
Shan-hai-kwan Railway ; and, finally, the smaller
cost of production and lower rates of freight of the
American and Japanese cotton fabrics would completely outdistance the Russian. Let us observe
with what artificial measures the Russians have been
meeting this situation. With a view to diverting
the tea trade from Vladivostok to Dalny, Russia
imposed an import duty of 3 rubles per pood from
August, 1902, and increased it in May, 1903, to
25.50 rubles,[1] which with other measures dealt a
crushing blow to the prosperity of Vladivostok.[2]
This must at least have stifled the transportation
of tea up the Amur, without, perhaps, affecting
the inroad of teas through the old Kiakhta and by

[1] The *Tsūshō Isan* for June 23, 1903, pp. 34–35. Pood =
36.112 lbs.; ruble = 51.5 cents.

[2] Under this and other differential measures the commercial
importance of Vladivostok is said to be fast passing away. Local
merchants made a strong plea of their case before M. Witte
when he traveled in the East in 1902, but on his return he reported to the Czar that the interests of the Empire demanded a
large sacrifice at Vladivostok for the sake of Dalny.

sea.[1] As regards the export trade at Niu-chwang, the Russians took advantage of the important fact that the Shan-hai-kwan Railway did not penetrate sufficiently north to reach some producing centres of Western Manchuria, while the waters of the Liao were navigable only 200 miles from the mouth, and were, together with the harbor itself, ice-bound from November till March. Dalny was nearly ice-free, and the Manchurian Railway was available through all seasons. The only competitors of the railroad would seem to be the small bean-carrying junks plying down the Liao, which were both owned and loaded by the same Chinese merchants. This competition the Russians met by greatly reduced freight rates of the railway, which made it possible for

---

[1] The effect of the new duties levied on tea at other places than Dalny is seen in the following comparative table. The figures for 1902 are taken from the U. S. *Monthly Summary* for January, 1904, p. 2420, and those for 1903 have been converted from data given in the British *D. and C. Reports*, Annual Series No. 3280.

In 1902, the Russian Empire took 882,893 out of the 1,519,211 *piculs* of tea exported from China, while in 1903 the corresponding amounts were 1,010,580 out of 1,677,530. The distribution of the imported teas to the Russian Empire, according to the routes, was as follows: —

| | 1902 | 1903 |
|---|---|---|
| *Via* Odessa and Batum | 206,699 *piculs* | 200,391 *piculs* |
| *Via* Kiakhta | 403,648 | 244,668 |
| To Russian Manchuria | 272,546 | 191,679 |
| To Port Arthur and Dalny | | 373,842 |

We presume that most of the teas exported to Russian Manchuria went through Niu-chwang. The table plainly shows an increased importation at Dalny at the expense of all other points. It is not known how much of the 373,842 *piculs* imported at Dalny and Port Arthur was reshipped to other ports not mentioned here. (*Picul* = $133\frac{1}{3}$ lbs. av.)

every 100 poods of Manchurian grain and beans
to be carried 600 miles between Harbin and Dalny
for about fifty-seven cents gold, or $10 per ton.[1]
From Dalny, heavily subsidized Russian boats transported Manchurian exports to Japan at a freight rate
which, in conjunction with railway rates, amounted
to the saving by the shipper of 4.50 *yen* per ton, as
compared with the railway-rates *plus* the freight-
rates of non-Russian vessels.[2] When the flour industry of the Russian towns in Manchuria is developed, Russian steamers may be seen carrying flour
from Dalny, not only to Japan, but to Chinese and
Eastern Siberian ports.  As for the import trade of
Manchuria, the Russians, who have ousted American
importers of kerosene oil at Vladivostok, seem to
be now by energetic methods slowly driving away
the same rivals from Chemulpo and from Dalny.[3]

[1] See the *Tsūshō Isan*, April 18 and August 3, 1903, and the
U. S. daily *Consular Reports*, January 21, 1904 (No. 1856).
Reduction apparently had not reached its minimum point. It
was unknown whether Dalny handled much of the Manchurian
export trade.

[2] The *Kokumin*, March 7, 1903. The ex-Japanese Consul at
Niu-chwang, Mr. K. Tanabe, doubts that Dalny will completely
displace Niu-chwang as an exporting centre. The latter is geographically the nature outlet for the grain from the Liao Valley,
and, in winter, the handling of this product is apt to be done
more at Mukden than at Dalny, the latter becoming in that case
a mere port of transit. Moreover, mercantile customs differ so
much at Niu-chwang and Dalny that it is not possible that the
conservative Chinese merchants should readily transfer their
business from the one place to the other. See Tanabe's conversation in the *Tōyō Keizai Zasshi* ("Oriental Economist"), No.
244 (September 25, 1902), p. 16.

[3] The central distributing station at Vladivostok has a capa-

Vastly more important as articles for importation
than kerosene oil are cotton yarn and textiles, which
are annually supplied from abroad to the value of
over 12,000,000 *taels*. By far the greater part of
sheetings, drills, and jeans comes from America.
The Russians were not unable to produce cotton
fabrics almost as good as the American goods, but
the trans-Siberian freight was twice as expensive
as the Pacific transportation, and could not be expected to be further reduced without great difficulty.[1] It was not impossible to suppose that the
Russian Government might ultimately apply to
Manchuria the system of granting a premium and
an additional drawback on textiles made from imported cotton, which had been in successful operation in Persia. There was no question but that,
together with the development of Manchuria under
Russian control, foreigners would lose most of their
import trade in lumber, butter, and flour, and here
again the Russian success must depend on the
exclusiveness of their policy.[2] Mr. H. B. Miller,

city of 600,000 poods, and the one to be built at Dalny will hold
1,500,000 poods, to which a special tank steamer will bring oil
from Batum. — The *Tsūshō Isan*, May 3, 1903. Americans
tried to build warehouses at Dalny, but were opposed by Russians. The importation of American kerosenes at Niu-chwang
decreased from 3,172,000 gallons ($410,500) in 1901 to 603,000
gallons ($77,000) in 1902, and the decrease was in no small
measure due to the Russian competition at Dalny.

[1] The *Tsūshō Isan*, October 23, 1903, pp. 1–21; the U. S.
daily *Consular Reports*, May 7, July 16, and August 28, 1903,
and February 23, 1904.

[2] See Mr. Miller's reports in the U. S. daily *Consular Reports*

the United States Consul at Niu-chwang, seems
to have made a delicate reference to this point
when he said, in his report dated December 5,
1903 : " The United States trade in Manchuria
with the Chinese amounted to several millions of
dollars per year, and was almost entirely imports.
It hâd grown very fast, and would have had an
extended and most substantial increase without the
Russian development, for the country was being
improved and extensively developed with a continual immigration from other provinces in China,
before the railway construction began." [1] Much has
been said regarding the oft-reiterated wish of Russia
to keep Dalny as a free port, but it is well known
that it has recently been placed under a protective

for January 21 and 24, and February 5 and 6, 1904 (Nos. 1856
1858, 1859, and 1870).

Mr. James J. Hill, in a recent speech at Minneapolis, said
that his great system of transportation, by taking advantage of
all conditions, and by carrying full loads both ways, had been
able to make a freight rate of forty cents a hundred pounds of
flour to the Orient, or one mill per ton-mile. According to him,
the effect of the growing exportation of wheat from the Pacific
coast to the East seems to have caused an advance in its price
at Minneapolis of five to seven cents per bushel. In view of these
facts, the possible exclusion of American flour from Manchuria
would not be without serious effects, especially if we consider
Mr. Hill's opinion that the success of Mr. Chamberlain's financial scheme would result in enabling Manitoba to supply all the
wheat needed in Great Britain, thus leaving in the United States
a large surplus of grain, for which other markets would have to
be developed. See the American *Review of Reviews* for February, 1904.

[1] The U. S. daily *Consular Reports*, February 15, 1904 (No.
877), p. 11.

tariff.[1] We are not in possession of the details of this tariff, but its general significance can hardly be mistaken when we see how the Russians have been reducing freight rates to the utmost, subsidizing their own steamers, and pooling together their great banking and railway facilities, all for the purpose, on the one hand, of developing Russian industries in Manchuria, and on the other, of monopolizing the bulk of its trade.

Not only in trade, but in colonization also, the Russians have been building up new cities and developing old ones under their exclusive policy with an unheard-of rapidity. Dalny is a good example of the former class. Still more conspicuous is the city of Harbin, the so-called Moscow of Asia, the geographical and commercial centre and headquarters of the railway work in Manchuria, which is said to have consisted of a single Chinese house in 1898,[2] but now contains 50,000 people.[3] Well might Count Cassini, as he did, refer, not only to the colonization, but to the general civilizing influence of the Russians in Manchuria in the following language : [4] " Through the pacific channels of diplomacy my government acquired privileges which, accepted in good faith, have been exer-

[1] The U. S. daily *Consular Reports*, January 19, 1904 (No. 1854). Also see *ibid.*, April 4, 1903.

[2] British Consul Hosie's report, the *British Parliamentary Papers* ("Blue Books"), *China, No. 1 (1900)*, p. 154.

[3] See U. S. daily *Consular Reports*, February 15, 1904 (No. 1877), and the *Tsūshō Isan*, October 8, 1903, pp. 42–43.

[4] The *North American Review* for May, 1904, pp. 683–684.

cised in a spirit of true modern progressiveness, until now the flower of enlightened civilization blooms throughout a land that a few years ago was a wild, and in many parts a desolate, seemingly unproductive waste. Before the signing of the treaty which I had the honor to negotiate in behalf of my Sovereign, giving to Russia railroad and other concessions in Manchuria, no white man could have ventured into that province without danger to his life. . . . Upon the basis of the rights to commercial exploitation thus peaceably obtained, Russia built a railway into and through Manchuria. She built bridges, roads, and canals. She has built cities whose rapid construction and wonderful strides in population and industry have no parallel, certainly in Europe and Asia, perhaps even in America. Harbin and Dalny are monuments to Russian progressiveness and civilization. These great undertakings, wonderful even in a day of marvelous human accomplishment, have cost Russia more than 300,000,000 dollars." Without stopping either to dispute the historical accuracy of Count Cassini's statement or to deny the wonderful work the Russians have accomplished in Manchurian cities, it seems pertinent to call our attention to the exclusive side of the Russian enterprise in this vast territory. Harbin is one of the so-called "depots," over eighty in number, which are found along the whole length of the Manchurian Railway, each one of which extends over several square miles, within which none but the Russians and Chinese have the right of permanent settlement.[1] Russia would not consent to the opening of Harbin (and, presumably, all other cities within the " depots " of the Manchurian Railway) to foreign trade. Even outside of these cities, the Russian Government appeared to be opposed to the opening of new ports, and when it was no longer politic to continue the opposition, Russia informed other Powers in 1903 that she had no intention of objecting to the opening of new treaty ports " without foreign settlements " in Manchuria.[2]

The meaning of all these protective and exclusive measures becomes plain, when it is seen that the complete control of the economic resources of Manchuria would give Russia, not only sufficient

---

[1] For the laborious process of obtaining permits to carry on business only for short terms in these great sites for future cities, see the *Tsūshō Isan*, September 18 (pp. 40–41) and November 23 (pp. 39–40), 1903.

At Dalny, however, Russia has welcomed the coöperation of all nationalities in its development, and has been rather disappointed at their comparative indifference. See Mr. F. Nakasawa's conversation in the *Tōyō Keizai Zasshi* (" Oriental Economist"), No. 262 (March 15, 1903), p. 13. The reasons for this modification at Dalny of the customary Russian policy are plain, for the port must be developed as rapidly as possible before the Russians can absolutely control its trade. Thus the importance of Dalny as a trading port brings to conspicuous prominence the universal contradiction of the Russian commercial policy in East Asia. Russia would exclude other trading nations from her possessions in order to control the trade, but is at the same time unable to develop it without either the coöperation of other people or some unnatural devices.

[2] See pp. 313 ff., below.

means to support Eastern Siberia, but also a great
command over the trade of China and Japan. The
latter country Russia might be able to reduce to dire
distress, when necessary, by closing the supplies
coming from Manchuria, upon which Japan will have
to depend every year more closely than before.[1] The
success of these great designs on the part of Russia
would depend upon how completely protective and
exclusive her Manchurian policy can be made.

Coming from Manchuria to Korea, we find the
economic position of the Russians in a totally different situation, for either their vested or even their
potential interests in the Peninsula were slight, excepting, perhaps, their already acquired timber concessions [2] on the northern frontier and the Kaiserling whale fishery on the northeastern coast. [3] It has

[1] On March 27, 1904, Russia declared that Niu-chwang was
under her martial law. This eventuality had been fully expected
by Japan. The gravity of the situation, however, may be understood, when we remember that the Russian law of neutrality considers food as among contraband goods, so that the supply of
millet, beans, and bean-cakes from Manchuria to Japan was
henceforth completely closed, until the Russians evacuated Niu-
chwang in July.

[2] These concessions were acquired by the Russians in 1896
when the Korean King was still living in the Russian Legation in
Seul. About May, 1903, after more than seven years' inactivity,
the Russians began to cut timber on a large scale along the Yalu
River, and subsequently made extensive improvements at Yon-
gampu at the mouth of the river. The political features of this
event do not concern us here. See pp. 263, 289 ff., 318 ff., below.

[3] Kaiserling is a successor to the two other Russians who, one
after the other, had been engaged in the whale fishery on the
Japan Sea for a long period of time. It was Kaiserling, however,
who extended the work, made an agreement with the Korean

been pointed out, however, that the fact that Dalny was not altogether ice-free made Russia covet Chemulpo or some other trade port on the western coast of Korea.[1] However that may be, it is safe to say that Russia's interests in Korea are slightly economic, but almost wholly strategic and political.

Let us sum up our discussion at this point, and compare the economic interests of Russia and Japan in Manchuria and Korea. In Manchuria, both Powers seek trade and colonization, with the important difference that Japan's interests are actually great and potentially greater, while those of Russia are both actually and potentially preponderant. A difference of greater moment lies, however, in the fact that, so far as her trade and industry are concerned, Japan's interests call for an equal opportunity there for all industrial nations, while Russia's interests may be maintained and developed only by a highly exclusive policy. In Korea, its opening for the trade, settlement, and enterprise of the Japanese is not only the most natural method of strengthening Korea herself, but also a primary condition for the life and growth of Japan. Russia's

Government, and was turning the business into an apparently successful enterprise. In 1901, his two vessels caught about eighty whales, which number was in 1902 increased to 300. — The *Tsūshō Isan*, September 28, 1903, p. 34.

[1] Mr. J. Sloat Fassett's article in the American *Review of Reviews*, for February, 1904, p. 174.

In the winter of 1902–3, ice at Dalny was six inches thick. — Mr. F. Nakasawa in the *Tōyō Keizai Zasshi* ("Oriental Economist"), No. 262 (March 15, 1903), p. 13.

economic interests there, on the other hand, may be
measured by the number of her resident subjects and
the extent of their enterprise, which are, outside of
Yongampo, next to nothing. Her interests, being,
as we shall soon see, mainly strategic and political,
demand here also a policy directly opposed to the
open door. If we now consider Manchuria and
Korea together, it may be said that Russia's economic interests are, even in Manchuria, rather for
her glory as a great, expanding empire than for any
imperative need of trade and emigration in that
particular part of her Asiatic dominion, while similar interests of Japan, primarily in Korea and secon-
darily in Manchuria, are vital, as they are essential
for her own life and development as a nation. The
case for Russia can, perhaps, never be understood
until her *political* issues are examined.

Politically, also, the interests of the two Powers
are found to be directly opposed to one another.
It has been rightly said that Manchuria is the keynote of the Eastern policy of Russia. Besides its
immense wealth still unexploited, Manchuria possesses the great Port Arthur, which is the only
nearly ice-free naval outlet for Russia in her vast
dominion in Asia, while the 1500 miles of the
Manchurian Railway, together with the Great Siberian Railway, connect this important naval station
with the army bases in Siberia and European Russia,
so that Manchuria alone would seem to be politically more valuable for Russia than the rest of her
Asiatic territories. Without Manchuria, Russia

would be left inclosed in the ice-bound Siberia, with no naval or commercial outlet during nearly five months of each year. With Manchuria, Russia's traditional policy, which has repeatedly failed since Peter the Great on the Baltic Sea and other European waters, as also on the Persian Gulf, — the policy of becoming the dominant naval power of the world, — would at last begin to be realized. The very importance of Manchuria for Russia, however, constitutes a serious menace to Japan and to the general peace of the Far East. In the first place, the Russian control of Port Arthur gives her a large measure of control over the water approaches to Peking, while the Mongolian Railway now reported to be in contemplation would bring Russian land forces directly upon the capital of the Chinese Empire. The very integrity of China is threatened, and a more serious disturbance of the peace of the world could hardly be imagined than the general partition and internal outbreaks in China which would follow the fall of Peking under the pressure of Russia from Manchuria and Mongolia. Not less grave is the fact that Manchuria is geographically and historically connected with the Peninsula of Korea,[1] which makes Russia's occupation of Korea a necessary adjunct of her possession of Manchuria. Geographically considered, there exists no abrupt change from the eastern part of Manchuria to the

[1] It is well known that at several times in history kingdoms have been built which extended over both sides of the present boundaries between Korea and Manchuria.

northern half of Korea,[1] which fact goes far to explain the Russian solicitude to obtain railway and other concessions between the frontier and Seul. Even more serious conditions exist on the southern coast of Korea, which contains the magnificent harbor of Masampo, which constitutes the Gibraltar between the Russian fleets at the ice-bound and remote Vladivostok and the incommodious and not altogether ice-free Port Arthur, with no effective means of connecting them. By controlling this coast, Russia would not merely possess a truly ice-free, and the best naval port to be found in East Asia,[2] but also at last feel secure in Manchuria and

[1] It is noticeable that the Russian diplomatic historian already referred to gives as a reason for the desirability of placing Korea under Russian protection the need of safe-guarding the frontiers of Russian territories adjacent to Korea. — The *Dōbun-kwai Hōkoku*, No. 49, p. 8.

[2] The Bay of Masampo, generally so-called, which lies between the Island of Koji and the Korean coast, is said to be deep and broad enough to hold the largest fleet, sheltered from winds from all directions. Several islands with sufficiently wide passages between them form a splendid gate to the bay, while the western extremity of the latter may be walked across, when the tide is low, from the Koji to the coast.

As to the Masampo reach or inlet, specifically, which is the head of the gulf, "its entrance, five cables wide, named the Gate, is perfectly free from dangers, and is available for all classes of vessels. On either side are treeless hills, bare in winter, but in summer covered with grass; these hills, near the entrance, slope steeply to the water's edge. The general depth over the reach is seven fathoms, but it shallows gradually as the town of Masampo is neared, until at one mile from the town the depth is four fathoms. . . . Anchorage may be had anywhere in Masampo reach, according to draught; a depth of three fathoms being found at half a mile from the town, and six to seven fathoms

complete her Far Eastern design of absorbing Korea
and China and pressing down toward India.  If, on
the contrary, another Power should control Masampo, it would be able to watch the movement of the
Russian fleets in their attempts to unite with one another, and also seriously impede the greatest hopes
of Russia's Eastern expansion.  From Japan's standpoint, the Russian occupation of this section of
Korea would not only possibly close Korea against
her trade and enterprise, but also threaten her own
integrity.  Only fifty miles away lie the Japanese
islands of Tsushima, which Russia has always cov-
eted, and which would have been hers had it not
been for the shrewd diplomacy of the late Count
Katsu.[1]  From Tsushima the mainland of Japan is
visible on the eastern horizon, so that the presence
of Russia at Masampo would arouse in the heart of
Japan the most profound feeling of unrest.  Russia must have Masampo, and Japan must not let her
have it.

In concluding our discussion of the vital issues,

at two miles below it." — The *Sailing Directions for Japan,
Korea, and Adjacent Seas*, published by the British Admiralty,
London, 1904, pp. 114–115.  Masampo is the best but not the
only good naval harbor on the southern coast of Korea.

[1] In 1861, when some Russian marines landed here and took
virtual possession of the islands, Awa Katsu, who was then one
of the officers appointed by the Yedo government to study the
possibility of organizing military forces after the Western model,
succeeded in setting the British Minister against the Russian
Minister about the Tsushima affair.  Russia was obliged to abandon the islands.  See the *Katsu Kaishū* (a life of Katsu), Tokio,
1899, iii. pp. 57–59.

both economical and political, which are at stake, it would seem that Manchuria is for Japan a great market as well as an increasingly important supply region of raw and food products and a field for emigration, while for Russia it is the keynote of her Eastern policy, and economically the most promising of all her Asiatic possessions. On the other hand, Korea is essential for Russia for the completion of her Manchurian policy,[1] and for strengthening enormously her general position in the East. For Japan, Korea is nothing short of one half of her vitality. By the opening or closing, strength or weakness, independence or fall, of Korea, would Japan's fate as a nation be decided. On the contrary, Russia, with Manchuria and ultimately Korea in her hands, would be able, on the one hand, to build up under her exclusive policy a naval and commercial influence strong enough to enable her to dominate the East, and, on the other, to cripple forever Japan's ambition as a nation, slowly drive her to starvation and decay, and even politically annex her. From Japan's point of view, Korea and China must be left open freely to the economic enterprise of herself and others alike, and, in order to effect that end, they must remain independent and become stronger by their internal development and reform.[2] Russia's interests are intelligible, as

[1] It is interesting to hear that Russian school text-books enumerate Korea and Manchuria among the Russian spheres of influence. — A letter from Tōsuisei, dated St. Petersburg, February 13, 1900, in the *Kokumin*, April 1, 1900.

[2] It is remarkable how little the spirit of Japan's policy, which

are Japan's, but unfortunately their desires are antagonistic to each other, so that a conflict between an open and an exclusive policy is rendered inevitable. The series of events during the past decades, particularly since 1895, which we shall narrate in this volume, has only served to bring this conflict into a sharp clash in arms.

. . . . . . . . .

In closing, it may not be entirely out of place to attempt a speculation upon the significance of the conflict, not to the belligerents, but to the world at large. From the latter's point of view, the contest may fairly be regarded as a dramatic struggle between two civilizations, old and new, Russia representing the old civilization and Japan the new.

the writer has attempted to express in this sentence, is understood among the people here. A vast majority of people, not excluding recognized writers and speakers on the East, seem to ascribe to Japan certain territorial designs, particularly in Korea. It is not remembered that Japan was the first country to recognize the independence of Korea, the cause of which also cost Japan a war with China. The present war with Russia is waged largely on the same issue, for it is to Japan's vital interest to keep Korea independent. From this it hardly follows that Japan should occupy Korea in order not to allow her to fall into the hands of another Power. If Korea is really unable to stand on her feet, the solution of the difficulty does not, in Japan's view, consist in possessing her, but in making her independence real by developing her resources and reorganizing and strengthening her national institutions. It is in this work that Japan's assistance was offered and accepted. It would be as difficult for any impartial student not to see the need of such assistance as to confuse it with annexation. It would, however, be entirely legitimate to regard the task as extremely difficult and dangerously prone to abuse. Further, see pp. 366 ff., below.

Two dominant features, among others, seem to characterize the opposition of the contending nations: namely, first, that Russia's economics are essentially agricultural, while those of Japan are largely and increasingly industrial; and, secondly, that Japan's strength lies more on sea than on land, while Russia represents an enormous contiguous expansion on land. It is evident that the wealth of a nation and its earning capacity cannot grow fast under a trade system under which it imports many and exports few manufactures.[1] The commercial prosperity of Russia depended formerly upon its nearness, first to the trade route with the Levant,

[1] Russian exports for 1900–2 are classified as follows (1000 rubles as unit): —

| Food-stuffs | Raw material | Animals | Manufactures | Total |
|---|---|---|---|---|
| 1900....381,174 | 269,806 | 17,902 | 19,553 | 688,435 |
| 1901....430,955 | 256,697 | 20,224 | 21,939 | 729,815 |
| 1902....526,189 | 258,267 | 21,558 | 19,263 | 825,277 |

It is seen that the exportation of food-stuffs was the largest in value and increasing, while that of manufactured articles was the smallest (2.5 per cent.) and, to say the least, stationary. Imports were as follows: —

| Food-stuffs | Raw material | Animals | Manufactures | Total |
|---|---|---|---|---|
| 1900....79,844 | 307,402 | 1,136 | 183,682 | 572,064 |
| 1901....84,349 | 288,107 | 1,495 | 158,993 | 532,944 |
| 1902....81,409 | 295,483 | 1,403 | 148,800 | 527,095 |

The importation of manufactures decreased, but also that of raw material did not increase, while, as shown above, the exportation of manufactures was slight and stationary. Figures have been taken from the *Tsūshō Isan* for November 25, 1903, which drew them from Russian official sources.

It is interesting to note the unfavorable conditions of the foreign trade of Russia's ally, France, in U. S. Consul Atwell's report in the daily *Consular Reports* for February 24, 1904 (No. 1884), who quotes from Georges Blondel.

and then to the free cities of Germany, but with
the fall of Constantinople and the decline of the
Hansa towns the business activity of Southern and
Baltic Russia has in turn passed away. Then, from
the time of Ivan the Terrible, she unified her European territory, and expanded eastward on land,
until she had embraced within her dominion much
of Central and all of Northern Asia. For such an
expansion Russia seems to have been particularly
fitted, for her primitive economic organization suf-
fers little from external disturbances, while the au-
tocratic form of her government enables her to
maintain and execute her traditional policy of expansion. But the real importance of her expansion
appears to be more territorial than commercial, for
the days of the land trade with the Orient are numbered. Even the great Siberian Railway would not
successfully divert the Eastern trade landward.[1] If
Russia would be prosperous, she must control the
Eastern sea by occupying northeast China and
Korea. Here she comes in conflict with Japan, the
champion in the East of the rising civilization.
The economic centre of the world has been fast
passing to America, where cotton, wheat, coal, and
iron abound, the people excel in energy and intelli-
gence, and the government is servant to the welfare
and progress of the people. Japan has joined the
circle of this civilization, ever since the influence
of the youthful nation of America was extended

[1] See the Supplementary Note to this chapter on pages 61–
64.

to her through Commodore Perry [1] and Townsend Harris, and the spirit of national progress through industry and education was eagerly adopted by her. To-day, Japan stands within the range of the interests of the British and American sea-power over the Pacific, Atlantic, and Indian oceans, while Russia, on the other hand, represents a vast expansion on land.

The historical bearing of the effects of the old civilization to the world may, perhaps, be best characterized by the one word — *unnatural*. Observe, first, the effect of the policy of land aggression on the internal affairs of Russia. The policy is costly. Hence the great incongruity between the economics of the people, which are agricultural, and the finance of her government, which would be too expensive even for the most highly advanced industrial nation. Hence, also, it is, perhaps, that the richer and more powerful her government becomes, the poorer and more discontented her people seem to grow. Her administration must naturally be maintained by the suspicion of her people and the suppression of their freedom,[2] and the suspicion and suppression must

[1] Documents of that time clearly indicate that the discovery of gold in California and the westward expansion of the American nation, as well as the growing prospects of the China trade and the increasing application of steam in navigation, were the motives which prompted the United States Government to open negotiations with Japan in 1853.

[2] To-day there seem to be about 84,500 public schools in Russia, of which 40,000 are under the jurisdiction of the Ministry of Education [compared with 30,157 public and private schools in Japan in 1902]. Toward the maintenance of the 40,000 schools,

become more exhaustive as the disparity widens between rulers and ruled.[1] Under these circumstances, a constitutional régime would not be possible, for a free expression of the popular will would be hardly compatible with a form of government which seeks to strengthen the state at the expense of the nation. Again, consider the unnatural situation of an agricultural nation competing in the world's market with industrial, trading nations which command a higher and more effective economic organization. If Russia would sell her goods, her markets abroad must be created and maintained by artificial means:[2] protective and exclusive mea-

the ministry appropriates only about $2,000,000, or a little over one eighth of the annual cost. The teachers number 172,000 [in Japan, 126,703, in 1902], and pupils and students, 4,568,763 [in Japan in 1902, 5,469,419]. 7,250,000 children of school age are without any education [while in Japan, in 1902, the ratio of attendance to the number of children of school age was 95.80 per cent. for boys and 87.00 per cent. for girls, or, on the average, 91.57 per cent.]. See the U. S. daily *Consular Reports* for February 8 and March 4, 1902 (Nos. 1871 and 1892), [and the *Kwampō*, April 8, 1904].

[1] As an evidence for this striking state of things the reader is referred to Dr. E. J. Dillon's article in the American *Review of Reviews* for October, 1904, pp. 449–454. The whole subject should be more carefully studied than it seems to have been thus far.

[2] " The whole northern part of *Asia Minor*, according to the treaty between Russia and Turkey, is now placed under such conditions that Russian capitalists have the area open to them, to the exclusion of foreign enterprise. A situation analogous is found in *Persia*, where the entire northern portion is acknowledged to be under the exclusive economic influence of Russia." — Consul Greener at Vladivostok, in the U. S. daily *Consular Reports*, April 22, 1903 (No. 1627).

sures must be pushed to such an extent as to distance all foreign competition, the interests of the consumer must be disregarded,[1] and those of the growing industrial nations must be sacrificed,[2] all for the sake of artificially promoting the belated manufactures in Russia.[3] From this unnatural state of things would seem to follow the Russian policy of territorial occupation and commercial exclusion in the East, and also her free use of the old-time intrigue in diplomacy; for it is Russia's fortune that she would not be able to compete freely with the new, growing civilization, whose open arts she cannot employ to her advantage, but to whose advanced standard of international morals she must appear to conform. Her position forbids her to

[1] For example, the normal freight per ton from Russia to Eastern Siberia would be about twenty-one rubles, while that from Japan or Shanghai is three or four rubles. If Russian goods were sold to the artificial exclusion of articles exported from nearer countries, the consumer's burden would be greatly increased.

[2] Count Cassini, the present Russian Ambassador at Washington, wrote, in the *North American Review* for May, 1904: " . . . But let us suppose for argument's sake that Russia, triumphant in this war, finds herself dominant in Manchuria. Japan, her enemy, could look for no favors; she could not expect to find encouragement for the importation of her manufactures " (p. 688).

[3] Continuing, the Count stated: "But Manchuria would require many things that Russia could not supply, or supply at figures reasonable enough to create a market. In Russia, agriculture is, comparatively speaking, more important than manufacturing, and those goods which are made in my country are not such as Manchuria would need. Russia, too, would be obliged to use the railway with its high freight tariffs. . . . " — *Ibid.*

have recourse to an open policy and fair play, and yet she cannot afford to overtly uphold the opposite principles.[1] On the other hand, the new civilization, represented in the present contest by Japan, relies more largely upon the energy and resources of the individual person, whose rights it respects, and upon an upright treatment by the nations of one another.

What is the goal of the warfare of these two civilizations? It is, it may be said, the immensely rich and yet undeveloped North China, of which Manchuria is a part, and to which Korea is an appendix. Over this territory, the interests of Russia and Japan have come to a clear and sharp clash, those of the former demanding the subjection and closure of this great portion of the earth's surface, and those of the latter imperatively calling for its independence and progress.

Whoever wins, the issues are momentous. If Russia should win, not only Korea and Manchuria, but also Mongolia would be either annexed by Russia or placed under her protection, and Japan's progress would be checked and her life would begin to fail. Russia would assume a commanding position over all the Powers in the East, while the trading nations of the world would be either largely or com-

[1] One can seldom find a more outspoken confession of a diplomacy consisting of a series of deliberate falsehoods than the chapters on the Russian relations with China, Korea, and Japan, in a diplomatic history by a Russian writer, as translated in the *Dōbun-kwai Hōkoku*, Nos. 45, 46, 48, 49, and 50 (August, September, November, and December, 1903, and January, 1904).

pletely excluded from an important economic section of Asia. The Siberian railway system might at last be made to pay, and Russia's exclusive policy would enable her and her ally France to divide the profit of the Eastern trade with the more active industrial nations. The old civilization would enjoy an artificial revival, under the influence of which China and Korea would be exploited by the victors and, for the most part,[1] closed against reformatory influences from abroad. All these momentous results would be in the interest of an exclusive policy incorporating principles which are generally regarded as inimical to freedom and progress. If, on the contrary, Japan should win, the doubtful importance of the Siberian Railroad as a carrier of the Eastern trade would in the mean time be further overshadowed by the Panama Canal, and it would be compelled to perform its perhaps proper function of developing the vast resources of Siberia and Manchuria. The Oriental commerce would be equally free and open to all; the Empires of China and Korea would not only remain independent, but, under the influence of the new civilization, their enormous resources would be developed and their national institutions reformed, the immense advantages of which would be enjoyed by all the nations

[1] The Russian diplomatic historian to whom frequent reference has been made frankly says that the feebleness and internal disorder of China are welcome conditions for the expansion of Russian influence in the Far East, and that it would be the height of folly to displace the weak China with a colonial possession of a European power. — The *Dōbun-kwai Hōkoku*, No. 48, p. 36.

which are interested in the East.  There would naturally result a lasting peace in the East and the
general uplifting of one third of the human race.
Japan's growth and progress after the war would
be even more remarkable than in the past.  In short,
East Asia would be forcibly brought under the influence of the new civilization, the effect of which would
not be without a profound reaction upon Russia
herself.  Humanity at large, including the Russians,
would thereby be the gainer.  The difference in the
effects of the outcome of the war, according to who
is the victor, would be tremendous.  Which will
win, the old civilization or the new?  The world at
this moment stands at the parting of the ways.

## SUPPLEMENTARY NOTE

### ON THE SIBERIAN RAILWAY [1]

ACCORDING to an estimate made by a Russian expert of
the carrying capacity of the great Siberian railway system,[2] the Siberian section alone will carry at least 190
million poods, and the Manchurian section from 100 to
150 million poods, making a total of 300 to 350 million
poods, approximately.  It is contended, however, that,
while the present conditions of the inhabitants of Siberia
and Manchuria make it possible for the railway to carry
only raw and crudely manufactured goods, these are the
very articles whose cost would easily be raised by the
long distance over which they have to be carried by rail.
In Europe, it never pays to carry these articles for a

[1] See p. 55, note 1, above.
[2] The *Shiberiya oyobi Manshū*, pp. 221–223.

longer distance than 2000 miles. Nor would it in Siberia, unless abnormal reductions are made in freight rates, or unless commerce and manufacture are artificially fostered in Siberia and Manchuria. It is supposed, therefore, that it would always be unprofitable to carry bulky, cheap goods between Europe and the East on the Siberian Railway. China's exports to Russia consist of such costly goods as teas and silks, which may be profitably transported by rail, but thus far even teas have only begun to be so transported under more or less artificial measures in favor of the railway traffic at the expense of the routes through Kiakhta, up the Amur, and by sea to Odessa. As to Russian imports into China, cotton and woolen goods and metals would never be carried by rail under normal circumstances.[1] The benefit of the eight thousand versts of the railway from Moscow to Dalny may be safely said to be as slight to the carrying trade as it is great to the travelers and postal service between Europe and the East.

The statistics for 1899 and 1900 show that the bulk of the Russian trade with China was carried on land, but that the land trade was decreasing and sea trade increasing. See the following table (unit 1000 rubles):[2] —

|  |  | Export | Import | Total | Ratio |
|---|---|---|---|---|---|
| 1899 | Land | 7,522 | 30,007 | 37,520 | 74 % |
|  | Sea | 4 | 13,508 | 13,512 | 26 |
| 1900 | Land | 6,678 | 29,779 | 36,457 | 69 |
|  | Sea | 24 | 16,166 | 16,190 | 31 |

It should be noted, however, that the period covered by the table is not only too short, but also precedes the opening of the Manchurian Railroad to trade, which took place only in 1903. Nor should it be overlooked that the figures indicate the China trade of *Russia* alone.

[1] The *Shiberiya oyobi Manshū*, pp. 223–225, 490–495.
[2] The *Tsūshō Isan*, July 8, 1903, p. 4.

Regarding the *European* trade with China in general, M. Sorokin, Assistant Director of Customs at Niu-chwang, is reported to have remarked that the freight per pood from Europe to the East was five rubles on land and 1.50 on sea.[1] Certain articles, such as glassware, tobacco, and the like, seem to be carried from Russia to China at two rubles by rail and one ruble by ships.[2] The sea route consumes nearly two months, but, for bulky merchandise, it would be impossible for the railway to compete with it.

It is interesting, in this connection, to remember that, from *America*, the freight between San Francisco and the Eastern ports has been reduced repeatedly during the last year, owing to the competition among the shipping companies, so that the charge for flour does not seem to be more than one mill per ton-mile, or forty cents a hundred pounds for 8000 miles.

During 1901, according to the latest statistics available, the deficit of the Ussuri branch of the Siberian Railway is said to have amounted to $435,162, and that of the entire railway to $11,330,000.[3]

.    .    .    .    .    .    .    .    .    .    .

In this connection, it is interesting to note that this view is further confirmed by no less authority than Count Cassini, the present Russian Minister at Washington, who, in his statement given on April 9, and published in the *North American Review* for May, 1904, said:

". . . Consider Russia's position commercially toward Manchuria with that of the United States. In this country [the United States] are made not only the very materials that would find a sale among the people of the

[1] The New York *Evening Post*, January 20, 1903.

[2] The U. S. daily *Consular Reports*, April 22, 1903 (No. 1627).

[3] The U. S. daily *Consular Reports*, February 24, 1904 (No. 1884).

province, but with American goods shipped by an all-water route, the cost of transportation would be much lower than the cost of carrying on the all-land routes to which Russia would be confined.  Should Russia ship by water to Manchuria from Odessa, the distance would still be too great to make competition with the United States successful.  From Moscow to Port Arthur the distance by rail is 5000 miles.  It is therefore easy to realize the privileged position of the United States in competing over an all-water route from the Pacific coast, with Russia over an all-rail route." [1]

[1] The *North American Review*, May, 1904, p. 688.

# CHAPTER I

## RETROCESSION OF THE LIAO-TUNG PENINSULA

THE way in which the momentous *issues* already discussed in the introductory chapter have been at work and have steadily culminated in the present conflict is with unusual clearness and in the most instructive manner illustrated by the *historic events* which led up to the outbreak of the war. The study of these events also appears essential for an intelligent understanding of the situation, for, in this crisis, as in many another in history, the contestants do not seem to be always conscious of even the more important issues at stake, while the events, in their main outlines, are patent to every one. The former may be found only by an analysis of facts, some of which are obscure, but the latter are narrated dramatically, from time to time as they occur or are published, in the press and in the diplomatic correspondence, so that it is little wonder that the events are often taken for the causes, even the significance, of the supreme fact to which they seem to point. The student should investigate the issues if he would know the meaning of the war, but, if he wishes to see something of the conscious attitude which the belligerents take toward the situation, perhaps no more profitable way can be found than in a study of the events through which the issues have been writing history.

The conflict of Russia and Japan was foreshadowed already in the middle of the past century, when the former began to claim some of the Kurile Islands and the whole of Sakhalien, upon parts of which Japan had long exercised vague sovereign rights.[1] Presently, in 1858, Muravieff " Amurski " succeeded in creating a common proprietary right with China over the vast territory lying between the Ussuri River and the sea.[2] The same territory was, only two years later, definitively annexed [3] to Russia through the skillful diplomacy of Ignatieff, Russian Minister at Peking, who, taking advantage of China's defeat at the hands of the allied forces of England and France, had won the favor of the Chinese Government by acting as mediator between it and the allies. The Eastern naval headquarters of Russia,

[1] See the negotiations of 1852, 1859, and 1862, and the treaties of 1855 and 1867, between Russia and Japan, regarding the Kuriles and Sakhalien. The *Tō-A Kwankei Tokushu Jōyaku Isan* (a collection of special treaties relating to Eastern Asia, compiled by the Tō-A Dōbun-kivai, Tokio, 1904. Cloth, 4°, xiv + xii + 812 + 70; hereafter abbreviated as *Tokushu Jōyaku*), pp. 1–8. This work, which is in Japanese and Chinese, is by far the most complete collection of the treaties and conventions concluded between Japan, China, and Korea, and other Powers. It also contains historical notes explaining the origin and nature of many important agreements.

[2] Treaty of Aigun, May 16, 1858, Article I.—*Ibid.*, pp. 200–202 (Chinese); W. F. Mayers's *Treaties between the Empire of China and Foreign Powers*, 3d edition, Shanghai, 1901, p. 100 (French).

[3] Treaty of Peking, November 14, 1860, Article I.— *Tokushu Jōyaku*, pp. 202–203 (Japanese); Mayers, p. 105 (French).

which had been transferred from Peterpavlofsk
in Kamchatka to Nicolaiefsk at the mouth of the
Amur, was now again moved further south to Vladivostok, founded in 1860, at the southern end of
the new territory. No sooner did the remote but
certain pressure from the expanding northern Power
begin to be felt in Japan than, in 1861, a Russian
man-of-war took possession of the Japanese islands
of Tsushima in the Korean straits, from which it
withdrew only at the instance of the British Minister, Sir Rutherford Alcock.[1] Half a dozen years
after, the island of Sakhalien was placed under
a common possession between Russia and Japan,
while, in 1875, the island was surrendered to Russia, Japan receiving in return the chain of sterile
Chishima Islands (the Kuriles).[2] This brought the
presence of Russia still nearer home to Japan than
before. On the other hand, Russia seemed to have
only begun her ambitious career in Eastern Asia,
for she could hardly be expected to be forever satisfied with her naval headquarters at Vladivostok,
a station which, situated as it was at the southern
extremity of her Oriental dominion, was so completely ice-bound during a large part of each year
that her fleet was obliged to winter in Japanese
harbors.

[1] See p. 51, note 1, above.
[2] See *Tokushu Jōyaku*, pp. 5-14. See a Russian view of these
affairs in the *Dōbun-kwai*, No. 50 (January, 1904), pp. 25-30.
See also Z. Nakamura, *Chishima Karafuto Shinryaku-shi* (history of Russian aggression in the Kuriles and Sakhalien),
Tokio, 1904.

Then followed a comparatively long period of inactivity on the part of Russia. When, however, in 1891, she finally resolved to build the Trans-Siberian Railway, the inadequacy of Vladivostok, not only as the Pacific naval harbor of the Russian Empire, but also as the terminus of the great railroad, became evident. To Russia a southern expansion toward an ice-free outlet seemed now a necessity. For the realization of this desire, an opportunity presented itself in a striking form, in 1895, at the end of the Chinese-Japanese war.

In order to obtain a clear understanding of this situation, it is necessary to return to the outbreak of hostilities and thence trace the evolution of Chinese diplomacy up to their close. At the unexpected dispatch of large forces by Japan to Korea, in June, 1894, the Chinese Government appealed to some foreign Ministers at Peking to bring pressure to bear upon Japan to withdraw her troops from the Peninsula. The Russian Minister is said to have observed that Russia would not be prepared to organize an armed coercion until Japan endeavored to exercise actual control over the Korean Kingdom, but might undertake to tender friendly advice to Japan to withdraw. England was reluctant, but as an appeal was again made to the Powers, she took the lead in persuading others to join in a concert to stay Japan's hand in Korea. The plan was, however, frustrated by the emphatic refusal of Germany to consider it. An ineffectual counsel was then made to Japan by a few of the Powers indi-

vidually, not to embark upon a war against China.[1]
A war, nevertheless, ensued, with a rare success
on the part of Japan. During the course of hostilities, China seems to have more than once[2] avowed
her impotence and requested the Powers to intervene, until her repeated reverses on land and the
well-nigh complete annihilation of her northern
squadron brought her to such straits that the
friendly Powers could no longer remain inactive.
Japan also intimated her willingness to negotiate
for peace. After the envoys whom China had sent
with insufficient powers had been twice refused by
Japan, Li Hung-chang, later to be joined by his
son-in-law, Li Ching-fang, arrived with plenary
powers at Shimonoseki, on March 19, 1895, where
he was received by the Japanese Plenipotentiaries,
Count Itō, Premier, and Viscount Mutsu, Foreign
Minister. It appears, however, that China had already signified to certain Powers her suspicion that
Japan desired the cession of a territory on the Chinese mainland. Before, therefore, Li Hung-chang
left the Chinese shores, the German Minister at
Tokio was instructed by his government to warn
the Japanese Foreign Office that certain Powers
had been contemplating assent to China's appeal
to interfere, and that the demand for a cession of
territory on the continent would be particularly
calculated to provoke such an intervention.[3]

[1] *Tokushu Jōyaku*, pp. 78–79, 719.
[2] See, for instance, the London *Times*, November 7, 1894, p. 5.
[3] *Tokushu Jōyaku*, pp. 79–80.

It was under these circumstances that negotiations were opened between the Chinese and Japanese Plenipotentiaries on March 20. It is unnecessary here to recount the story of an abortive attempt made on Li's life by a fanatic, and of the consequent armistice for twenty days. At Li's recovery, the Japanese terms for peace were proposed on April 1, which with amendments became the basis of the final Treaty [1] signed at Shimonoseki on April 17. It provided, among other things, for the absolute independence of Korea, the cession to Japan of the Liao-tung Peninsula, Formosa, and the Pescadores, and an indemnity of two hundred million *taels*. Of the ceded territories, the Liaotung being situated, as it were, in a position to hold a key at once to Peking, Manchuria, and Korea, its cession to Japan was probably calculated, from the latter's point of view, first, to render any renewed attempt of China to dominate Korea impossible, and, secondly, to establish an effective barrier against the southern expansion of Russia.[2]

Naturally, the progress of the peace negotiations had been watched with keen interest by the European Powers. Particularly alert was Russia, whose press deprecated so early as March 31 the alleged intention of Japan to secure territory on the main-

---

[1] For the text of this treaty, see the *Treaties and Conventions between the Empire of Japan and Other Powers*, compiled by the Foreign Office, Tokio, 1899, pp. 377 ff.; Mayers, pp. 181–184; U. S. 54th Congress, 1st Session, *House Documents*, vol. i. pp. 200–203; etc.

[2] *Tokushu Jōyaku*, pp. 43–45, 80.

land, and which, as soon as Li Hung-chang communicated to her early in April the terms proposed
by Japan and appealed to her to interfere, discerned
in those terms a great turning-point of her own
career in the East. She must at once have realized
the grave danger to the entire future of her Eastern
policy from Japan's occupation of the Liao-tung
Peninsula, as well as the immense advantages which
her own possession of the same territory would confer upon herself. Nor did the Korean independence,
which the new treaty secured, fail to be interpreted
by the Russian press as an exclusive protectorate
to be exercised by Japan over the Kingdom. "Russia," wrote the *Novoe Vremya* about April 20,
" cannot permit the protectorate over Korea which
Japan has secured for herself by the conditions
of the treaty. If the single port of Port Arthur
remain in possession of Japan, Russia will severely
suffer in the material interest and in the prestige of
a Great Power." [1] It was just the time to intervene.
China had shown herself impotent, and had appealed
for intervention, and Japan was an exhausted victor. By one clever stroke Russia might coerce the
latter and ingratiate herself with the former. She
would, however, perhaps have thought twice before
she acted, had it not been for the active assistance rendered to her by France and Germany.
At a council, it is said, Russian naval and military
authorities concluded that Russia alone could not
successfully combat Japan, which, however, might

[1] The London *Times*, April 22, 1895, p. 5.

be coerced if Russia coöperated with France. An active communication of views now ensued between the Foreign Offices of St. Petersburg, Berlin, Paris, and London. The diplomatic correspondence of the day is still withheld from the public view, but it is well-known that France readily acceded to the Russian desire for a joint intervention, and Germany suddenly changed her former attitude toward Japan and allied herself with the two intervening Powers; while Great Britain, which had more than once acted in favor of China, altered her course to the opposite direction by declining to admit that Japan's terms of peace were prejudicial to her own interests. The reasons avowed by Germany and France for their assistance to Russia would seem to be rather unconvincing, unless one takes for granted the existence of certain unexpressed motives for the act. Germany claimed to have found in the terms of peace a future menace to the political and economical interests of Europe, for those terms "would constitute a political preponderance of Japan over China," to use the language of "an evidently inspired article" of the *Cologne Gazette*, "and would exercise a determining influence on the development of China's economic condition, and of the sway of Japan in that country. From this it is concluded that Japan is endeavoring to post herself as a sentry, as it were, before all the chief important routes of China. As Japan commands, by Port Arthur and Wei-hai-Wei, the approach to the Yellow Sea, and, by Formosa and the Pescadores, the

chief commercial route to China, it is taken to be
desirous of encircling her with a firm girdle, in
order, if necessary, to seclude her completely
from the world. The European Powers, therefore,
wish to ward off in time any steps prejudicial to
their interests." [1] Nor did the reasons brought forward by France seem to be more germane to her
own interests than those of Germany were to hers.
The *Débats* wrote, on April 31, that all the clauses
on the occupation of continental territory were impossible for Europe to recognize. Moreover, Port
Arthur, with a strip of territory round it in the
hands of the Japanese, would be a menace for
the independence of Korea, as much as for the
security of Peking. The *Temps* also said that
Japan's predominance over China, which would be
the ultimate result of the arrangement, was " a constant menace for the interests of Europe. It was a
serious blow dealt at the rights of the immediate
adjacent Powers. . . . A European concert was
now a duty toward civilization." Perhaps it is safe
to say that, so far as France was concerned, her
desire to oblige her political ally was a more real
ground for her coöperation with the latter than any
other presented in her press. As for Germany, her
Foreign Minister then remarked, it is said, that
Japan had never requited the favors Germany had
done her during the war, but had, on the contrary,
deliberately concluded with China a treaty containing provisions not only excessively favorable to

[1] The London *Times*, April 22, 1895, p. 5.

Japan, but also prejudicial to the political and economic interests of Europe. This remark, again, hardly explains the suddenly changed attitude of Germany. Perhaps it is well to surmise that there existed deeper and more complex diplomatic reasons, upon which it would be idle here to speculate. The declination of Great Britain to join in the concert may more easily be accounted for. China, which she had at first favored, had not only been inclining toward Russia, but had shown herself by her incompetency less worthy of trust than the ambitious Japan. The latter had also secured in the treaty certain commercial and industrial privileges in South China which would be even more advantageous to Great Britain than to Japan, while, on the other hand, the former had little reason to suppose that Japan's retention of the Liao-tung was designed to imperil China and Korea. On the contrary, the presence of Japan at the strategic position on the mainland might prove an effective check upon Russia, whose cause Great Britain was the least inclined to advocate. She therefore stood aloof from the joint intervention, and her conduct provoked a bitter resentment in the Russian and French press.[1]

The plan of intervention seems to have matured between Russia, France, and Germany by April 20, and, on April 23, their representatives at Tokio separately presented brief notes at the Foreign Office. These notes, accompanied as they were by the verbal

[1] *Tokushu Jōyaku*, pp. 81–82.

profession of each of the Governments, particularly the German, of its friendly motive in the act, intimated that Japan's retention of the territory was considered by them as not only imperiling the Chinese Capital, but also making the Korean independence illusory, and, consequently, prejudicial to the permanent peace of the Far East.[1] The treaty of Shimonoseki had been signed on April 17, and the exchange of its ratifications fixed for May 8. The Japanese Government had to answer the three Powers within the fifteen days between April 23 and May 8, for, whatever its decision regarding the Liao-tung, it would be unwise to postpone the ratification of the treaty with China.[2] In the mean time, the Eastern fleets of the three Powers were augmented and concentrated, and made ready, if need be, for an immediate and concerted action, Russia going even so far as to prepare the army contingents in the Amur region for quick mobilization. Unknown as it was how thoroughly the Powers were determined, in case Japan should refuse to consider their counsel, to appeal to force of arms, none the less real was their idea of coercion, as well as the

[1] The German note, which was accompanied by a Romanized translation into Japanese, is said to have contained a statement to the effect that Japan was weak, Germany was powerful, and Japan would surely be defeated in case she should go to war with Germany. This peculiar sentence was, at the protest of the Japanese Foreign Office, expunged from the note. — *Tokushu Jōyaku*, p. 86.

[2] To the last moment Russia, it is said, persisted in advising China to postpone the ratification.

exhaustion of Japan's resources.   On the other hand, the common interests of Japan, Great Britain, and the United States had not developed to such an extent as to justify their united resistance against the intervening Powers.   Japan seems to have complied with the Powers' wishes so far as to agree to retrocede the Liao-tung save the small peninsula of Kinchow containing Port Arthur, but the Powers declined for evident reasons to accede to the proposed compromise.   The British Foreign Minister also urged Japan to make to the susceptibilities of Europe all concessions compatible with her dignity and her permanent interests.[1]   The Japanese Government, after holding repeated conference before the Throne and with military councilors,[2] definitely resolved, on May 4, to relinquish, for an additional monetary consideration from China,[3] all of the Liao-tung.   Evidently time was too limited and the occasion too inopportune for Japan successfully to induce China to pledge not to alienate in the future any part of the retroceded territory to another Power.   On May 10, the entire nation of Japan beheld with deep emotions the simultaneous publica-

[1]   The London *Times*, May 3, 1895, p. 5;   M. de Blowitz's correspondence, dated Paris, May 2.

[2]   The declaration made in November, 1903, by a person intimately associated with Marquis Itō, who was the Premier during the war. — The *Kokumin Shimbun*, November 10, 1903.

[3]   Germany is said to have undertaken, when her note was presented, to guarantee a monetary consideration from China.   By the treaty between Japan and China, concluded on September 22, the sum was fixed at 30,000,000 *taels*.

tion of the treaty of Shimonoseki, which had been
ratified in its original form, and of a special Imperial decree countersigned by all the Ministers of the
Cabinet, announcing that a desire to insure a permanent repose of the Orient had compelled Japan
to go to war, and that the same desire had now
prompted the three Powers to tender to Japan their
present friendly counsel, which the Emperor, for
the sake of peace, had accepted.[1]

The historical significance of this memorable incident deserves special emphasis. It is not too much
to say that with it Eastern Asiatic history radically
changed its character, for it marks the beginning
of a new era, in which the struggle is waged no
longer among the Oriental nations themselves, but
between sets of interests and principles which characterize human progress at its present stage, and
which are represented by the greatest Powers of the
world. China's position as a dominant exclusive
force was no sooner overthrown in Korea than it
was replaced by that of another power of a like
policy and with aggressive tendencies. Moreover,
the area opened to the advance of Russia covered

---

[1] *Tokushu Jōyaku*, pp. 81–87. As has been said, the diplomatic correspondence of the day has not been published by any
of the Powers concerned. The information briefly given in the
text has been culled from, besides *Tokushu Jōyaku*, the leading
articles of the *Tokio Nichi-Nichi Shimbun* (Tokio Daily News),
a semi-official organ of the Japanese Government at the time,
as quoted in the *Nisshin Sen Shi* (history of the Japan-China
war, Tokio, 1894–5, 8 vols.), vol. viii. pp. 141–171. These articles give a minute and careful account of the diplomacy of the
day, and may largely be relied upon as authentic.

not only Korea, but also Northern China and beyond, and the new aggressor was the very power which had thirty years before created a restless feeling among the Japanese, by extending toward them through Primorsk and Sakhalien its already enormous contiguous dominion. The influence of Russia was now brought face to face with that of Japan, each with a promise to extend against, and perhaps to clash with, the other. With the movement of Russia there traveled from Europe to East Asia her sympathetic relations with France, while against this practical alliance stood the increasing common interests and sympathies of Japan, Great Britain, and the United States; Germany remaining as a free lance between the two groups of Powers. This remarkable accession, in both area and agents, of the new activity in the East was heralded in, to all appearance, not gradually, but with a sudden sweep. And gravely ominous was its opening scene, representing at once a pretended good-will toward a feeble empire and an armed coercion of a proud nation whom coercion would only stimulate to greater ambition.

It now remains for us to interpret the effects wrought upon Japan by the intervention of the three Powers, for the sentiment of the nation seems to be so universally and persistently misunderstood as to have caused even some of the natives to misconstrue their own feelings. It is generally supposed that the conduct of the Powers in depriving Japan of her prize of victory excited in her breast a deep

feeling of revenge, but this view seems to evince
too slight an understanding of the characteristics
of the nation. Also, the prevailing sense of pity
manifested by friendly foreigners toward Japan for
her alleged misfortune appears entirely misplaced,
for, on the contrary, she has derived an inestimable
benefit from the experience. Let us explain. The
most obvious lesson drawn by the best minds of
Japan, and unconsciously but deeply shared by
the entire nation, was neither that the Powers were
acting upon a principle altogether different from
their professed motive, for that was too plain to
every one; nor that she must some day humiliate
the very Powers which had brought coercion upon
her, because it was well known that their self-in-
terest had demanded it, as hers would, were she in
their place. Japan suddenly awoke to an absorbing
desire which left little room for the question of
national revenge. It became to her as clear as daylight that the new position she had acquired in the
Orient by her victory over China could be maintained, and even her independence must be guarded,
only by an armament powerful enough to give her
a voice among the first Powers of the world. If
she would not retire into herself, and finally cease
to exist, she must compete with the greatest nations,
not only in the arts of peace,[1] but also in those of

---

[1] It will be remembered that Japan had in 1894 revised her
treaties with the Powers, and thereby freed herself from the yoke
of consular jurisdiction and placed the foreign residents within
her domain under the jurisdiction of her own law, and also
largely restored her tariff autonomy.

war. Moreover, a far vaster conflict than she had
ever known in her history, excepting the Mongol
invasion of the thirteenth century, was seen to be
awaiting her. It is perhaps characteristic of modern
Japan that she scarcely has time to breathe. The
only course to save her seemed to be, now as at any
other recent crisis of her life, to go forward and
become equal to the new, expanding situation. As
soon as her supremacy in the East was assured,
Japan thus found herself confronted with a task
hitherto almost unpremeditated, and henceforth began an enormous extension of her military forces,[1]
as well as a redoubled activity in all other lines of
national progress.[2]

[1] The position which the military and naval expenditures
have occupied in the finance of the Japanese Government
since the war of 1894–5 may be gathered from the following
table (unit, 1000 *yen; yen* = 49.8 cents):—

| | Total revenue of the Government | Total expenditures of the Government | Army and navy expenditures | Ratio of the last two |
|---|---|---|---|---|
| 1894–5[1] | ,... 98,170 | 78,128 | 20,662 | 26.4 % |
| 1895–6[1] | ....118,432 | 85,317 | 23,536 | 27.6 |
| 1896–7[1] | ....187,019 | 168,856 | 73,248 | 43.4 |
| 1897–8[1] | ....226,390 | 223,678 | 110,542 | 49.3 |
| 1898–9[1] | ....220,054 | 219,757 | 112,427 | 51.1 |
| 1899–1900[1] | ....254,254 | 254,165 | 114,212 | 44.9 |
| 1900–1[1] | ....295,854 | 292,750 | 133,113 | 45.4 |
| 1901–2[1] | ....274,359 | 266,856 | 102,360 | 38.3 |
| 1902–3[2] | ....297,341 | 289,226 | 85,768 | 29.7 |
| 1903–4[3] | ....251,681 | 244,752 | 71,368 | 31.7 |
| 1904–5[3] | ....229,855 | 223,181 | 69,433 | 31.1 |

[1] Settled accounts.          [2] Actual account on October 31, 1903.
[3] Estimates in the budget.    All based on the Fourth *Annual*.

[2] To take only a few tangible instances, Japan's national
budget grew more than three-fold during the ten years before
1903, her foreign trade in 1903 was 263% as large as it was in
1894, her private companies increased from less than 3000
in 1894 to 8600 in 1902, with a corresponding growth of their

What is less obvious, but still more important, is — it is questionable if there is in the entire range of Japan's national life another point less understood abroad but more essential for an insight into the present and future of the Extreme Orient than this — the increased enthusiasm of Japan in her ardent effort to strengthen her position in the world by basing her international conduct upon the fairest and best-tried principles of human progress. The effort is not free from occasional errors, but the large issue grows ever clearer in Japan's mind. A study of her past would seem to convince one with overwhelming evidence that her historic training has produced in Japan moral and material characteristics eminently fit for the pursuit of such a policy. However that may be, the subsequent evolution of her interests at home and abroad seems, by a fortunate combination of circumstances, to have irrevocably committed her to this course; for not only does a common policy along these lines draw her and the Anglo-Saxon nations closer together, but it is therein also that the vital promise of her future seems to lie.[1] And it may be added, the consciousness of this powerful unity of moral and material life seems to have infused a thrilling new force into that historic love of country of the

authorized capital from less than 200 million to 1,226.7 million *yen*, and her population itself has increased perhaps by 12%. A decisive development has also taken place in both the internal politics and the international relations of Japan.

[1] See our Introduction.

Japanese nation.[1] It is to the intervention of 1895 and the situation that ensued that Japan owes the hastening of all these results.

[1] An attempt has been universally made during the present war to explain the apparent contempt of death of the Japanese soldier as due to his low estimate of human life, or else to his fatalistic view of the world. It may be seriously doubted whether these explanations are tenable. At least it may be said that in no other case would the sons of Japan so fearlessly and cheerfully face death. It is impossible to discover in them a less fear of death than in other nations. Life is dear, but it is sacrificed to a cause which is considered higher than life. It was the primary lesson in the education of the *samurai* to choose death when it saved honor and when life was selfish. This view of life has now been transferred from the narrow sphere of the individual person or fief to the large field of the entire nation, whose cause, it is believed, represents the best postulates of human progress. It would, perhaps, be legitimate to criticise the incidental abuse of this feeling, or to question whether the same loyalty might not be transferred to a still higher region than the state, but the subject must first be understood by the critic.

# CHAPTER II

## THE "CASSINI CONVENTION" AND THE RAILWAY AGREEMENT

REGARDED, however, from a broader point of view, no one could predict a happy consequence of so ominous a beginning, as has been described, of the new Eastern situation. By her successful intervention, Russia had conferred upon China a signal favor, for which a reward was expected; but the reward, again, assumed such a form that it at the same time served as a new favor looking toward a fresh reward, so that the final resultant of the repeated process proved altogether out of proportion to the initial deed of patronage. The first step of this process was a 4 per cent. loan[1] to China of 400,000,000 francs at 94⅛, and payable in thirty-six years, beginning with 1896. Not only were these liberal terms attended by no security, but also the interest was guaranteed by a special edict of the Czar.[2] The loan was issued principally from Paris in July, 1895,[3] and the in-

---

[1] See Henri Cordier, *Histoire des relations de la Chine avec les puissances occidentales*, 1860–1902 (3 vols.), vol. iii (Paris, 1902), pp. 305–306. The loan contract, dated June 24, 1895, appears in *Tokushu Jōyaku*, pp. 660–667.

[2] *Tokushu Jōyaku*, pp. 667–668.

[3] Cf. Art. 15 of the contract.

come was intended to cover one half [1] of China's indemnity to Japan.[2] In order to facilitate the transactions in connection with this loan, as well as to promote the commercial relations between Russia and Eastern Asia, the Russo-Chinese Bank was organized late in 1895. In August, 1896,[3] the Chinese Government was induced to contribute 5,000,000 *taels* toward the capital of the Bank, which seem to have been paid out of the new loan.[4] Later in the same year, Prince Ukhtomsky, president of the Bank, who had come to Peking with an immense number of costly presents to be distributed among the members of the Court, succeeded in securing the consent of the Chinese Government to the Statutes of the Bank, which were subsequently published on December 8.[5] The privileges of the

[1] The other half, £16,000,000, was supplied by some British and German subjects by the contract of March 11, 1896, at 5% interest, and repayable in thirty-six years. Another £16,000,000 loan was later supplied by the same parties. — *Tokushu Jōyaku*, pp. 668–673.

[2] 5,000,000 *taels* were, however, as will be seen below, used for another purpose.

[3] The contract dated August 25, 1896. — *Tokushu Jōyaku*, pp. 640–641.

[4] According to a Peking correspondent to the *Kokumin* (May 30, 1904), the Chinese Government had been paying the stipulated 4% interest for this sum to the French creditors, but the Bank had never repaid the interest to China. Moreover, the Niu-chwang branch of the Bank, since the Russians occupied the port in August, 1900, had been receiving the returns of the Chinese maritime customs there, which finally amounted to about 5,000,000 *taels*. Neither the principal nor the interest of this sum had been paid by the Bank to the Chinese Government.

[5] *Tokushu Jōyaku*, pp. 642–660.

institution as enumerated in these Statutes included the receiving of tax returns, management of local finances, coining, payment of the interests of the public bonds, and construction of railways and telegraph lines in China, in so far as concessions should be made by her Government to the Bank. The latter now has more than thirty branches and agencies in East Asia, and this professedly private corporation has since proved to be a great instrument through which the Russian Government has obtained from China enormous concessions in Manchuria.

Before we examine the nature of these concessions, it is important to observe what took place between Russia and China through the official channels. On March 27, 1896, the Eastern world was startled to see the publication in the *North China Daily News* of a treaty of defensive alliance concluded earlier in the same year between Russia and China. The Japanese Government had already, on March 16, been assured by the Foreign Office at St. Petersburg that the treaty did not exist.[1] It is not clear whether the denial referred to the particular treaty in question or to any treaty of alliance whatsoever. However that may be, the reported agreement[2] was of the most serious character, as will be gathered from the following abstract. In recognition of the service rendered by Russia regarding the matter of the Liao-tung Peninsula and of the

---

[1] *Tokushu Jōyaku*, p. 231.

[2] The Japanese text appears in *ibid.*, pp. 231–234.

loan, the Chinese Emperor desired to conclude with
Russia a treaty of alliance ; and, consequently, it
was agreed, in secrecy, that, if Russia should come
in conflict with other Asiatic Powers, she should be
allowed to make free use of any port or harbor on
the Chinese coast, and, in case of urgent need, levy
troops from among the Chinese people.  If a protest
should be made by other Powers, China should
answer that she was powerless to resist Russian
demands.  If she should desire even to render active
assistance to Russia against the common enemy, she
might do so, but this point required further discussion.  In view of the great disadvantages of the ice-
bound naval harbors of Russia, China agreed to
allow her in time of peace a free use of Port Arthur,
or, if the other Powers should object, of Kiao-chau.
If the latter should be found inadequate, Russia
might choose any harbor on the coast of Kiang-su
and Che-kiang.  If, on the other hand, China should
be at war with another Power, Russia should en-
deavor to effect a compromise between the belligerents, and, if the effort should fail, it should be the
duty of Russia openly to assist China and thereby
strengthen the alliance between the two Powers.  In
regard to Manchuria, Russian military officers should
be free to travel along the eastern frontiers of the
Sheng-king and Kirin Provinces and to navigate
the Yalu and other rivers, the object being either to
further trade or to patrol the frontiers.  When the
Siberian Railway was completed, a branch line might
be constructed under the joint control of China and

Russia, passing through the Provinces of Heilung and Kirin, and reaching Ta-lien or some other place selected by Russia. In order to protect this line, Russia might possess near Talien-wan an island and the opposite shore, fortify them, and station there her squadron and military forces. If a war should arise between Russia and Japan concerning Korea, China should allow Russia to send her troops toward the Yalu, so as to enable them to attack the western boundary of Korea.

No matter whether any treaty of alliance had been signed between China and Russia early in 1896, significant events soon followed which gave rise to rumors of grave import. When it was resolved by China to send Wang Tsz-chun to St. Petersburg as special envoy to attend the coronation of the Czar, which was to take place in May of the same year, M. Cassini, Russian Minister at Peking, is said to have intimated that no one but Li Hung-chang was acceptable to Russia as the representative of the Chinese Emperor. Li's pro-Russian proclivities had been well known, but he had up to this time been in disgrace for having concluded the treaty of Shimonoseki so unfavorable to China. He now regained his favor with the Court, and started on his mission to Russia, presumably taking with him the draft of the Russo-Chinese convention which M. Cassini had framed. The convention is reported to have been signed, to avoid suspicion of other Powers, not at St. Petersburg, but at Moscow, and, on the Russian

side, not by M. Lobanoff, Foreign Minister, but by
M. Witte, Minister of Finance. When, however,
the agreement was referred to the Yamên at Peking for ratification, a large majority of the Chinese
Ministers are said to have disapproved the terms of
Li's treaty, until the strenuous efforts of M. Cassini
turned the tide and the convention was ratified by
the Emperor on September 30, 1896. This is the
celebrated "Cassini Convention."[1] Let us now examine the more important of its contents. The preamble explicitly referred, as also did the treaty of
alliance already summarized, to the favors done to
China by Russia at the close of the recent war.
The body of the convention falls, in its substance,
into two large divisions, namely, the Articles (1–6)
relating to railway concessions in Manchuria, and
those (8–11) in regard to the disposition of certain
ports on the Chinese littoral. Russia was allowed
to extend the Siberian Railway to Vladivostok
across Manchuria *via* Aigun, Tsitsihar, Petuna,
Kirin, and Kun-chun (Art. 1). As regards the projected Chinese railroad between Shan-hai-kwan and
Mukden, if China should find it inconvenient to
build it, Russia might furnish capital and construct
the line, China reserving to herself the option of
buying it after ten years of Russian management
(Art. 2). Another Chinese line in contemplation
between Shan-hai-kwan and Port Arthur and Talien-wan *via* Niu-chwang, and its appurtenances,

[1] *Tokushu Jōyaku*, pp. 234–236. A French translation is
found in Cordier, *Histoire*, vol. iii. pp. 343–347.

COUNT CASSINI

*Russian Minister at Washington, and formerly at Peking*

should be built in accordance with the general railway regulations of Russia (Art. 4). The fifth Article was striking : All the railways built by Russia
in the Chinese territory were to be protected by
the local Chinese authorities, but in the more remote regions, where the necessary protection was
not available, Russia was allowed, in order to afford
a better protection to her railroad and property, to
station special battalions of Russian infantry and
cavalry. Regarding the ports, it was agreed that
Russia might lease Kiao-chau for fifteen years for
the use of her squadron, but, in order to avoid suspicion by other Powers, she should not immediately
occupy the harbor or seize the points commanding
it (Art. 9). In view of the strategic importance of
Port Arthur and Talien-wan and their adjacent territories, China should in haste provide for their
adequate defense and repair their fortification, and
Russia should render all necessary aid for the protection of the two harbors, and should not allow
any other Power to attack them; if, for urgent
necessity, Russia should engage in a war, China
should allow her, to enable her to attack the enemy and defend her own position with greater
ease, temporarily to concentrate her military and
naval forces in those harbors (Art. 10). So long,
however, as Russia was not involved in hostilities,
China should retain all rights in the control of
Port Arthur and Talien-wan, and Russia should
not interfere with them in any manner (Art. 11).
In addition to these Articles, it was provided that,

if China should desire to reorganize the entire army of Manchuria on the European basis, she should engage the services of Russian military instructors (Art. 8). In the matter of mining, Russian and Chinese subjects might, with the consent of local authorities, work all kinds of minerals in the Heilung and Kirin Provinces, and in the Long White Mountains (Art. 7).

Such are the contents, in brief, of the much debated "Cassini Convention," the existence of which has been as often alleged as denied. The reported document may well be unauthentic, at any rate in several important particulars. Its main interest consists, however, not so much in the question of its literal authenticity, as in the important facts, (1) that the subsequent course of events is largely foreshadowed in its contents, and (2) that high Russian authorities have obtained, or at least claimed, certain privileges which cannot be found in all the other Russo-Chinese contracts that are known to us, but are in one way or another reflected in the present convention. The universal belief in the diplomatic world appears to be that, if the published text of the Cassini Convention is untrustworthy, some of its substance must have been contained in an agreement which Li Hung-chang signed in Russia in 1895, and in some later secret agreements. Nor is it impossible to substantiate this belief from evidence of undoubted authenticity. Thus M. Pavloff, the Russian *Chargé d'Affaires* at Peking, said, on October 8, 1897, to Sir Claude MacDonald, the British Minister, that "shortly after the return of Li Hung-chang from his mission to St. Petersburg, the Chinese Government had informed the Russian Minister that they had no intention of continuing the Northern line [beyond Shan-hai-kwan toward Kirin], but if at any time they did continue it, owing to the particularly friendly relations existing between the Russian and Chinese Governments, they would in the first instance address themselves to Russian engineers and employ, if necessary, Russian capital." [1] It will at once be observed that this closely corresponds to Article 3 of the Cassini Convention. On this ground, M. Pavloff considered it a "contravention of the agreement" [2] on the part of the Chinese Government that the latter allowed British subjects, on June 7, 1898, to furnish capital and the chief engineer for the extension of the Northern line, and, repeatedly and in a manner highly irritating to the British and Chinese Governments, demanded the replacement of Mr. Kinder and his staff with Russian engineers.[3] It was again in the same spirit that Russia succeeded in inducing England to insert in the ad-

[1] *The British Parliamentary Papers, China, No. 1 (1898)*, Dispatch No. 14, pp. 5-6. Cf. *China, No. 2 (1899)*, No. 2, in which M. Pavloff claims to have secured in December, 1897, a repetition of this pledge.

[2] See *China, No. 2 (1904)*, Nos. 28-29, modified Article 12. Sir Ernest Satow, however, denied that any such agreement existed. See *China, No. 2 (1904)*, No. 30, March 19, 1901.

[3] See *China, No. 1 (1898)*, Nos. 13, 38, 26, 43, 111, 113, 115, 117, 121; *China, No. 2 (1899)*, Nos. 2, 9, 10, 52, 65; *China, No. 1 (1900)*, No. 321.

ditional clauses of the Anglo-Russian railway agreement of April 28, 1899, a statement to the effect that the Russians might extend the Manchurian Railway in a southwesterly direction through the region traversed by the Northern Chinese line built with British capital,[1] Count Muravieff explaining that M. Witte attached importance to the insertion of this clause.[2] Well he might, for no sooner was the Agreement concluded than Russia pressed China, though without success, for the concession for a railway reaching directly to Peking itself.[3] Again, if the provision in the Cassini Convention that China should with all haste repair the fortification of Port Arthur, with the assistance of Russia, and, in case of necessity, turn it over to the use of the latter's fleet (Art. 10), was false, it was not long before Count Muravieff could declare, in December, 1897, that an " offer " had been made by the Chinese Government to allow the Russian squadron to winter at the port.[4] More significant still was M. Pavloff's remark to Sir Claude MacDonald, that " he must tell him frankly that the Russian Government intended that the provinces of China bordering on the Russian frontier must not come under the influence of any nation except Russia." [5] Sir Claude pointed out

[1] *China, No. 2 (1899)*, No. 138.
[2] *China, No. 1 (1900)*, No. 148.
[3] *Ibid.*, pp. 112, 116, 120, 132, 160, 180, 214–215.
[4] *China, No. 1 (1898)*, Dispatch No. 37, pp. 12–13, Goschen to Salisbury.
[5] *China, No. 1 (1896)*, p. 6, Conversation on October 18, 1897.

that Kirin, the probable terminus of the extension line, to which M. Pavloff had objected, was more than two hundred miles from the Russian frontier, but the *Chargé* had evidently marked out the entire Manchurian provinces as a Russian sphere of influence. It may be said that this claim even exceeded the Cassini Convention and verged to the less trustworthy treaty of alliance. The attention of the reader may, however, be called to a still more direct evidence than the veiled remarks of M. Pavloff. In the official statement accompanying the text of the Russo-Chinese Convention of April 8, 1902, which was published in the *Official Messenger* of April 12, occur the following words : " The Chinese Government, on their side, confirm all the obligations they have previously undertaken toward Russia, and particularly the provisions of *the 1896 agreement*, which must serve as a basis for the friendly relations of the neighboring Empires. By this *defensive agreement*, Russia undertook in 1896 to maintain the principle of the independence and integrity of China, who, on her side, gave Russia the right to construct a line through Manchuria, and to enjoy the material privileges which are directly connected with the above undertaking." [1] It is impossible to find any one contract concluded in 1896 which either might be considered a " defensive agreement " or contains the points enumerated in the quoted passage. The so-called Cassini Convention alone contains the provisions about the railway,

[1] See *Tokushu Jōyaku*, pp. 274–275.

as well as Articles 9 and 10, which may be said to
" maintain the principle of the independence and
integrity of China." [1]  The coincidence becomes
even more striking when we consider, together with
the Convention, the reported treaty of defensive
alliance of 1896, which may be regarded, if any,
the preliminary plan of the Convention. It is also
interesting to note that when Dr. George Morrison,
the noted Peking correspondent of the *Times*, had
an interview with Prince Ching on March 19, 1901,
and directly referred to the supposed existence of
a series of secret agreements between Russia and
China, beginning with the one which Li Hung-
chang negotiated during his mission in St. Petersburg, the Prince " assented without the slightest
demur." [2]  Finally, we are in possession of a vague
statement made by Count Cassini himself, who, in
1904, referred to the treaty " giving to Russia railroad and other concessions in Manchuria," which,
said he, " I had the honor to negotiate [at Peking]

[1]  See *Tokushu Jōyaku*, pp. 274-275.

[2]  The *Times*, March 20, 1901, p. 5. This evidence, however,
cannot for a moment be considered equivalent to the others
which have been cited. Not only is it silent about the contents of
the agreements, but also the "assent" of the Prince may be due
to some misunderstanding. In the same article, Dr. Morrison
goes on to say: "I have reason to believe that the original Russian draft promised China protection only against Japan, but
was modified at the request of the Chinese to include protection against aggression by all foreign Powers. China invoked its
provisions after Germany seized Kiao-chau, but Russia turned a
deaf ear." This statement is again as vague as the reported text
of the treaty of alliance of 1896. It is to be regretted that the
writer did not explicitly state his "reason."

in behalf of my Sovereign."[1] The agreement of September 8, 1896, to which we shall presently turn, "giving railway and other concessions in Manchuria," was concluded between the Chinese Minister at St. Petersburg and the Russo-Chinese Bank, and, unless Count Cassini negotiated it at Peking at the same time that the Chinese Minister did at the Russian capital, it may be inferred that the former, in his quoted statement, referred to a "Cassini Convention." It is not at all impossible, however, that both he in China and Mr. Hu in Russia took part in the negotiations which resulted in the conclusion of the agreement of September 8, 1896.

Taking all these indications together, it seems almost safe to aver that at least two important items of concessions — namely, railway grants and the use of some ports for strategic purposes — must in some form have been secured by Russia after 1896, and before the actual lease of Port Arthur and Talien-wan in 1898. It is needless to say that these two objects, railways and ports, possessed a political meaning of the greatest moment, the ports affording the Russian navy a commanding point on the Pacific coast, and the railways ultimately connecting that point with the army bases in Siberia and European Russia.

Of these two items, it was the railways that first emerged from the state of a preliminary to that of a final agreement between Russia and China. And

[1] The *North American Review* for May, 1904, p. 683.

it was here that the Russo-Chinese Bank played a
great rôle for the Russian Government, for the
Agreement of August 27 (September 8), 1896,[1] providing for the construction by the Russians of a
railway through Manchuria connecting the Trans-
Baikal and South Ussuri lines of the Siberian railway system, was concluded between the Chinese
Minister at St. Petersburg and the Bank. The latter undertook to organize the Eastern Chinese[2]
Railway Company with its accounts separate from
those of the Bank (Art. 1). It is instructive to note
that it is stated in the preamble of this Agreement
that the Chinese Government "intrusted"[3] the
Bank to undertake the construction of the line, and
that the government agreed to contribute 5,000,000
*taels* toward the capital of the Company.[4] The

---

[1] *Tokushu Jōyaku*, pp. 495–498 (a Japanese translation). The
present writer is also in possession of the Chinese text. He is not
aware that its European translation has ever been published. Its
contents are found in Alexander Hosie, *Manchuria*, pp. 43–44.

[2] The Manchurian provinces are called "the Chinese Eastern
Three Provinces," and hence the name of this railway and of the
Company. It is essential to keep this line in mind apart from the
Chinese Northern railway system referred to on pages 156–157.

[3] "Of her own volition," as Cassini added. See the *North
American Review* for May, 1904, p. 683.

[4] According to Art. 12, these 5,000,000 *taels* were to be returned to the Chinese Government as soon as the line was in
running order. It will be remembered that the government was
responsible for the contribution of an equal amount of money to
the capital of the Russo-Chinese Bank. It is probable that the
money has been transferred from the Company to the Bank, so as
to make it pay two bills, the one after the other. It has already
been reported that the money was originally paid out of the
Russo-French loan of 1895. If this report is true, the whole ar-

Russian troops should be transported by the railway without obstruction and at half-fare (Arts. 8
and 9). Upon the basis of this Agreement were promulgated by the Government of the Czar Statutes [1]
providing for the construction and operation of the
railway. Nothing can better betray than these two
documents, the Agreement and the Statutes, that
the enterprise was only in a very limited sense an
undertaking of a private company. In the first
place, the capital of the Company was divided into
share-capital and bond-capital, the former, not guaranteed by the Russian Government, being limited
to only 5,000,000 rubles, while the latter, which
was officially guaranteed, could be indefinitely
expanded according to necessity.[2] It in fact had
already before the present war swollen to the enormous sum of over 270,000,000 rubles.[3] In the second place, the operation of the railroad was placed
upon the uniform basis of the Siberian system, and
under the management of a board whose nominal

rangement may be characterized as extremely clever on the part
of Russia.  Cf. p. 84, note 4, above.

[1] Confirmed by the Czar on December 4/16, presented to the
Ruling Senate on December 8/20, and finally published in the
*Bulletins des Lois* on December 11/23, 1896. See an English
translation of their text in the *British Parliamentary Papers,
Russia, No. 1 (1898)*, and *China, No. 1 (1900)*, pp. 57–61; a
Japanese translation in *Tokushu Jōyaku*, pp. 495–500. At the
further extension of the railway by the agreement of March 27,
1898, supplementary statutes were promulgated on February 5,
1899. See *ibid.*, pp. 516–520.

[2] Articles 10–16.

[3] Page 32, above.

president was a Chinese,[1] but whose vice-president, who was to assume the actual direction, was under the supervision of the Minister of Finance.[2] Finally, but not the least in importance, was the provision regarding the protection of the railway and its employees and the policing of the lands assigned to the road and its appurtenances. The former duty was to be performed by the Chinese Government, but the latter " was confined to police agents appointed by the Company. The Company shall for this purpose draw up and establish police regulations." [3] In these police agents, ostensibly to be employed by the Company, one may discern the origin of the famous " railway guards," later called the " frontier guards," whose existence has become an important problem since 1902 in connection with the Russian evacuation of Manchuria. It should also be noted that this provision concerning the police agents does not appear in the corresponding Article in the text of the Agreement between China and the Bank, upon which the Statutes were based, so that one is at a loss to know what was the conventional ground for this Russian law, unless, indeed, it was the so-called Cassini Convention, which was alleged to have provided for the organization of Russian infantry and cavalry battalions

[1] The Chinese Minister to St. Petersburg at that time was appointed the first president.

[2] Articles 18–27 ; Agreement, Article 1.

[3] Article 8. Compare Art. 5 of the Agreement, which contains merely the former part of this arrangement, i. e., the protection of the railway and its appurtenances by the Chinese Government.

in order to protect Russian interests in the more remote parts of Manchuria.

It was agreed that the line should, after eighty years, come under the possession of the Chinese Government, which might also buy up the road and its appurtenances after thirty-six years.[1] It is interesting to see that it also provided that during the eighty years of Russian management, all commodities carried between China and Russia by the railway should pay in China duties one third less than the ordinary import and export duties in that Empire,[2] a provision hardly reconcilable with the open door principle, and explicitly contrary to the principles proposed by the United States to the Powers two years later.[3]

The Eastern Chinese Railway Company was organized in February, 1897, and the first sod of the Manchuria Railway was cut with great ceremony on the eastern frontier of the Kirin Province on August 28, 1897.

To some this railway concession may have appeared at first to have been intended merely to reduce the time and expense of completing the eastern section of the Siberian Railway by allowing it to pass across Manchuria through a route shorter and easier than the one along the Amur and Ussuri rivers. Such a belief was, however, soon dispelled, or rather, modified, by the acquisition by Russia of the lease

[1] The Agreement, Art. 12; the Statutes, Art. 2.
[2] The Agreement, Art. 10; the Statutes, Art. 3.
[3] See p. 150, note 1, below.

of the greatest naval harbor in the Yellow Sea, and, simultaneously, of the right to join this naval basis by a new railway with the main Manchurian line, so as to make complete the connection between Port Arthur and the army centres in Siberia and Russia. The Russian lease of this port was, however, preceded by and modeled after the German lease of Kiao-chau, which should therefore receive our brief attention first.

# CHAPTER III

## KIAO–CHAU

KIAO-CHAU, in the Province of Shan-tung, was, as will be remembered, a port marked in the so-called Cassini Convention for the use of the Russian squadron. Its value as a commercial and strategical *point d'appui*, as well as the greatness of the mineral wealth of Shan-tung, must have been as well known to the Germans as to the Russians.[1] How it happened that Russia forsook this important position, or, more accurately, how Germany succeeded in securing its lease without a protest from Russia, still remains to be explained. It is known, however, that the offers which had been made by China, perhaps in recognition of Germany's service in the Liao-tung affair,[2] of a docking and coaling station on the

[1] Herr von Richthofen, now the Foreign Minister of Germany, and the greatest authority on Chinese geology, wrote an article in the *Kolonialzeitung* of January 6, 1898, describing the mineral resources of the province, and concluding that the Power which possessed Kiao-chau would control the coal supply in northern Chinese waters. See *China, No. 1 (1898)*, p. 21. The same authority had shown years ago the advantageous position of Kiao-chau.

It will also be remembered that during the Chinese-Japanese war, war-vessels of several Powers were temporarily anchored here, so that the superb position of the port was familiar to every one.

[2] "Considering that there has never been any disagreement

southern coast, had been declined by Germany;[1] and also that Germany's own attempts to secure a point on the Lappa Island near Amoy, and later in Amoy itself, had never materialized. As to Kiao-chau, the desire of Germany for its possession had henceforth been often observed by the Chinese Minister at Berlin,[2] but, for the realization of the desire, either the time was not ripe, or the susceptibilities of Russia had to be considered. Toward the latter half of 1897, however, the German Government seemed to have concluded that a general partition of China was now a likelihood, for which emergency Germany should prepare herself by obtaining a powerful foothold on the littoral. Observe the following statement made, in a retroactive manner, after the lease of Kiao-chau had been acquired, by Herr von Bülow in the Reichstag, on April 27, 1898 : " Mention has been made of the partition of China.  Such a partition will not be

existing between China and Germany, and that the German Government came to the assistance of China in securing the evacuation of the Liao-tung Peninsula by the Japanese for which she has never been recompensed ; and further, as England, France, and Russia have taken maritime ports in the East, and as Germany has no port as a rendezvous for her vessels and for a coaling station, her position is not equal to the other great Powers." — The Tsung-li Yamên's memorial to the Throne, translated in Mr. Denby's dispatch of March 9, 1898 (U. S. 55th Congress, 3d Session, *House Documents*, vol. i, p. 189). The same sentiment may have prompted the Tsung-li Yamên to make the offers stated in the text.

[1] *China, No. 1 (1898)*, No. 25.

[2] U. S. 55th Congress, 3d Session, *House Documents*, vol. i. p. 189.

brought about by us, at any rate. All we have done
is to provide that, come what may, we ourselves shall
not go empty-handed. The traveller cannot decide
when the train is to start, but he can make sure not
to miss it when it does start. The devil takes the
hindmost. . . . In any case, we have secured in
Kiao-chau a strategical and political position which
assures us a decisive influence in the future of the
Far East. From this strong position we can look
on with complacency on the development of affairs.
We have such a large sphere of action and such important tasks before us that we have no occasion to
grudge other nations the concessions made them.
German diplomacy will pursue its path in the East
as everywhere else — calmly, firmly, and peacefully.
We will never play the part of mischief-maker ; nor
will we play that of Cinderella." [1] Before this glorious consummation was reached, Germany must have,
it is presumed, made diplomatic efforts to conciliate
Russia, and it is in this connection that it is alleged
by some that the two Powers then matured between
themselves a compromise whereby Germany should
not be molested in her possible attempt to seize
Kiao-chau at the first opportunity, and Russia, in
her turn, should be free to follow the precedent and
demand of China a lease of Port Arthur.[2]

However that may be, an opportunity for Germany's action came when, as is well known, two
German Catholic priests were murdered by a mob

[1] *China, No. 1 (1899)*, p. 67.
[2] *Tokushu Jōyaku*, p. 355.

in the Kü-ye District, in Shan-tung, on November 1,
1897. The late Provincial Governor, Li Ping-hing,
who had recently been transferred to Sz-chwan,
was suspected of having instigated the crime. The
Peking Government at once ordered a strict search
for the culprits, and in three weeks the local authorities succeeded in arresting four of the guilty
persons.[1] It was too late. Three German men-of-
war had arrived at Kiao-chau, about November 17,
to be joined later by several others, and landed
600 marines, who seized the Chinese barracks of
the port.[2] As the Tsung-li Yamên had received
no previous communication from the German authorities regarding the demonstration, it " could
only surmise that Kiao-chau had been seized on
account of the murder of the German missionaries."[3] The German Minister at Peking, Baron von
Heyking, then presented six demands, including
the punishment of the late Governor Li, an indemnity for the murdered, and the preference for
German capital and engineers in the future railway
and mining enterprises in the Province of Shan-tung
— the desire for the lease of Kiao-chau being still
veiled, — and these demands were, with some modifications, accepted by China. At this time, however, Prince Henry of Germany, whom the Kaiser
had bade farewell at Kiel in his celebrated "mailed
fist" speech, was on his way to China with his

---

[1] *China, No. 1 (1898)*, No. 3.          [2] *Ibid.*
[3] *Ibid.*, No. 2. Cf. *House Documents*, op. cit., pp. 187–189, a
memorial of the Yamên to the Throne.

squadron. As soon as he arrived, Baron von Heyking presented the long concealed demand for a
lease of the bay and the surrounding promontories of
Kiao-chau. In the face of the strong position and
forces commanded by Germany, China had no choice
but to yield.[1] When she was finally, on March 6,
1898, prevailed upon to sign the Agreement with
Germany, the Government of the latter declined to
publish anything but its first section containing the
use and lease of Kiao-chau,[2] and the contents of
its other two sections concerning the railway and
mining privileges granted to Germany[3] in the Shan-
tung Province, as well as a separate agreement
concerning the direct reparation for the crime of
Kü-ye, have not, so far as is known, been officially
given to the world from Berlin.[4]

The act of Germany was a *débâcle*, and in the
concessions she wrested from China were involved
questions of grave importance and far-reaching
consequences. In the first place, was not the lease
of á commanding port in reality an infringement
of the territorial sovereignty of the Chinese Empire? In the second place, how could the prefer-

[1] The lease was later fixed for ninety-nine years. The leased
territory covers about 540 square kilometres (208.4 square miles),
including about 80,000 inhabitants.

[2] *Das Staatsarchiv*, Band 61, No. 11518.

[3] Meyers, pp. 281–282; *China, No. 1 (1899)*, No. 65; *Tokushu Jōyaku*, pp. 359–360, 363–365.

[4] For the extraordinary proceedings of the German Minister
in his dealings with the Chinese Government, see *China, No. 1
(1898)*, Nos. 5, 6, 17, 20, 34, 35, 40, 53, 70, 73, and 113. Also
see *Tokushu Jōyaku*, pp. 355–357.

ence given to Germany in the future railway and mining operations in one of the richest of the eighteen Provinces be reconciled with the principle of the equal opportunity for the economic enterprise of all nations in China? If the action of Germany could be, as it soon seemed to be, used by other Powers as a precedent, would not the consequences for the cause, to say the least, of the fair treatment and mutual harmony in China of the nations among themselves be disastrous? It is interesting to observe the attitude taken toward this incident by Great Britain, the Power which possessed the greatest interest in insisting upon, as well as strongest power to enforce, the two cardinal principles of the world's diplomacy in China, namely, the territorial sovereignty of the Chinese Empire and the equality therein of economic opportunity for all nations. Official dispatches of the day clearly indicate that, on the one hand, Germany made efforts to allay the susceptibilities of Great Britain, and that, on the other, the British remonstrances were not only so mollified as to be ineffective, but were also turned in such a direction as only to add to the dangers of the situation. Let us observe how this was done. It was repeatedly declared, during the negotiations between Germany and China, by the German Representatives at Peking and London and by Herr von Bülow himself, that the northern port of Kiao-chau had been chosen for its remoteness, for one thing, from the regions in which England was directly interested ; that nothing was being

done during the negotiations with China which
would be embarrassing to Great Britain ; that Germany was raising no objections to the British terms
of the Anglo-German loan to China now under consideration ; that the management of the new colony
would be found to be liberal, for the German Government was convinced that the British system of
colonization was the right one ; and that the Kaiser
and his Government were strong partisans of a good
understanding between Germany and England.[1]
Beside these assurances from Germany, it is interesting to note that, on December 1, 1897, Sir
Claude MacDonald wrote from Peking to the Marquess of Salisbury : " If the German occupation of
Kiao-chau is only used as a leverage for obtaining
satisfactory reparation . . . for the murder of the
German missionaries, the effect on the security of
our own people will be of the best. If, on the other
hand, the German object is to secure Kiao-chau as
a naval station, under cover of their demands for

[1] See *China, No. 1 (1898)*, Nos. 39, 49, 74. It is interesting to
observe that when, in order to restore the balance of power in the
Gulf of Pechili, which had been disturbed by the lease of Port
Arthur by Russia, England demanded the lease of Wei-hai-Wei,
she took pains to explain to Germany that her acquisition of the
port, the meaning of which was purely military, would in no way
interfere with the German interests in Shan-tung, and that there
would be no attempt to make railway connections with Wei-hai-
Wei. An interesting diplomatic correspondence followed this
explanation, which it is hardly necessary to describe. What is
emphasized here is that England, in negotiating the lease of Wei-
hai-Wei, largely reciprocated the cordiality Germany had shown
in her occupation of Kiao-chau. See *China, No. 1 (1899)*, Nos.
2, 8, 9, 10, and 31.

reparation, it is by no means clear that their acquisition of it will prejudice our interests." [1] Whether or not this idea was indorsed by the British Government, Sir Frank C. Lascelles, the Representative at Berlin, said to Herr von Bülow, on December 30, "That, so far as he knew, Her Majesty's Government had raised no objection to the German ships going to Kaio-chau. Should, however, a demand be put forward for exclusive privileges, or should other countries seek to take possession of Chinese ports, it would probably become necessary for Her Majesty's Government to take steps for the protection of her vast interests in China." [2] In this last sentence is seen a curse of China's foreign relations, that is, the idea of the balance of power — a balance between foreign nations on her ground and at her expense. An offending Power would not retrace its steps, and another Power would virtually recognize them by itself demanding counterbalancing rights from China, which might expect

[1] *China*, No. 1 (*1898*), p. 20.

[2] *Ibid.*, p. 14, No. 39. Sir Claude MacDonald had already written to the Tsung-li Yamên, on December 10: "I have the honor to inform your Highnesses and your Excellencies that I have received telegraphic instructions from Her Majesty's Government to address the Yamên with regard to the concession in Shan-tung which it is reported that the German Government has asked from China. I am directed to state that Her Majesty's Government will demand equality of treatment for British subjects according to the treaty rights possessed by Great Britain, and that Her Majesty's Government will require compensation on any points in respect to which those rights may be disregarded."— *Ibid.*, p. 28, inclosure in No. 70.

other Powers also to follow suit with little regard
to her primary rights of sovereignty. Germany
could scarcely have felt the force of the British protest which was, indeed, rather directed to China than
to Germany. The latter secured what she asked,
and made Kiao-chau as free a port as her treaty-
tariff system would allow ;[1] but German claims to
the sole right of railroad and mining concessions
in the province were speedily emphasized by the
organization of the *Schan-tung Eisenbahngesell-
schaft*, with a capital of fifty-four million marks,
and also of the *Deutsche Bergbaugesellschaft*.[2]

[1] See *China, No. 1 (1899)*, p. 240, No. 322; *China, No. 1
(1900)*, pp. 12–13, 35, 146–147, 106, 233, and 241–244.

[2] It is unnecessary to recount the painful negotiations in
1898–9 concerning the Tien-tsin-Ching-kiang railway concession, in which the German claim in Shan-tung was strongly presented, and had to be recognized to a large extent by the British
Government. See *China, No. 1 (1900)*, pp. 14, 16, 17–18, 33,
118, 121, 175, 180.

# CHAPTER IV

## PORT ARTHUR AND TALIEN-WAN

As has been said, it appears impossible at the present state of our knowledge to trace the exact connection of Russia with the German occupation of Kiao-chau.[1] What is of more direct interest to our study, and is more easily established by evidence, is the fact that, with the plea that she could not be denied what had been granted to Germany,[2] Russia closely followed the latter's example,[3] and, under similar terms to hers,[4] demanded a lease of Port

[1] Cf. *China, No. 1 (1898)*, Nos. 1 and 15. China seems to have requested Russia to advise Germany to reconsider her action. Later, Russia is said to have reported that she had failed to change the mind of the Kaiser.

[2] Count Muravieff's remark to Sir N. O'Conor, the British *Chargé* at St. Petersburg, on March 28, 1898. — *China, No. 1 (1898)*, No. 125.

[3] Kiao-chau was occupied on November 17, three Russian war-vessels came to Port Arthur on December 18, 1897 ; the German-Chinese Agreement was concluded on March 5, the formal demand by Russia was presented about the 7th, and granted on the 27th of the same month, 1898.

[4] *Ibid.*, pp. 42–43, Nos. 95, 96, 98, 100. It is interesting to note that, on February 4, 1902, when negotiations were in progress between Russia and China, the former supporting large exclusive demands made by the Russo-Chinese Bank in Manchuria, M. Lessar, the Russian Minister, said that his Government was merely asking for privileges similar to those of Germany in Shan-tung. — U. S. 57th Congress, 2d Session, *House Documents*, vol. i. p. 274.

Arthur and Talien-wan, and also a railway concession between a point in the Manchurian line granted in 1896 and the ports. Recent years have seldom seen a situation so instructive of the character of the Far Eastern diplomacy in general, and of Russia's method in particular, as the foreign relations in China which culminated in the conclusion of the Russo-Chinese Agreement of March 27, 1898. These relations were also unusually complex, owing to the position which England held therein, whose vast interests in various parts of China were at once brought in many-sided contact, not only with Russia, but also with other Powers interested in China.

On December 20, 1897, a report reached the British Foreign Office that three Russian men-of-war had arrived at Port Arthur, and that three others were expected at Talien-wan and three more at Port Arthur.[1] Two days later it was officially explained by Count Muravieff " that the step taken was entirely a question of convenience for the ships, and had absolutely no connection with the occupation of the bay of Kiao-chau by Germany." The Count added " that there had always been a difficulty about keeping more than a certain number of men-of-war at a time in Japanese ports, and that, consequently, the Imperial Government had been glad to accept the offer of the Chinese Government to allow the Russian squadron to winter at Port Arthur. This arrangement was all the more

[1] *China, No. 1 (1898)*, p. 9, No. 231.

convenient as that port was within an easy distance
of Vladivostok, and had an arsenal where their
ships could undergo all necessary repairs. Moreover, it was an advantage that Port Arthur was
quite free from ice in the winter, though this fact
was not so important now, as Vladivostok was at
present furnished with an exceptionally powerful
ice-breaker, which it was hoped would make that
port available for egress and ingress during the
winter months. In fact, Vladivostok remained, as
heretofore, their centre in the Far East, and the
headquarters of their land and sea forces, so that
the mere fact of the Russian squadron wintering
at Port Arthur made no change whatever in the
situation." [1]  On the same day that this pacific declaration was made, it was reported, as it was later
confirmed by Chinese authorities, that Russia was
offering to China a 4 per cent. loan of 16,000,000
pounds at 93, an extremely favorable term, to pay
off the balance of the Japanese indemnity. The
suggested security was the income of the land tax
and *likin*, besides which Russia was said to have demanded as *quid pro quo* all future railway concessions in Manchuria and North China, as well as the
succession of a Russian subject to Sir Robert Hart
as Inspector-General of the Maritime Customs.[2]  It

---

[1] The statement made by Count Muravieff, on December 22,
1897, at his diplomatic reception, and reported by Mr. W. E.
Goschen. — *China*, *No. 1 (1898)*, pp. 12-13, No. 37.

[2] See *Ibid.*, Nos. 26, 43, 62. At the same time, M. Pavloff, the
Russian *Chargé* at Peking, demanded the dismissal of Mr.

was on this occasion that M. Pavloff, claiming that
the Tsung-li Yamên had promised to employ Russian engineers and Russian capital in the construction of any railway between the Great Wall and
the Russian frontier, undertook to record the alleged promise and express his gratification, and,
seeing that the Yamên did not reply, took it for
granted that the matter was settled, and notified
the St. Petersburg Government to that effect.[1] Nor
did the Russian Representatives at Peking fail
thereafter to appeal to this agreement concluded by
M. Pavloff in so striking a fashion, whenever China
opened any discussion with another Power regarding any subject connected with railways north of
Shan-hai-kwan. In the mean time, an Anglo-German syndicate had made an offer, last June, of a
loan for the same purpose, and now Sir Claude
MacDonald strongly supported a scheme of a new
loan presented by the Hong-kong and Shanghai
Bank, a British concern, in competition with the
Russian proposals.[2] One of the terms of the British loan as matured between the Bank, Sir Claude,
and the Marquess of Salisbury, was the opening of
Talien-wan to foreign trade.[3] The British Minis-

Kinder, British chief engineer of the Northern Railway. — *Ibid.*,
No. 38; cf. Nos. 111, 115, 117.

[1] M. Pavloff's own story to Sir Claude MacDonald, on March
17, 1898. — *China, No. 2 (1899)*, No. 2.

[2] *China, No. 1 (1898)*, No. 26.

[3] *Ibid.*, Nos. 30, 32, 43, 46. Some of the other terms were: (1)
the maritime and native customs, salt tax, and *likin*, as security;
(2) a railway from the Burmese frontier to the Yang-tsze valley;

ter's intention obviously was, among other things, to forestall the possible Russian occupation of this port as well as Port Arthur.[1] The significance was well understood by the Tsung-li Yamên, which was, however, afraid to embroil China with Russia, for the latter's *Chargé d'Affaires* " had protested, under instructions from his Government, against its [Talien-wan's] opening in the strongest manner, and had warned the Yamên that it would incur the hostility of Russia by doing so." [2] The reason for

(3) a guarantee against the cession of territory in the Yang-tsze valley to any other Power; (4) the opening of some other ports; (5) the pledge that so long as the British trade with China was larger than the trade of any other nation, the inspector-general of customs should always be an Englishman; (6) a freer internal navigation; etc. These terms seem to have been framed so as to protect British interests in China strictly within the scope of the most-favored-nation principle. The demand for the opening of Talien-wan and Nanning strongly prejudiced England against Russia and France, while the Burma-Yang-tsze Railway was unpleasing to France, and the non-alienation of the river valley was sometimes regarded by Russia as a counterpart of her own claims beyond the Great Wall. The whole story of the loan negotiation, as well as that of the Northern Railway extension loan, is highly interesting and important in the recent history of China, but we are here concerned with the bearing of the first loan on the development of the Manchurian question.

[1] It is highly interesting to note that during the latter part of 1903, when Russian aggression in Manchuria and on the northern frontier of Korea was feared, the American and Japanese Governments, with the moral support of the British, made successful efforts to open Mukden, Tatung-kao, and Antung to foreign trade. This proposition had met a strong Russian opposition, which also delayed, till after the outbreak of the present war, the opening of Wiju on the Korean border.

[2] *China, No. 1 (1898),* Nos. 51, 57.

this strenuous opposition was, on January 19, 1898, explained by the Russian Ambassador at London, who " urged very strongly that if we [the British Government] insisted on making Talien-wan an open port, we should be encroaching on the Russian sphere of influence, and denying her in the future that right to the use of Port Arthur to which the progress of events had given her a claim." These remarks were significant in showing how foreign was the idea of the open door to the Russian policy in Manchuria. When Lord Salisbury asked the Ambassador, in the same interview, what possible objection he could have to making Talien-wan a free port if Russia had no designs on that territory, the latter replied " that without any such designs it was generally admitted that Russia might claim a commercial *débouché* upon the open sea, and that in order to enjoy that advantage fully she ought to be at liberty to make such arrangements with China as she could obtain with respect to the commercial régime which was to prevail there." Here is a clear indication that Russia had little faith in the compatibility of other nations' commercial welfare in China with her own, or, in other words, in the ability of her people and the efficiency of their economic organization to compete with other nations in an open market. Else, she would not object to the opening of a port to the world's trade. Lord Salisbury reminded the Russian Representative that "the most-favored-nation clause forbade China to give Russia at Talien-wan more favorable

terms with regard to customs duties than she gave
to other treaty Powers." [1]    England's position,
which was repeatedly shown to Russia, was that it
was natural that Russia should open a port for
her commerce on the coasts of the North Pacific,[2]
but that it would be a contravention of the treaty
rights [3] of other nations to make of the port an
exclusive market for Russian trade. Under these
persistent representations, Count Muravieff at last
declared, on January 28, through M. de Staal,
Ambassador at London, that any (tout) [4] commercial outlet secured by Russia " would be open to
the ships of all the great Powers, like other ports
on the Chinese mainland. It would be open to the
commerce of all the world, and England, whose
trade interests are so important in those regions,
would share in the advantage." [5]    Then what was
meant by "open"? M. de Staal stated on February 10: "I cannot in any way anticipate the
decisions of my Government, which, in the event

[1] *China, No. 1 (1898)*, No. 59.

[2] *Ibid.*, Nos. 72, 76, 123, etc.

[3] The most-favored-nation clause is referred to, which —
sometimes in general and sometimes in specific terms, and sometimes reciprocal and conditional, but nearly always unilateral
and unconditional — is inserted in the treaty of China with each
Power. See Mayers, op. cit.

[4] A dispute arose later between the Russian and British Governments on this word "any" (*tout*). The latter interpreted it to
mean any port secured by Russia in China, while the former
claimed that the Czar's Government had never promised to open
Port Arthur to foreign trade. — March 13, 1898; *China, No. 1
(1898)*, pp. 47–48, No. 114.

[5] *Ibid.*, No. 76.

of acquiring an outlet in Chinese waters, naturally remains free either to establish a *porto franco* [i. e., a port where goods imported are exempt from all import dues] there, or to assimilate the port in question to the treaty ports of the Chinese littoral." [1] It will be seen later that, through the Imperial Order of July 30 (August 11), 1899,[2] Russia declared Dalny a "free port" in the sense of a *porto franco*, under certain conditions. In the face of these elastic conditions, one would be slow, in spite of the Order, to admit that the question stated by M. de Staal in the quoted passage has been definitively settled by his government one way or the other, or in a third alternative.[3]

Up to this point, namely, about February 10, 1898, one can follow the gradual withdrawal of Lord Salisbury's position. He at first seemed to have accepted Sir Claude MacDonald's suggestion to insist upon the opening of Talien-wan as a condition of the British-Chinese loan, but, evidently at the Russian opposition, presently contented himself with giving the following instruction to the British Minister at Peking: "You are not bound to insist on making Talien-wan a treaty port if you think it impracticable, though we give it up with regret. Would it be possible to obtain a promise of such a concession if ever a railway was made to that port? You should maintain demand for opening of other

---

[1] *China, No. 1 (1898)*, No. 83.

[2] See p. 133, below.

[3] Compare the Russian reply to Secretary Hay's note of September, 1899, pp. 135–138, below.

ports." [1] Then, when the Chinese Government was so pressed by the opposition of Russia and France as to declare on January 30 that unless England pledged herself to offer protection to China against Russia, she could not consent to accept the loan,[2] Lord Salisbury's policy receded further than before. He now made representations to Russia not to infringe the most-favored-nation treatment in Talien-wan, if she should lease the port. It is needless to say that such a direct request to Russia was tantamount, on the part of England, to abandoning the desire of securing the opening of the port from China, which, save for Russian threats, was willing to comply with the desire; and to acquiescing in and even recognizing Russia's right to lease the port, instead of opening it as a treaty port. Under these circumstances, it was not strange that the British Government was met by Russia with the ambiguous phrase, " open port," which, in spite of Lord Salisbury's attempt[3] to interpret it in the sense of a *porto franco*, was found, in M. de Staal's statement of February 10, already quoted, to be still more uncertain than it appeared when it was first declared. Russia seemed to have gained all that England lost, but it was a mere prelude to a far more serious situation which was still to develop.

It would have been plain to any one, had he

---

[1] On January 17. — *China, No. 1 (1898)*, No. 56.  Cf. No. 62.

[2] *Ibid.*, Nos. 65, 69, 75, 78, 79.

[3] In his speech before the House of Lords on February 8.  See *ibid.*, Nos. 82, 83, 87; the *Parliamentary Debates*, 4th Series, vol. 53, pp. 40–41.

been susceptible to certain unmistakable signs, that Russia's desires in Manchuria were more extensive than the mere acquisition of a lease of a commercial outlet on the Yellow Sea. The same Count Mura-vieff, who had said three weeks before that the pre-sence of Russian ships at Port Arthur late in 1897 was purely for the sake of wintering there, and that the fact that Port Arthur was ice-free was not very important, now declared, on January 12, 1898, that when the Russian fleet had left the port, after win-tering there, the Chinese Government had given the Russians a prior right of anchorage — *le droit du premier mouillage*.[1] The question so gently broached was more clearly pronounced a week later, when M. de Staal strongly maintained that the open-ing of Talien-wan would result in an encroachment upon the Russian sphere of influence, and in " deny-ing her in the future that right to the use of Port Arthur to which the progress of events had given her a claim." [2] In the face of these official remarks, it would be impossible to deny that Russia wished to use, not only Talien-wan, but also Port Arthur, and the latter for purposes clearly other than com-mercial. Yet the British Government does not seem to have taken any action in the matter, but, on the contrary, its tacit recognition of Russia's demand of the lease of Talien-wan was not of a nature to dis-courage her design upon Port Arthur. On Febru-ary 14, China made concessions to Great Britain regarding internal navigation, the non-alienation of

[1] *China, No. 1 (1898)*, No. 54.   [2] *Ibid.*, No. 59.

the Yang-tsze Provinces, and the appointment of an Englishman to the inspectorate-general of customs so long as the British trade was preponderant in China ;[1] on the 19th, the preliminary agreement of the British loan was signed ;[2] and March 6 saw the conclusion of the German agreement concerning the lease of Kiao-chau and privileges in the Province of Shan-tung. Russia immediately seized this opportunity in bringing forward her long cherished design, for, on March 7, it was simultaneously reported in the London *Times* and by Sir Claude Mac-Donald, soon to be confirmed by the Tsungli-Yamên and admitted by Count Muravieff, that M. Pavloff was pressing the Peking Government to grant the lease of Port Arthur and Talien-wan and the railway concession from Petuna on the trans-Manchurian Railway to the ports.[3] The report appears to have made a profound impression upon the British Government, which, on the day it was received, was compelled to say that, if the Russian demands were granted, " her influence over the Government of Peking would be so increased, to the detriment of that of Her Majesty's Government, that it seemed desirable for them to make some counter-move. The best plan would perhaps be, on the cession of Wei-hai-Wei by the Japanese [who had been holding it, according to the treaty, pending the final payment of Chinese indemnity], to insist on the refusal of a lease of that port on terms similar to those granted

[1] *China, No. 1 (1898)*, No. 85.     [2] *Ibid.*, No. 88.
[3] *Ibid.*, Nos. 95, 96, 99, 100, 101, 103.

to Germany." [1] This view was sounded, it is true, to the British Minister at Peking, and not to the Russian Government, but the latter was not to encounter an effective protest from a government which had so soon made up its mind that the protest might fail and be compensated by itself reproducing the evil at China's expense.[2] At any rate, Count

[1] *China, No. 1 (1898)*, No. 95 (Salisbury to MacDonald).

[2] The Russian Government soon had occasion to gauge the strength of the British protest, for, on March 8, Sir N. O'Conor made a striking statement to Count Muravieff, as will be seen in the following report (*ibid.*, No. 108, O'Conor to Salisbury): "I alluded, as no doubt his Excellency was aware, to the junction of the Burmese and Chinese railway systems. This demand became at once still more necessary and reasonable if greater privileges of the same kind were accorded to Russia in the Liao-tung Peninsula, as they had apparently already been accorded in Manchuria. Count Muravieff did not, however, respond to these remarks beyond saying that he supposed the Burma-Chinese line would, in this case, descend to the valley of the Yang-tsze." The Count's remark may be considered a sufficient reply, when it is seen in connection with another remark he made a few moments earlier. When Sir N. O'Conor alluded to the objectionable features of leasing Port Arthur, the Foreign Minister reminded him that British interests were principally represented in the neighborhood of the Yang-tsze. Russia would evade the British protest by turning England's attention to her own sphere, in which Russia had little interest, and would not object to a British repetition there of Russia's conduct in Manchuria. Muravieff must have thought that O'Conor, by his reference to the Burmese Railway, now voluntarily threw himself into his net. Russia later succeeded in inducing England to conclude the Anglo-Russian railway declaration of April 28, 1899, delimiting in a negative manner the railway spheres of the two Powers in China, Russia pledging not to seek concessions and not to obstruct those of the British in the Yang-tsze valley, and England pledging similarly in regard to Russian concessions beyond the Great Wall. (See *China, No. 2 (1899)*, No.

Muravieff deemed it now safe to declare, beginning with March 8, that no alternative had been left to Russia, under the uncertainty attending the development of affairs in the Far East and other circumstances, but to demand a cession both of Talien-wan and Port Arthur, the former only to be opened to foreign trade; that one of these ports without the other would be of no use to Russia, while the use of both was of vital necessity to her; and that the lease would not interfere with the sovereign rights of the Chinese Empire. To the last pledge was added, probably at the persistent representations of England, that the treaty rights acquired by the Powers in China would be respected.[1]

The distinction made by Count Muravieff between Port Arthur and Talien-wan at once brought home to the British Government the gravity of the situation. The first impulse on the part of Lord Salisbury was to fall back upon M. de Staal's statement of February 10, that any (*tout*) port which Russia might acquire on the Chinese coast should be

138.) The Russian Government naturally considered the conclusion of this agreement as a diplomatic victory over the British, and seemed to have interpreted its terms as implying that all the territory beyond the Great Wall was the Russian sphere, not only of railway concessions, but also of general interests and influence. Already in May of the same year, M. Pavloff renewed his demand at Peking for the concession of a Russian railway to be built directly to the Chinese capital, thus even overreaching the limit set in the British agreement of less than a fortnight previous. See *China, No. 1 (1900)*, pp. 112, 116, 120, 129, 132–133, 214–215.

[1] *China, No. 1 (1898)*, Nos. 101, 105, 108, 110, 114, 120, 149.

open to the foreign trade.[1] Count Muravieff, however, explained that the statement applied only to
Talien-wan, but no promise had been made regarding Port Arthur.[2] On March 15, however, he was
authorized by the Czar to give to Sir N. O'Conor
" an assurance that both Port Arthur and Talien-
wan would be open to foreign trade, like other
Chinese ports, in the event of the Russian Government's obtaining a lease of these places from the
Chinese Government." The Count intimated next
morning that it would be desirable for the British
Government not to repeat this assurance in the
House of Commons, for " it might be considered as a
want of courtesy toward the Chinese Government,
who had not yet formally agreed to give the Russian
Government a lease of the ports in question." [3]

Presently, however, the British Government
awoke to the conviction that Port Arthur was " not
a commercial harbor," and " it was doubtful whether
it could be converted into one." " But," stated the
Marquess of Salisbury, " though not a commercial
harbor, Port Arthur supplies a naval base, limited
indeed in extent, but possessing great natural and
artificial strength. And this, taken in connection
with its strategic position, gives it an importance in
the Gulf of Pechili and therefore at Peking, upon
which, in their representation to Japan at the close
of the war with China, the Russian Government
laid the greatest emphasis. . . . The possession,

[1] *China, No. 1 (1898)*, No. 104.
[2] *Ibid., No.* 114.                         [3] *Ibid.*, No. 120.

even if temporary, of this particular position, is
likely to have political consequences at Peking of
great international importance, and the acquisition
of a Chinese harbor notoriously useless for commercial purposes by a foreign Power will be universally
interpreted in the Far East as indicating that the
partition of China has begun. . . . It may, perhaps, be proper to observe that a great military
Power which is conterminous for over four thousand miles with the land frontier of China, including the portion lying nearest to its capital, is never
likely to be without its due share of influence on
the councils of that country. Her Majesty's Government regard it as most unfortunate that it has
been thought necessary, in addition, to obtain control
of a port which, if the rest of the Gulf of Pechili
remains in hands so helpless as that of the sovereign Power, will command the maritime approaches
to its capital, and give to Russia the same strategic advantage by sea which she already possesses
in so ample a measure by land." [1]  In this spirit,
the British Government asked Count Muravieff
through Sir N. O'Conor, on March 23, to reconsider the advisability of pressing demands upon
China in regard to Port Arthur.  England would not
object to the Russian lease of an ice-free commercial harbor connected by rail with the trans-Siberian

---

[1] *China, No. 1 (1898)*, No. 138.  The Marquess did not refer
to a matter of enormous importance, that the proposed railways
would *connect* the immense land and sea forces of Russia, which
he emphasized.

Railway, but questions of an entirely different kind were opened if Russia obtained control of a military port in the neighborhood of Peking. England, on her part, was prepared to give assurances that beyond the maintenance of the existing treaty rights she had no interests in Manchuria, and to pledge herself not to occupy any port in the Gulf of Pechili as long as other Powers maintained the same policy.[1] To this protest, so plainly attended by a second wish of Great Britain to make a counter-move when the prime move of Russia could not be checked, Count Muravieff made, on March 23, a firm reply, refusing absolutely to admit that the integrity of the Chinese Empire was violated by the proposed lease of Port Arthur, and repeating his assertion that the possession of that harbor was a question of vital necessity to Russia. Sir N. O'Conor confessed the futility of his protest.[2] About the same day, M. Pavloff informed the Peking Government that Russia could not consider the question of Port Arthur and Talien-wan apart, and insisted upon their lease before the 27th, failing which, Russia would take hostile measures.[3] Now England definitely resolved, on March 25, to obtain speedily the lease of Wei-hai-Wei in terms similar to those granted to Russia for Port Arthur, and ordered the British fleet to proceed from Hong-

[1] *China, No. 1 (1900)*, Nos. 123 and 133.

[2] "I cannot say that my efforts were successful. . . . I was unable to induce his Excellency to modify his views." — *Ibid.*, Nos. 125 and 132.

[3] *Ibid.*, No. 126.

kong to the Gulf of Pechili,[1] and, three days later, notified the Russian Government that she would retain her entire liberty of action to take steps to protect her interests, and to diminish the evil consequences which she anticipated.[2] On the preceding day, however, a Russo-Chinese Agreement had been signed, incorporating all the points upon which Russia had insisted and against which England had vainly protested. Count Muravieff at once briefly announced to the Powers the successful conclusion of the Agreement;[3] and, when the British Government called upon him to fulfill his promise to give a written assurance of Russia's declared intention to respect the sovereign rights of China and the treaty privileges of the other Powers in the leased territory, he calmly replied that what was interpreted as promises was in fact " very confidentially " expressed views, and that " the time was not opportune " for making the assurances public. Russia would not, he added, so " abuse the lease granted by a friendly Power " as " to arbitrarily transform a closed and principally military port into a commercial port like any other." [4] The triumph of Russia was tardily followed, on April 3, by the promise England secured from China to lease Wei-hai-Wei to her for the same period as Port Arthur,[5] thus again substituting for an effec-

---

[1] *China, No. 1 (1900)*, No. 129.    [2] *Ibid.*, No. 138.

[3] *Ibid.*, Nos. 134, 136, and 137.

[4] Cf. *ibid.*, Nos. 135, 137, 138, 139, 140, 149, and 151.

[5] *Ibid.*, No. 144. The agreement was signed at Peking on July 1. See *Treaty Series*, No. 14, 1898.

tive prevention of evils the " balance " [1] and retali-
ation between the Powers at the expense of China.[2]

[1] "Balance of power in Gulf of Pechili is materially altered
by surrender of Port Arthur by the Yamên to Russia. It is therefore necessary to obtain," etc. — Salisbury to MacDonald,
March 25; *China, No. 1 (1898)*, No. 129. Cf. also *China, No. 1
(1899)*, No. 2.

It should be said, in justice to Great Britain, that at first, when
the Chinese Government intimated toward the end of February
that they would lease Wei-hai-Wei to her if she would accept it,
Lord Salisbury considered such an offer premature, for his Government "aimed at discouraging any alienation of Chinese territory." — *Ibid.*, Nos. 90 and 91.

[2] Two other instances may here be cited to further illustrate
the policy of the British Government during this critical period
of time. (1) Soon after the appearance of Russian war-vessels at
Port Arthur, Admiral Buller, of the China station of the British
navy, arrived at Chemulpo with seven ships, on December 29,
and ordered the "Immortalité" and "Iphigenia" to proceed to
Port Arthur. The former was, on January 10, ordered to leave
for Chefu. The presence of the British boats created "a bad
impression" on Russia, which requested England to avoid dangers of conflict in the Russian "sphere of influence." The British Government explained that the ships had been sent by the
Admiral without instruction from the Admiralty, and would soon
leave, " in ordinary course of cruising." It was added, at the
same time, that British ships had a perfect right to proceed to
Port Arthur. It was reported at one time that the two boats had
been ordered away from Port Arthur under protest from Russia.
— *Ibid.*, Nos. 31, 48, 52, 63, 66, 68. (2) On March 8, Sir Claude
MacDonald was informed by the Tsung-li Yamên that the only
reason given by M. Pavloff for the demand of the lease of the
two ports was to "assist in protecting Manchuria against the
aggression of other Powers." Probably England and Japan were
meant, and the Yamên was fully alive to the absurdity of this
pretext, but was unable to resist the Russian demands. It therefore begged earnestly that the British Government would assist
it by giving a formal assurance to the Russian Government that
England had no designs on Manchuria. It does not seem to have

In this connection, it may be noted that the Russian Government considered, according to Count Muravieff, " that China owed them this [the lease of the ports] for the services they had rendered her in her war with Japan, and these services must be properly requited." [1] It was no matter of surprise to Japan that Russia now secured for herself the most strategic portion of the territory, the retention of which by Japan was, three years ago, declared by the same Power to be imperiling the position of Peking, rendering Korean independence nominal, and interfering with the permanent peace of the Far East. When it was announced by Russia, in December last, that Port Arthur had been lent to her by China only temporarily as a winter anchorage, the Japanese Government merely " credited this assurance, and accordingly took note of it." [2] When the negotiations for the lease were in progress, the Japanese Government made no protest, and when they were consummated, it manifested no appreciable sentiment. At the same time, it quietly approved of the British lease of Wei-hai-Wei, [3]

been thought necessary by the British Government to give such an assurance. See *ibid.*, Nos. 100 and 109.

[1] *China, No. 1 (1898)*, No. 114 (O'Conor to Salisbury, March 13).

[2] *Ibid.*, No. 29.

[3] "The Japanese Government," said Baron Nishi, Foreign Minister of Japan, confidentially, to Sir Ernest Satow, about March 20, "had been anxious that China should be able to maintain her position at Wei-hai-Wei, but if she found it impossible to do so, Japan would have no objection to its being held by a Power disposed to assist in maintaining the independence of

which the Japanese troops had still held pending
the final payment of the Chinese indemnity.  Then
they speedily evacuated the port in favor of England, leaving behind them every accommodation to
the successor.[1]

The Agreement concluded, on March 15/27,
1898, between Li Hung-chang and the Russian
*Chargé*, M. Pavloff, has never been published by
the Russian Government, and the only sources to
which we can turn are an English translation of a
Chinese *précis* forwarded by Sir Claude MacDonald
more than a month after the conclusion of the
Agreement,[2] and the Chinese text that appears in

China." — *China, No. 1 (1899)*, No. 35.  Cf. also Nos. 49, 79,
81, 107, etc.

[1] *Ibid.*, Nos. 85, 112, 118, 231, 238.
Russia had undertaken to request Japan to promise that
China would secure Wei-hai-Wei after the Japanese evacuation,
but Japan declined to make such a pledge. — *Ibid.*, No. 30.  In
April, 1902, the control of Wei-hai-Wei was transferred from
the Admiralty to the Colonial Office.  The mouth of the harbor is
so large that it would require an enormous expenditure and large
forces to fortify and defend it adequately.  At the time when England leased the port, she was hardly inclined to let financial considerations thwart her effort to restore her prestige so abruptly
foreshadowed by that of Russia.  In 1902, however, the lately
concluded Anglo-Japanese agreement of alliance rendered the
fortification of Wei-hai-Wei no longer necessary.  See *Tokushu
Jōyaku*, pp. 172–173.

[2] *China, No. 1 (1899)*, pp. 127–129, No. 187, dated Peking,
April 29.  Regarding this *précis*, Sir Claude says: " It bears
every sign of foreign authorship, and the original cannot have
been drafted by a Chinese.  I have no doubt that the document
correctly represents the sense of the original agreement, for it
fully corresponds with what I have been able to learn of the contents of the latter."  M. Cordier also relies on this *précis* in his

the *Tō-A Kwankei Tokushu Jōyaku Isan*.[1] Port
Arthur and Talien-wan, with their adjacent waters,
were leased to Russia for twenty-five years, subject
to renewal by mutual agreement, the lease not affecting the sovereign rights of China (Articles 1
and 3); within the leased territory, Chinese citizens
might continue to live, but no Chinese troops should
be stationed, and the responsibility of military affairs should be vested in one Russian officer, who
should not bear the Chinese title of governor-general or governor (Article 4); Port Arthur would be
a naval port open only to the Russian and Chinese
men-of-war, but closed against the commercial and
naval ships of other nations, while Talien-wan, except the portion used exclusively for naval purposes,
would be a trading port open freely to the merchant
vessels of all nations (Article 6); the Russians
would be allowed to build forts and barracks, and
provide defenses (Article 7); there should be a neutral territory to the north of the leased ground, which
would be administered by Chinese officials, but into
which no Chinese troops should be sent without
consulting the Russian authorities (Article 5); the
railway contract of 1896 might be extended so as
to cover a branch line to Talien-wan and, if necessary, another line between Niu-chwang and the
Yalu, but the construction of the railways should

*Histoire des relations de la Chine avec les puissances occidentales*,
vol. iii. pp. 362–364.
  [1] *Tokushu Jōyaku*, pp. 244–245. This Chinese text naturally clears up some points which are obscure in the *précis*.

not be made a ground for securing territory (Article 8). Sir Claude Macdonald presented also, on June 14, what he believed to be an authentic version of the Special Russo-Chinese Agreement concluded on April 25 (May 7), 1898, to supplement the Agreement of March 15.[1] It defined the extent of the leased territory, and of the neutral territory to the north of the former (Articles 1 and 2).[2] Within the latter, it was agreed, no ports should be open to the trade of other nations, and no economic concessions made to them, without Russian consent (Article 5). At Kin-chow, the administration and police were to be Chinese, but the military, Russian (Article 4). Regarding railways, it was provided that Port Arthur and Talien-wan should be the termini of the conceded line, along which no railway privileges should be given to other nations. Russia would, however, have nothing to say if China herself should undertake to construct a railway from Shan-hai-kwan to a point near the Russian line (Article 3).

[1] See *China, No. 1 (1899)*, p. 188, No. 273. Also Cordier, *Histoire*, vol. iii. pp. 365–366. A Japanese version obtained from the Foreign Office at Tokio appears in *Tokushu Jōyaku*, pp. 246–247. The Special Agreement was supplemented by another Agreement concluded on April 25 (o. s.), 1899.

[2] The boundary of the leased territory began with the northern side of A-tang Bay (Port Adams), on the west coast of the Liao-tung Peninsula, and passed through and included the A-tang Mountains, ending near Pi-tse-wo, and including the adjacent waters and isles. The northern limit of the neutral ground started at the mouth of the Kai-chow River, passed north of Yuyen-ch'êng and along the Ta-yang River, and ended at and included its mouth.

These agreements were accompanied by some characteristically pacific and magnanimous utterances by the Czar, professing his firm friendship with China, extolling the wise decision of the Son of Heaven in granting the lease, and emphasizing that the direct communication by means of the great Siberian Railway with the hitherto closed-up country would largely contribute to the peaceful intercourse of the peoples of the East and West, to which task Russia was called by Divine Providence.[1]

The leased territory was named Kwan-tung[2] by the Russians, and the Provisional Regulations for its administration were published at St. Petersburg through the *Bulletin des Lois* of August 20 (September 1), 1899.[3] By these regulations, the Kwantung region was placed under the jurisdiction of the Ministry of War, with its chief seat of administration at Port Arthur (Articles 4 and 6). The Administration was headed by a Governor, appointed and removed at the immediate will of the Czar, who was also Commander-in-Chief of the army forces of the territory and entered into immediate communication with the commander of the cis-Amur region, and in addition commanded the navy at Port Arthur

---

[1] See the Czar's telegraphic message to the Chinese Emperor, on March 15/27; and his Imperial orders of March 17/29 and July 30/August 11. *China, No. 1 (1899)*, pp. 20–21, 1–2, and 262–263.

[2] Meaning, presumably, east of Shan-hai-kwan.

[3] See *China, No. 1 (1900)*, pp. 292–293, 304–311, and 335. Also the *Tsūshō Isan* (Japanese Consular Reports), April 28, 1904, pp. 33–46.

and Vladivostok ; the latter port, however, retained its Commander of the port, who was subservient to the Governor (Articles 3, 7, 12, 13, and 14). In matters concerning frontier and foreign relations, the Governor directly communicated with the Russian Representatives at Peking, Tokio, and Seul, and with the Russian military and naval agents (Article 22). At the creation on August 13, 1903, of a Vice-regency in this region, which will receive attention later, it became necessary to make some changes in the administrative rules, which had not been completed at the outbreak of the present war.

Talien-wan being mainly open to foreign trade, its organization and administration were set on a separate basis from the rest of the Kwan-tung. At the instance of M. Witte, then the Minister of Finance, an Imperial Order was promulgated on July 30 (August 11), 1899, ordering that near Talien-wan a new town named Dalny should be built, which was simultaneously declared a free port under the following conditions, namely, that the importation and exportation of merchandise should be allowed free of customs dues in Dalny within the limits determined, and liable to modification, by the Minister of Finance ; but that goods imported into Russia from Dalny should pay the regular import duties in force in the Russian Empire.[1] By the Provisional Regulations already referred to of August 20 (September 1) of the same year, the organization of Dalny was assigned to

[1] See *China, No. 1 (1900)*, pp. 262–263.

the Eastern Chinese Railway Company, under the
chief direction of the Minister of Finance, and its
administration was intrusted to a Prefect, to be
appointed and dismissed by Imperial orders and
subordinate to the Governor of the Kwan-tung
(Articles 99 and 101).[1]  It is already well known
that Dalny, now covering about 100 square versts
in area, was, according to M. Witte's plan, intended
to be the commercial terminus of the great Siberian Railway, and eventually the mercantile outlet
on the Pacific of the vast Russian Empire.  Before
the war, the works at Dalny, including its large
docks and piers, had cost already nearly 20,000,000
rubles.  Part of this immense expenditure was to
have been met by the income of the public sales at
auction of land-lots, held three times since 1902, in
spite of the fact that the twenty-five year lease of
the territory to Russia would hardly justify her in
alienating portions of it permanently.[2]

[1] *China, No. 1 (1900)*, pp. 308–311.

[2] Conditions at Dalny since its foundation are minutely described by M. Suzuki, agent of the Japanese Foreign Office in
the *Tsūshō Isan* for April 23 (pp. 39–49), 28 (pp. 32–46), May 3
(pp. 37–49), 8 (pp. 42–55), 12 (pp. 36–42), and 18 (pp. 33–37),
1904.

# CHAPTER V

## SECRETARY HAY'S CIRCULAR NOTE

It is unnecessary for us to describe how, between 1897 and 1899, other so-called spheres of influence and of economic concessions than those already mentioned were marked out in China by the Powers, for, important as they are in the general history of the modern East, they have little bearing upon our immediate subject. It suffices to recall that the process was begun by the German seizure of Kiaochau; that unfortunately Great Britain felt obliged to have recourse to the policy of the balance of power; and that no other " sphere " had the grave significance and the evil forebodings of the Russian territory of the Kwan-tung in Manchuria. It was during this period that a Power whose position was so unique as to justify the act appealed to the other interested Powers, in September, 1899, to make declarations that they would observe the principle of the equal economic opportunity for all nations in their respective spheres of interest in China. The principle thus proposed by the United States was stated to imply (1) non-interference with the treaty rights and vested interests of each other; (2) the maintenance of the Chinese treaty tariff, except in " free ports," under the Chinese man-

agement; and (3) no differential treatment in the
harbor duties and railway charges, in the spheres.
The phrase " leased territory " was used in connection with only the first of these three points,
while the words " spheres of interest " were applied
to all three, so that it was uncertain whether the
second and third points were intended by Secretary
Hay to cover the leases, as well as the spheres.[1]
In reply to this proposition, Great Britain, which
had stronger reason than the United States to in-
dorse a policy which had originated with her and
which she had long upheld in China at enormous
cost, and Japan expressed their unequivocal adherence to the proposed principle.  Germany, France,
and Italy also assented, all except Italy, however,
with the natural reservation that the desired declarations would be made if all other interested Powers
acted likewise.[2]  As regards the question whether
the three points applied to the leases and spheres
alike, it is interesting to note that Germany, France,
and Great Britain replied, in effect, in the affirmative, Germany using the expression " its Chinese
possessions," and France employing the phrase
" the territories which were leased to her."  The
statement used by Great Britain was the most
explicit and comprehensive, for she mentioned " the
leased territory of Wei-hai-Wei and all territory in
China which may hereafter be acquired by Great

[1] *China, No. 2 (1900)*, No. 1.
[2] *Ibid.*, Nos. 2, 3, 4, and inclosures 1, 2, 3, 4, and 5, in
No. 5.

Britain, by lease or otherwise, and all 'spheres of interest' now held, or that may hereafter be held in China." Beside these assurances, the Russian assent was highly significant, which, with the reservation similar to that of the other Powers, stated : " As to the ports now opened, or hereafter to be opened, to foreign commerce *by the Chinese Government*,[1] and which lie *beyond* the leased territory to Russia, the settlement of the question of customs duties belongs to China herself, and the Imperial Government [of Russia] has no intention whatever of claiming any privileges for its own subjects to the exclusion of foreigners." But " in so far as the territory leased by China to Russia is concerned, the Imperial Government [of Russia] has already demonstrated its firm intention to follow the policy of the 'open door' by creating Dalny (Talienwan) a free port; and *if at some future time that port, although remaining free itself, should be separated by a custom-limit from other portions of the territory in question*, the customs duties would be levied, in the zone subject to the tariff, upon all *foreign* merchants without distinction as to nationality. With the conviction," the Russian note concluded, " that this reply is such as to ratify the inquiry made in the aforementioned note [of the United States], the Imperial Government is happy to have complied with the wishes of the American Government, especially as it attaches the highest value to anything that may strengthen

[1] The italics in the quotations are the author's.

and consolidate the traditional relations of friendship existing between the two countries." [1]  On the
strength of the various replies from the Powers,
however, the United States Government considered
that " the Declaration suggested by the United
States on that subject [i. e., the proposals about
the Chinese trade] had been accepted by those
Powers," and regarded the assent given by them
" as final and definite." [2]  It is interesting to note
that no Power made a formal declaration [3] suggested by Secretary Hay, who, however, seems to
have deemed the replies with reservations as equivalent to such a declaration.  It is problematical
whether this exchange of notes did in the slightest
degree have the effect of changing the actual situation, at least so far as Russia was concerned.

[1] *China, No. 2 (1900)*, inclosure 6 in No. 5.
[2] *Ibid.*, No. 5, White to Salisbury, March 30, 1900.
[3] Cf. *ibid.*, No. 6.

# CHAPTER VI

## THE OCCUPATION OF MANCHURIA

WE have given only an incomplete account of the manner in which certain Powers seemed, during the years 1897 and 1898, to vie with one another in transgressing, in effect, the principle of the territorial integrity of the Chinese Empire, to which they at the same time professed their adherence. Another principle, however, — that of the open door, or of the equal opportunity in China for the commercial and industrial enterprise of all nations, — was, as we have seen, not as openly ignored even by the most aggressive Powers. The time arrived, in 1900, when the observance of both principles appeared to be the only safeguard against a general partition of China and an internal revolution through the length and breadth of the vast Empire. The story of the Boxer trouble is too fresh in every one's memory to need to be retold. It was during this insurrection, and during the march of the allied forces toward Peking and the long negotiations which followed it, that all the Powers concerned repeatedly and unequivocally pledged themselves to one another to maintain the two cardinal principles of Chinese diplomacy. It now belongs to us to relate, however, that it was

in the midst of this reiterated promise of fair play
that the most acute stage of the Manchurian question was reached. Evidence is abundant to show
that Russia was inclined greatly to underestimate
the seriousness of the troubles in North China,
where a concerted action of all the interested
Powers was imperative, while in Manchuria, which
Russia had for years regarded as her sphere of influence,[1] she carried forward aggressive measures
with great rapidity and on an enormous scale.
Thus, even so late as June 20, when the railway
communication of Peking with Tientsin had been
cut for three weeks;[2] when Prince Tuan and his
anti-foreign counselors swayed the Court, and the
Tsung-li Yamên had long proved utterly impotent
to cope with the situation;[3] when the 6000 Chi-

[1] It may reasonably be said that the meaning of the intervention of Russia, France, and Germany, in 1895, in regard to
Japan's claim upon the Liao-tung Peninsula may be gathered,
in a retroactive way, from Russia's conduct in Manchuria since
1896. At any rate, M. Pavloff declared, in October, 1897, that
"the Russian Government intended that the provinces of China
bordering on the Russian frontier must not come under the influence of any nation except Russia." — *China, No. 1 (1898)*, p. 6.
This declaration throws light not only on the trans-Manchurian
railway concessions and the lease of ports, but also on Russia's
action respecting the Northern Railway extension and the consequent Anglo-Russian agreement of April, 1899. In May, 1898,
there were already 200 Russian soldiers in Kirin, and in December, 2000 in Port Arthur and Talien-wan, while many Cossacks
guarded railway construction, and many barracks were being
hurriedly built, so that there were sufficient indications even
before 1900 that Russia regarded Manchuria as her sphere of
influence.

[2] May 29. — *China, No. 3 (1900)*, No. 5.

[3] Cf. *China, No. 4 (1900)*, No. 1 (June 5).

nese soldiers sent against the Boxers around Tientsin betrayed themselves into inaction ;[1] when the
international relief corps of marines led by Admiral Seymour had already been forced backward ;[2]
when the Boxers had at last poured into Peking[3]
and held the foreigners in siege for a week, killing
many Chinese as well as the Japanese Chancellor
Sugiyama ;[4] and when the Taku forts had been
taken by the allied squadron,[5] only to infuriate
the anti-foreign sentiment all over North China ;[6]
when no news had been received by him even from
Tientsin and Taku for the past four days,[7] and after
he had dispatched 4000 Russian soldiers for the
disposal of M. de Giers at Peking,[8] — Count Muravieff still held an optimistic view, and supposed that
the trouble would be over within two weeks, saying
that Middle and South China were under a greater
peril than the North.[9] This last assertion, which he
made more than once,[10] is significant when we consider that Middle and South China included regions
where British interests were predominant. Although

[1] *China, No. 3 (1900)*, No. 94; *No. 4 (1900)*, No. 1 (June 8).

[2] *China, No. 3 (1900)*, No. 219 (June 16–26).

[3] *Ibid.*, No. 133; *No. 4 (1900)*, No. 2 (evening, June 13).

[4] *China, No. 3 (1900)*, No. 122 (June 13).

[5] *Ibid.*, Nos. 132, 148, 157, and 186 (June 17).

[6] *Ibid.*, No. 157.

[7] *Ibid.*, No. 159. It is true that some of these events had not
been known to Muravieff, but enough news had reached him to
show the extreme gravity of the situation.

[8] *Ibid.*, No. 149 (June 16).

[9] *Ibid.*, No. 159. Also see Nos. 43, 45, 48, 65, 58, 114, 120, all
indicating the optimistic view of the Count.

[10] Cf. *ibid.*, No. 120 (June 13).

Russia persistently declared her firm intention to act in concert with other Powers in North China, it is not altogether impossible to suppose, as it has been alleged, that she was not unwilling to divert the attention of Great Britain and others from North China, where Russia would not have hesitated, if possible, to render her sole assistance to China to suppress the insurrection.  At least, Russia declared it to be one of her objects in China to "assist the Chinese Government in the work of reëstablishing order so necessary in the primary interest of China herself ; "[1] at least, the pro-Russian Li Hung-chang expressed, on June 22, an otherwise inexplicable confidence in his ability to restore peace.[2]  The real

---

[1] *China, No. 3 (1900)*, No. 149 (June 16).  In the Czar's reply to the Chinese Emperor's appeal for a friendly intervention, it was stated that "the efforts of Russia had but one object in view, namely, to assist in the reëstablishment of order and tranquillity in the Chinese Empire, and, inspired by their traditional friendship for China, the Imperial Government have decided to render to the Chinese Government every assistance with a view to repressing the present troubles."  From the Russian Official Gazette, as reported by Sir Charles Scott on August 2, 1900; *China, No. 1 (1901)*, No. 105.  It is noteworthy that Russia had raised objections to sending large forces from Japan to the relief of Peking, one reason being that she supposed they would be commissioned, not only to rescue the Legations, but also to suppress rebellion and restore peace in Peking and Tientsin. — *Ibid.*, No. 29.

[2] *Ibid.*, No. 175.  A writer of diplomatic history of Russia, himself a Russian, considers that the anti-foreign uprising was owing to the conduct of other Powers [presumably in sending Christian missionaries], in which Russia had never participated; and that, therefore, it was purely accidental that she took part in the Boxer campaign.  See the *Tō-A Dōbun-kwai Hōkoku*, No. 48, pp. 35–36.

siege and firing of the Peking Legations had begun two days before, on June 20, the day when Count Muravieff uttered his optimistic remarks at St. Petersburg. The latter died the next day, and was succeeded in the Foreign Ministry by Count Lamsdorff. On June 26, the Russian Government ordered the mobilization into Manchuria of six large corps of troops from Hailar, Blagovestchensk and Habarofsk, Vladivostok and Possiet, and European Russia.[1] One estimate put the number of the Russian soldiers who had arrived in Manchuria by August at 30,000.[2] It is not easy to determine whether Russia took the offensive in the great Manchurian campaign which now began, or whether hostile acts of the Chinese precipitated it, but it seems safe to say that rumors of impending dangers had been abundant before the Russian troops poured into the territory,[3] and also that the dispatch of the

[1] *Tokushu Jōyaku*, p. 258. It is said that M. Witte was at the time opposed to sending so large forces into Manchuria.

[2] The *Kokumin*, March 8, 1901.

[3] But how soon before the order of mobilization is unknown. Writing on June 29 from St. Petersburg, Sir Charles Scott said that the Russian Government was alarmed by some news received on that day of the serious disturbances which had occurred near the Manchurian Railway, and it was rumored that the Boxers were attacking and destroying the line north of Mukden, and had cut off telegraphic communications with Vladivostok. "The Chinese Legation [at St. Petersburg] is much alarmed by this report," continued the British Ambassador, "as they had been seriously warned that the slightest movement against the safety of the Russian line would be followed by an instant and forcible action by Russia." — *China, No. 3 (1900)*, No. 240.

latter apparently provoked more extensive outrages of the rioters than would otherwise have been the case. We hear of the destruction of the railway and burning of religious establishments near Liao-yang and Mukden only from the end of June and beginning of July,[1] and the alleged determination of the Chinese troops to drive out all Russians from Manchuria was reported in the Russian *Official Messenger* toward the middle of July.[2] Just at this time riots occurred in the Liao-tung and its vicinity, communication by the Amur ceased, and Blagovestchensk was suddenly bombarded by the Chinese, followed by the slaughter of thousands of Chinese inhabitants by the Russian soldiers under General Gribsky.[3] Toward the south and east, the depot of Ninguta was destroyed, and several Russians were murdered at An-tung, about July 20. The Russian troops, many of whom had now arrived at different points in Manchuria, captured Hun-chun on July 27, Argun on July 30, Haibin on August 3, and Aigun and San-sin soon afterward.[4] Even the treaty port of Niu-chwang had also been seized, for which conduct the British and American consular agents could not find sufficient justification. On August 5, the port was

[1] The *Kokumin*, March 8, 1901, etc.

[2] *China, No. 1 (1901)*, No. 47.

[3] There were other cases reported of the slaughter of non-combatants. The aggregate of those people killed was said to have reached 25,000. See *Tokushu Jōyaku*, p. 261, which gives a list of these cases in detail.

[4] The *Kokumin*, March 8, 1901, etc.

COUNT LAMSDORFF
*Russian Foreign Minister*

placed under the civil administration of Russian authorities, under which injustice and disorder were said to have much increased.[1] It was on August 14, the day when the allied forces had almost reached Peking, that General Groderkoff in command of the northern army of the Manchurian invasion wrote to the Minister of War at St. Petersburg : " Fifty years ago Nevelskoy raised the Russian flag at the mouth of the Amur, on its right bank, and laid the foundation for our possessions on that great river. Now, after hard fighting, we have taken possession of the right bank, thus consolidating the great enterprise of annexing the whole of the Amur to Russia's dominions, and making that river an internal waterway and not a frontier stream, whereby free and unmolested navigation of that artery through one of the vastest regions of the Empire has been secured." Indeed, by the time when the Peking Legations were relieved, the major part of Manchuria had been reduced under a military occupation by Russia.[2] This may be said to mark a new stage in the development of the Manchurian question, for no

[1] See the reports of the British Consuls Hosie and Fulford and the American Consul Miller, in *China, No. 5 (1900)*, p. 47 ; *No. 2 (1904)*, pp. 29–33, etc.; and the 57th Congress, 2d Session, *House Documents*, vol. i. pp. 147–158. At one time the relations between the American sailors and citizens and the Russian authorities were wrought up to a high tension, and Mr. Miller used so strong language in his correspondence with the latter that he had to be warned by Minister Conger of Peking and Assistant Secretary Pierce at Washington.

[2] See *Tokushu Jōyaku*, pp. 258–262.

longer was this vast territory a mere sphere of Russian influence; it was a prize of conquest.[1] The problem for the Government of the Czar henceforth seemed to the outside world to be not so much how it might tighten its hold upon Manchuria, as how it might convert the temporary occupation into a permanent possession.

[1] Count Lamsdorff said on November 22, 1903, to Mr. Kurino, Japanese Minister at St. Petersburg, that " Russia once took possession of Manchuria by right of conquest. . . ." The *Kwampō*, March 24, 1904, supplement, p. 8.

# CHAPTER VII

## NORTH CHINA AND MANCHURIA

THE problem stated at the close of the last chapter forms an index to a period of Eastern diplomacy the singular features of which hardly find a parallel in the world's history. The affairs of the Extreme Orient had in general advanced to such a stage that no single Power could again seek to enforce its will without due regard to the interests of some other Powers. The Russian problem in Manchuria was, as will be seen after a little reflection, of such a nature that it could hardly be literally propounded before the world. The absorption of a vast and rich territory in China by a Power whose policy was known to be aggressive would at once arouse a determined protest of the Powers which were, from interest and from conviction, committed to the principles of the integrity of the Chinese Empire and the open door therein as the best means of insuring a lasting peace in the Far East. The Manchurian question had to be developed under a disguise until it would be, if ever, safe to cast aside the veil. Hence began Russia's long, laborious effort to explain to the critical world certain crude facts and deeds in Manchuria in the terms of some refined foreign phrases — phrases

whose significance in this particular case her rivals
well knew, but which they could not repudiate so long
as they themselves upheld the principles indicated by
those phrases. However, the moment a complex diplomatic machinery relies upon subterfuges for its
success, its ingenuity will be taxed to the utmost,
or its unity will be in danger. For it will not be
easy to make the entire body of diplomatic agents
speak the same untruths at all places and at all
times. As soon as one pretext is uncovered, another
must be invented, as it were, on the spur of the
moment, in order to cover the retreat from the
last one — a necessary change which might render
a quick readjustment of the entire organism to the
newly created situation almost impossible. It would
indeed have been one of the most striking feats of
the government of a nation, if the artful diplomacy
of Russia had been able to combat successfully to
the end, with the enemy's weapon, the straightforward statecraft of the partisans of fair play.
Let us now observe in the remaining chapters of
this work how this process went on, and how it
finally defeated itself, — how ingenuity gave place
to threats, and how diplomacy ended in war.

As has been suggested, Russia avowed that a
point in her policy in China at the outbreak of the
Boxer trouble was to assist the friendly Government
of that Empire in suppressing the insurrection and
restoring the normal order.[1] When, however, in

[1] The circular note addressed to the Powers on June 3/16,
*China, No. 3 (1900)*, No. 49; the letter to the Chinese Gov-

spite of Count Muravieff's inclination to regard this matter lightly, all the Powers concerned deemed the situation grave enough to justify sending forces to the rescue of their Representatives and subjects in Peking, it became necessary for Russia to act in concert with the others, instead of alone assisting China. Russia promptly, on June 16,[1] declared her intention to coöperate with the other Powers, and claimed, about a month later, to have proposed to the Powers the following "fundamental principles as their rule of conduct in relation to events in China," which principles were agreed to by the majority of the Powers : [2] (1) Harmony among the Powers ;

ernment on June 11/24, *China, No. 2 (1904)*, p. 18 ; the Czar's reply to the Chinese Emperor, *China, No. 1 (1901)*, No. 105, etc.

The Emperor had sent a specially worded personal message to each of the heads of the French, German, Russian, British, American, and Japanese nations, once about July 19 and again on October 14, that is, before and after the capture of Peking by the allied forces. In each case the Emperor made a special appeal to the person addressed, and begged him to take the initiative in coming to China's assistance in solving the situation. The various replies are highly instructive. It seems that the Czar supposed that he had alone been singled out by the Chinese Empire for the first special plea, and answered accordingly.

See *China, No. 1 (1901)*, Nos. 1, 51, 56, 61, 78, 79, 105, 113, 252; *China, No. 5 (1901)*, Nos. 5, 24, 72, 108, 134, 174, 197; *China, No. 2 (1904)*, p. 18; 56th Congress, 2d Session, *House Documents*, vol. i. pp. 293–296.

[1] *China, No. 3 (1900)*, No. 149.

[2] These principles, says Lord Salisbury, on July 15, "have never been accepted by Her Majesty's Government, nor have we as yet discussed with other powers the circumstances to which those principles might possibly apply." — *China, No. 1 (1901)*,

(2) the preservation of the *status quo* in China prior to the trouble; (3) the elimination of everything which might conduce to a partition of China; and (4) the reëstablishment by common action of the legitimate central Government at Peking, which would be able of itself to guarantee order and tranquillity in that country.[1]  Probably before these pro-

No. 44.  Secretary Hay thought that the Russian *Chargé's* oral communication was "not explicit enough" to enable him to comment upon the so-called fundamental principles of Russia.—*Ibid.*, No. 114.  Later, about July 30, Mr. Hay replied to Russia by referring to his own circular note of July 3, and said that he deemed it "premature to forecast the means of bringing about those results [i. e., the restoration of order and responsible government in China]."—*Ibid.*, No. 140.  It is particularly remarkable that two of the Powers most interested in the principles proposed by Russia should be so conservative when the question was propounded by that Power.

[1] *China, No. 2 (1904)*, pp. 1 and 18.

It is interesting to compare these "fundamental principles" of Russia with the principles laid down in Secretary Hay's circular telegraph addressed to the Powers on July 3, or probably some days before the Russian note: "  . . . The purpose of the President is, as it has been heretofore," it said, "to act concurrently with the other Powers, first, in opening up communication with Peking and securing the American officials, missionaries, and other Americans who are in danger; secondly, in affording all protection everywhere in China to American life and property; thirdly, in guarding and protecting all legitimate American interests; and fourthly, in aiding to prevent a spread of the disorders to the other provinces of the Empire and a recurrence of such disorders.  It is, of course, too early to forecast the means of attaining this last result; but the policy of the Government of the United States is to seek a solution which may bring about permanent safety, and peace to China, preserve Chinese territorial and administrative entity, protect all rights guaranteed to friendly Powers by treaty and international law, and safeguard for the world the principle of equal and impartial trade with all

positions were penned by Count Muravieff, orders
had been issued by Russia to mobilize large forces
into Manchuria. In this territory and in North
China, events progressed rapidly in the next few
weeks, and, by the middle of August, the Legations
had been relieved, and the three Eastern Provinces
had largely fallen into the hands of the Russians.
It is essential to bear in mind this dual state of affairs, for henceforth it appeared that the best efforts
of Russian diplomacy were made at once, in one
sense, in reconciling to one another, and, in another
sense, in insisting upon, the widely different situa-
tions of Manchuria and of North China. On the one
hand, the principle of the integrity of China applied
to both regions alike, but, on the other, Russia
steadily declined to admit that Manchuria was within
the sphere of the concerted action of the Powers.
Thus, in her famous circular of August 25,[1] she declared, in regard to Manchuria, where " temporary
measures " of military occupation " had been solely
dictated by the absolute necessity of repelling the
aggression of the Chinese rebels, and not with interested motives, which are absolutely foreign to the
policy of the Imperial Government," that, as soon as

parts of the Chinese Empire."—The 56th Congress, 2d Session,
*House Documents*, vol. i. p. 299. It will be observed that the
American note is not only probably earlier in date, but also
much wider in scope, than the Russian propositions, for the
former contains the open door principle, among others, which
receives no reference in the latter. It should be remembered,
however, that the American note was not a proposition to the
other Powers.

[1] *China, No. 1 (1901)*, No. 256.

peace was restored and the security of the railway was assured, " Russia would not fail to withdraw her troops from the Chinese territory, provided such action did not meet with obstacles caused by the proceedings of other Powers." [1] From these words it was evident that Russia would not allow the Manchurian question to be discussed by the Powers, for she would withdraw from it, as she had occupied it, on her own initiative, and with no interference from others. More important still was the fact that Russia, from this time on, pledged to evacuate Manchuria under the apparently reasonable conditions — of the question of the fulfillment of which, however, Russia would be the sole judge — that peace and security was restored in the territory, and that other Powers did not interfere with her intentions. As regards North China, the circular bespoke a striking action on the part of Russia. Of the two original intentions of Russia, namely, the rescue of the Russian subjects in Peking and the assistance to China to restore peace, the first had now been accomplished, but the second was hindered by the absence of the Imperial Court from the capital. In these circumstances, Russia, seeing no reason for maintaining the Legations and allied forces in Peking, would now withdraw M. de Giers and the Russian troops

[1] Statements of similar import occur in the *Official Messenger* of August 13, in the instructions given on October 25 by Count Lamsdorff to the Russian Representatives abroad, and those on December 28 by General Kuropatkin to the governors-general of the Amur and Kwan-tung Provinces. See *Tokushu Jōyaku*, pp. 259-260.

to Tientsin.  It was explained later [1] that, while the
action of Russia was not a technical proposition to
the other Powers, their concurrence in these measures would conduce to the return of the Court to
the capital and facilitate the settlement of the affair
between the allies and China.  It is interesting to
see that at the same time the Chinese Representative
at St. Petersburg urgently begged Li Hung-chang
to memorialize the Throne to the effect that an edict
should be issued to show China's severity and ability to maintain order when the European troops were
withdrawn, and the intention of the Court to return
shortly.  The adoption of this course, it was thought,
would allay the apprehensions of the allies regarding the withdrawal of their troops from Peking.[2]

[1] Cf. *China, No. 1 (1901)*, Nos. 267, 300, 314, 315.

Also see the most interesting Russian document, quoted in
*China, No. 2 (1904)*, p. 20.  One of its passages reads as follows:
"It must not be forgotten that an attack on the ancient tradi-
tions of the Chinese and on the prestige of their Government
might be attended by the most disastrous consequences ; all the
more so that the international troops cannot occupy indefinitely
the capital of a country of 400,000,000 inhabitants, whose right
to live at home as they please can hardly be questioned."

[2] *China, No. 1 (1901)*, No. 306.  Also see No. 313.

On August 19 and 21, Li Hung-chang wired to Wu Ting-fang
to urge upon the United States Government that, inasmuch as
the declared purpose of the allies to relieve the Legations had
now been accomplished, they should suspend hostilities, withdraw their troops, and appoint envoys to negotiate with China.
See *ibid.*, No. 239, and the 56th Congress, 2d Session, *House
Documents*, vol. i. pp. 197, 288–290.  We may naturally infer either
that Li sent similar telegrams to Russia, or that Russia had consulted Li before the circular was sent to the Powers, the general
tenor of thought is so alike in the telegrams and in the circular.

The Russian declaration, so far as it regarded North China, in spite of her avowal that she would act strictly in concert with the other Powers, was as surprising to some of the latter as it must have been pleasing to China.[1] As might be expected, the Powers, except France, doubted the practicability of so early an evacuation of Peking.[2] A similar proposition by Russia, dated September 17, so far as the withdrawal of the Legations to Tientsin was concerned, came to the same result.[3] Russia, on her part, actually withdrew her troops to Tientsin, but when peace negotiations were opened at Peking in October, her Minister was obliged to be present there. In the mean time, the different status in which Russia held Manchuria from North China was made evident by the vigorous prosecution of the campaign in the former. Ninguta, Kirin, and Tsitsihar fell

[1] Russia herself was conscious of the fact that others attributed to her the motive of ingratiating herself with China at a critical moment by taking, separately from the other Powers, an action favorable to China.  See *China, No. 2 (1904)*, pp. 19–20.

[2] See *China, No. 1 (1901)*, Nos. 275 (Austria); 280, 322, 328, (France); 309 (Italy); 281, 293, 305, 317, 318, 321, 327, 335, 378, 383 (England); 307; *No. 5 (1901)*, Nos. 110, 124, 127 (Japan); *No. 1 (1901)*, Nos. 270, 315 ; 56th Congress, 2d Session, *House Documents*, vol. ii. pp. 304–305, 378–379, 205 (the United States).  As a matter of fact, the Boxers still roamed about Peking, and the Chinese Court, which had fled to Ta-yuen, was still under the control of Prince Tuan and his associates.  A hasty withdrawal of troops from Peking would have been disastrous in its effect upon the foreigners and native Christians.

[3] See *China, No. 1 (1901)*, Nos. 356 (Russian proposition); 371, 395, 401 (England); 398 (Italy); *No. 5 (1901)*, No. 128, (Japan); *House Documents*, op. cit., vol. i. pp. 203–204, 305–306, 381–382.

into the Russian hands about the same time as the evacuation of Peking was announced; Liao-yang was taken late in September, and Mukden and Tieh-ling early in October. Fêng-hwang-Chêng and An-tung were captured even so late as December. On September 7, a solemn thanksgiving was held at the site of the burned town Sakhalin on the right bank of the Amur across Blagovestchensk, in which General Gribsky delivered a speech, and the high priest Konoploff was reported to have said : " Now is the cross raised on that bank of the Amur which yesterday was Chinese. Muravieff foretold that sooner or later this bank would be ours." [1]

[1] *China, No. 1 (1901)*, No. 375.

# CHAPTER VIII

## THE ANGLO–GERMAN AGREEMENT

WHEN we recall that even before 1900 Russia desired to control the railway enterprises, not only in Manchuria, but also on the right side of the Liao River, it is not altogether strange that, simultaneously with the occupation of Manchuria, the northern Chinese line was seized by her troops. This action, however, did not stop at the Great Wall. Had it not been for the protest of Great Britain, the Russians would have seized the entire line from Niuchwang up to Peking. During the latter part of June, they captured the Tientsin depot, burned the office, destroyed the safe and the documents it contained, and seized land, some tracts of which had been owned by British subjects.[1] On July 8, the Northern Railway was seized and the British engineer, C. W. Kinder, and his staff were turned out,[2] and, in spite of the dissent of the British and American commanders, the Admirals of the allied Powers voted on July 16 that the Russians should manage the railway.[3] In August, the Russians claimed also the line between Tong-ku and Shan-

[1] *China, No. 7 (1901)*, Nos. 21, 76, 81, 84, 86, 95, 103, 149, 153, 154, 174, 187, 189.
[2] *Ibid.*, Nos. 1 and 7.    [3] *Ibid.*, Nos. 2, 7, 9.

hai-Kwan, on the one hand, and the one between
Tientsin and Peking, on the other, thus completing the control of the entire connection.[1] British
protests were in a measure waived by the new
Commander-in-Chief of the allied forces, Count
von Waldersee, who early in October assigned the
repair of the section up to Yang-tsun to the Russians.[2] About this time, fifty miles of railway
material belonging to a British firm were seized at
Niu-chwang by the Russians,[3] followed by the seizure
of the collieries at Tong-shan and Lin-si hitherto
operated by the Chinese Engineering and Mining
Company.[4] Other incidents followed, greatly to the
annoyance of those whose interests had been invested in the works. It was at this juncture that,
on October 16, 1900, an Agreement was signed
between the Governments of Great Britain and
Germany, upholding the principle of the open door
in China (Article 1), disclaiming territorial designs
upon China on the part of the contracting Powers
(Article 2), and supplemented by the following
Article (3), embodying the well-known principle of
the balance of power at China's expense : " In case of
another Power making use of the complications in
China in order to obtain under any form whatever
such territorial advantages, the two contracting
parties reserve to themselves the right to come to a

[1] *China, No. 7 (1901)*, Nos. 11, 14, 19, 20, 22, 23, 25, 30, 35,
36, 57, 60, 103.
[2] *Ibid.*, Nos. 24, 27, 37, 38, 43, 50, 54, 55, 66, 68.
[3] *Ibid.*, Nos. 39, 77.           [4] *Ibid.*, 40, 78.

preliminary understanding as to the eventual steps to be taken for the protection of their own interests in China." [1] This is the notorious Anglo-German Agreement, the fate of which has been an object of much ridicule among writers upon Chinese affairs of recent years. The diplomacy which had resulted in the conclusion of this Agreement has not been made known to the public, but as to the circumstances which had caused the two Powers to negotiate, it may safely be inferred that, so far as the British side was concerned, the Russian conduct in North China was a potent factor.[2] As to the deeper causes on both sides for the extraordinary *rapprochement*, it is easy to speculate upon but unsafe to asseverate them.[3] The Agreement further stated that other interested Powers should

[1] The *British Parliamentary Papers, Treaty Series*, No. 1, 1900.

[2] On November 1, Lord Salisbury wrote to the British *Chargé* at St. Petersburg in unusually outspoken language, as follows: "In the event of the Russians making any complaint of our having concluded the Anglo-German Agreement without previously consulting them, you should dwell on the fact that the conduct and language of Russian officers in the Far East, in respect to the Chinese railway from Niu-chwang to Peking, and the way in which the property of British subjects on that railway has been dealt with by the Russian military authorities, has caused much perplexity to Her Majesty's Government. The Russian Government have given us many satisfactory assurances with respect to their intentions in these matters, but the little attention paid to the avowed policy of the Russian Government by officers on the spot has deterred us from fuller communication." — *China, No. 7 (1901)*, No. 45.

[3] See, for instance, the explanation offered in *Tokushu Jōyaku*, pp. 384–386.

be invited to accept the principles recorded in it
(Article 4). It is interesting to see how this peculiar combination of the principles of (1) the open
door, (2) the integrity of China, and (3) a balance between the Powers on the Chinese ground,
was viewed by the other Powers. Japan joined the
Agreement on October 29, as a signatory, but not
as an adhering State.[1] France, Austria, and Italy
recognized as identical with their own all of the
principles proposed,[2] while the United States did
likewise with the first two, but expressed itself un-
concerned with the third.[3] As for Russia, she seized
this opportunity to indulge her diplomatic sarcasm.
She declared that, from her point of view, the
Agreement " did not perceptibly modify the situation in China," and the second principle perfectly
corresponded with Russia's intentions, as " she was
the first to lay down the maintenance of the integrity of the Chinese Empire as a fundamental principle of her policy in China." Her reply to the
first principle was delicately expressed, as follows :
It " can be favorably entertained by Russia, as this
stipulation does not infringe in any way the *status
quo* established in China *by existing treaties*." [4] In
other words, the open door may or may not apply
to other places not yet covered by the existing

---

[1] *China, No. 5 (1901)*, Nos. 4 and 7, inclosure 2.

[2] *Ibid.*, Nos. 6, 8, and 9.

[3] The 56th Congress, 2d Session, *House Documents*, vol. i.
p. 355.

[4] The italics are the author's.

treaties and still open to whatever development might take place. The evil genius of the third Article of the Anglo-German Agreement was not less skillfully answered by Russia : " The Imperial Government, while referring to its Circular of the 12th (25th) August, can only renew the declaration that such an infringement [by another Power] would oblige Russia to modify her attitude according to circumstances." [1] From these words, it was plain that outside of the two contracting Powers, the Agreement could not exercise great influence, and least upon Russia, which declined to observe any new feature in the instrument. The virtue of the Agreement was, moreover, seriously impaired by the insincerity of one of its parties, and by the consequent difference of views between themselves. The document was openly talked about in Germany as the Yang-tsze Agreement, it being meant that Great Britain thereby pledged herself to abstain from annexing the Yang-tsze Provinces, hitherto considered, much to the jealousy of Germany, as a British sphere of interest.[2] More momentous was the question whether the Agreement included in its scope, not only the eighteen Provinces, but also Manchuria. The answer would, of course, depend upon whether both parties would consider, under the provision

[1] *China, No. 5 (1900)*, No. 5.

[2] Also see the debate in the House of Lords, on August 6, 1901, between Earl Spencer and the Marquess of Lansdowne. The *Parliamentary Debates*, Fourth Series, vol. 98, pp. 1351–1365.

of the third Article, that they alike possessed "their own interests" to protect in Manchuria. Seen in this light, it is not strange that, in the opinion of Lord Lansdowne, the "Agreement most unquestionably extended to Manchuria, which is part of the Chinese Empire," [1] while, from Count von Bülow's point of view, "The Anglo-German Agreement had no reference to Manchuria." "I can imagine nothing," he added, "which we can regard with more indifference" than Manchuria. [2] Evidently Germany had entered into the Agreement with different motives from those of Great Britain, and perhaps also with less zeal, if zeal there was.

[1] At the House of Lords, on August 6, 1901. The Japanese Government, also, in its reply to a question of a member of the National Diet, interpreted the Agreement to apply to the whole of the Chinese Empire. — *Tokushu Jōyaku*, p. 389.

[2] At the Reichstag on March 15, 1901. — The London *Times*, August 6, 1901, p. 7. He is also said to have declared to the Russian Representative at Berlin that Manchuria was outside of the sphere of German commercial rights, and consequently had no relation with the Anglo-German Agreement. It was reported even that Manchuria was originally mentioned specifically in the British draft of the Agreement, but the word was struck out at the request of Germany, and the more abstract phrase, "spheres of influence," was used therefor. — *Tokushu Jōyaku*, pp. 388–389.

# CHAPTER IX

### A *MODUS VIVENDI:* THE ALEXIEFF–TSÊNG AGREEMENT

In the mean time, the Chinese Court [1] having largely emancipated itself from the sway of the reactionary Prince Tuan and his associates, the Representatives at Peking of the eleven interested Powers had agreed in September to open discussions among themselves of the terms of peace to be presented to the Chinese plenipotentiaries, Prince Ching and Li Hung-chang.[2] The German Government, however, proposed, as a prerequisite of peace negotiations with China, a drastic measure demanding the surrender to the Powers of the chief culprits of the recent trouble. The proposition meeting little encouragement from other Ministers, Germany presented a

---

[1] The Court had fled toward Ta-yuen-Fu before the allied troops reached Peking, and thence started toward Si-ngan-Fu, the capital of many a historic dynasty, on October 1.

[2] Russia had early advocated accepting Li as plenipotentiary, while other Powers were still skeptical of the nature of his credentials. See *China, No. 1 (1901)*, Nos. 254, 356, 368, 371, 398, 401; *China, No. 5 (1901)*, Nos. 5, 31, 111, 112, 128, 216; U. S. 56th Congress, 2d Session, *House Documents*, vol. i. pp. 203–204, 305–306, 381–382. It was not till September 20 that Li entered Peking. Prince Ching had arrived there September 3. The appointment of the Prince as a plenipotentiary is said to have been partly due to Japanese influence.

new condition on October 3. The latter was, however, supplanted by the basis for negotiations formulated on September 30 and presented five days
later to the Powers by the French Minister.[1] His
proposals, to which Russia immediately assented,[2]
and which with important amendments [3] and addi-
tions became the basis of the Protocol signed on
September 7, 1901, comprised the following six
points : (1) the punishment of the chief offenders
designated by the Representatives of the Powers at
Peking ; (2) maintenance of the prohibition of the
importation of arms into China ; (3) indemnities for
the foreign governments, societies, and individuals ;
(4) establishment of a permanent legation guard at
Peking ; (5) dismantlement of the Taku forts ; and
(6) military occupation of two or three points on
the road from Tientsin to Taku, so as to keep open
the passage between Peking and the sea. It is
needless for us to follow the negotiations which
proceeded at Peking after these proposals were
made by France, but it is important to observe that
the French propositions were limited, in the first
place, to North China, and, in the second place, to
those questions in North China which concerned all
the Powers alike. The significance of all this, or at
least of the prompt assent of Russia,[4] may well be

[1] *Documents diplomatiques : Chine, 1899–1900*, No. 327
(p. 174). Also see *China, No. 5 (1901)*, pp. 5, 46, 53–54.

[2] *China, No. 5 (1901)*, No. 17.

[3] For the Japanese amendments, see *ibid.*, Nos. 60, 151, 178.

[4] Russia openly declared in her *Messager Officiel* of March 24
(April 6), 1901, that the Russian views regarding the settlement

inferred from the opposition as readily offered by
the latter when Germany [1] and Japan,[2] respectively,
urged that a proper mention should be made in the
peace protocol of China's consent to repair the
murder of Baron von Ketteler and the Chancellor
Sugiyama. Russia maintained that "proposals of
this nature, serving principally as a satisfaction to
be given to private views of one State, ought not to
enter into the common programme of the collective
demands, which had as their object the interests of
all the Powers collectively and the reëstablishment
of a normal state of affairs in the Celestial Empire." [3]
" In the Chinese question it is advisable," said the
*Official Messenger* of St. Petersburg, " not to lose
sight of the necessity of distinguishing clearly the
questions which interest each of the Powers in particular and those which affect the interests of all the
Powers in general." [4] This distinction had been fundamental in the Russian diplomacy in China since
1900, for, if one question of the former class was
allowed to be dealt with in the common deliberation
of the Representatives of all the Powers, why should
not another question of the same class be similarly
treated? Or, in other words, if the Sugiyama affair was referred to the collective council, the argu-

of the trouble in North China, as distinguished from Manchuria,
had " served the French Government as a basis for the elabo-
ration" of the latter's propositions. — *China, No. 2 (1904)*,
pp. 20–21.

[1] November 5. — *China, No. 5 (1901)*, No. 117.
[2] November 28. — *Ibid.*, Nos. 178 and 198.
[3] *China, No. 2 (1904)*, p. 21.          [4] *Ibid.*, p. 20.

ment that the Manchurian problem should be solved solely by Russia, without intervention of the other Powers, would lose much of its force.[1] The ultimate failure of Russian diplomacy — for diplomacy has failed when it ends in a war, and, if Russia does succeed, her success will be that of force, not of diplomacy — may be said to be largely due to the evident contradiction of this fundamental distinction between North China and Manchuria, upon which she sought to build her entire diplomatic structure in this crisis. As a matter of fact, it was as impossible to deny the profound interest felt by Great Britain and the United States, and, above all, by Japan, in the economic development of Manchuria, as it would have been to exclude Russia from the community of the Powers in North China. It should be remembered that Russia herself persistently maintained that the principle of the integrity of China applied also to Manchuria, and she would have hardly antagonized other Powers had she expressed an equally clear adhesion to the principle of the open door, and made efforts to carry out pledges regarding both principles.

Events soon took place, however, which made other Powers skeptical of Russia's sincerity in her profession of even the principle of the integrity of

[1] Russia allowed the question of the indemnity in Manchuria to be dealt with at the general conferences at Peking together with the indemnity respecting North China. In the matter of the punishment of guilty local officials, from the discussion of which Russia abruptly withdrew herself, the representatives of the other Powers included Manchuria in their consideration.

the Chinese Empire. The new question thus thrust upon the attention of the Powers was of an extremely grave nature, for if the sovereignty of Manchuria should eventually pass into the hands of Russia, the treaty rights that other nations had acquired therein from China might rightfully be terminated by Russia. Whatever her ultimate objects, it was hardly politic for her to approach the difficult Manchurian question at the time and in the manner selected by her. Dr. George Morrison reported to the *Times* on December 31, 1900, and Sir Ernest Satow, the British Minister at Peking, confirmed it as authentic,[1] that the delegates of Admiral Alexieff and the Tartar General Tsêng-chi, of Mukden, had signed, in November last, an agreement whereby Russia consented to return to the Chinese the civil government of the Southern Province of Fêng-tien (Sheng-king) in Manchuria, on the following conditions : —

1. " The Tartar General Tsêng undertakes to protect the province and pacify it, and to assist in the construction of the railroad.

2. "He must treat kindly the Russians in military occupation, protecting the railway and pacifying the

[1] *China, No. 2 (1904)*, No. 5 (January 4, 1901). Sir Charles Scott, Ambassador at St. Petersburg, reported on January 5, that it appeared to be generally believed there that "some provisional agreement, such as that indicated, had been concluded by Russia with the local authorities in Manchuria, and that she might eventually acquire by treaty the right to finish building the railway line through Manchuria to Port Arthur, and to protect it herself, the rights of the Russo-Chinese Company being transferred to the Russian Government." — *Ibid.*, No. 4.

province, and provide them with lodging and provisions.

3. "He must disarm and disband the Chinese soldiery, delivering in their entirety to the Russian military officials all munitions of war in the arsenals not already occupied by the Russians.

4. "All forts and defenses in Fêng-tien not occupied by the Russians, and all powder magazines not required by the Russians, must be dismantled in the presence of Russian officials.

5. "Niu-chwang and other places now occupied by the Russians shall be restored to the Chinese civil administration when the Russian Government is satisfied that the pacification of the provinces is complete.

6. "The Chinese shall maintain law and order by local police under the Tartar General.

7. "A Russian Political Resident, with general powers of control, shall be stationed at Mukden, to whom the Tartar General must give all information respecting any important measure.

8. "Should the local police be insufficient in any emergency, the Tartar General will communicate with the Russian Resident at Mukden, and invite Russia to dispatch reinforcements.

9. "The Russian text shall be the standard." [1]

In brief, the province was to be disarmed, its military government to be in the Russian hands, its civil government to be placed under the supervision of a Russian Resident, with additional duties on the part of the Chinese to provide for the Rus-

---

[1] The London *Times*, January 3, 1901, p. 3. In this and other reports Dr. Morrison seems to have translated from Chinese texts.

sian military and to protect Russian properties. The last provisions were coupled with the right of the Russians to supply reinforcements, if the Chinese local police should prove insufficient. The probable significance of this measure will be fully discussed in connection with the Russo-Chinese Convention of April 8, 1902. As regards the Agreement now under discussion, Dr. Morrison opined that it would necessarily be followed by similar agreements with reference to the other two of the three Eastern Provinces,[1] and then all Manchuria would be " a *de facto* Russian protectorate, Russia by a preëxisting agreement having already the right to maintain all necessary troops for the protection of the railway." It is needless to say that the report of this Agreement caused universal amazement in the diplomatic world. It soon became known [2] that the Chinese delegate who signed it at Port Arthur had received no authorization to do so from the Peking Government.[3] But the Japanese Government, hearing from a reliable source that so late as the beginning of February, Russia was pressing China to ratify the Agreement, under-

[1] The Russian *Official Messenger* of April 6, 1901, stated that "temporary agreements in writing (*modus vivendi*) respecting the reëstablishment of the local civil administration in the *three Provinces* of Manchuria were, before all else, concluded between the Russian military authorities and the Chinese tsian-tsiouns [Generals] of the three Provinces."— *China, No. 2 (1904)*, p. 22.

[2] *China, No. 2 (1904)*, No. 5 (January 4).

[3] The Tartar General Tsêng-chi was degraded for this offense, but Russia succeeded in reinstating him. — *The Times*, February 20, 1901, p. 5.

took to express its opinion to the Chinese Minister at Tokio, that the conclusion of any such agreement would be a "source of danger" to the Chinese Government, and that no arrangement affecting territorial rights of the Empire ought to be concluded between the Chinese Government and any one of the Powers.[1] At the instance of Japan, Great Britain also made precisely the same representation to China,[2] Germany following the example in slightly different language,[3] and the United States also reminding China of "the impropriety, inexpediency, and even extreme danger to the interests of China, of considering any private territorial and financial engagements, at least without the full knowledge and approval of all the Powers now engaged in negotiation."[4]

It has often been reported in the press that the Agreement was never ratified by either China or Russia. Before, however, any of the protests of the Powers reached the Peking Government, Count Lamsdorff had, on February 6, "very readily" ex-

---

[1] *China, No. 2 (1904)*, No. 8.

[2] *Ibid.*, No. 13 (February 13).

[3] The opinion of the German Government was that China "should not conclude with any Power individual treaties of a territorial or financial character *before* they can estimate their obligations toward all the Powers as a whole, and *before* the compliance with such obligations is accepted." — *Ibid.*, Nos. 12, 13.

[4] *Ibid.*, No. 19 (February 19).

What action the remaining Powers took is not shown in the Blue Books. Austria-Hungary and Italy are said to have also protested.

plained the situation to the British Ambassador at St. Petersburg. He said it was quite untrue that any agreement which would give Russia new rights and a virtual protectorate in Southern Manchuria had been concluded or was under discussion with China, but " the Russian military authorities who had been engaged in the temporary occupation and pacification of that province had been directed, when reinstating the Chinese authorities in their former posts, to arrange with the local civil authorities a *modus vivendi* for the duration of the simultaneous presence of Russian and Chinese authorities in Southern Manchuria, the object being to prevent the recurrence of disturbances in the vicinity of the Russian frontier, and to protect the railway from the Russian frontier to Port Arthur." " Some of the details of the proposed *modus vivendi* had been sent for consideration to St. Petersburg, but no convention or arrangement with the central Government of China or of a permanent character had been concluded with regard to Manchuria, nor had the Emperor any intention of departing in any way from the assurances which he had publicly given that Manchuria would be entirely restored to its former condition in the Chinese Empire as soon as circumstances admitted of it." [1] A careful reading of this statement, as typical of the many declarations made by Russia in regard to Manchuria, will show how untenable is the popular view that she persistently falsifies. There is here a fair admission that a *modus vivendi*

[1] *China, No. 2 (1901).*

was under way between the Russian military officers in Southern Manchuria and the local Chinese authorities, and that it was not of a permanent nature, nor was it concluded with the central Government at Peking, and both of these points accord with the reported facts. Nor can one deny the cogency of the argument that Russia would evacuate Manchuria " as soon as circumstances admitted of it." What constituted the objectionable feature of the affair, from the standpoint of the interested Powers, must have been that, inasmuch as Count Lamsdorff would not publish the terms of the *modus vivendi*, it was not possible for them to satisfy themselves that it contained nothing which would render impossible the consummation of " circumstances " favorable for evacuation, and eventually tend toward a " permanent" possession of the territory by Russia. As matters stood, it would be as natural for the Powers to entertain such a doubt, as it was for Russia to deem it necessary to declare, in her circular of August 25, 1900, that she would withdraw from Manchuria if, for one thing, no obstacle was placed in her way by the action of other Powers. The doubt of the Powers was rather intensified, if at all, by the further explanation by Count Lamsdorff on February 6, that "when it came to the final and complete evacuation of Manchuria, the Russian Government would be obliged to obtain from the central Government of China an effective guarantee against the recurrence of the recent attack on her frontier and the destruction of her railway, but had no intention of seeking this guarantee in any acquisition of territory or of an actual or virtual protectorate over Manchuria, the object being to simply guarantee the faithful observance in the future by China of the terms of the agreement [agreement between the Chinese Government and the Russo-Chinese Bank, September 28, 1896 ?], which she had been unable to fulfill during the disturbances. The terms of this guarantee might possibly form the subject of conversation here between Count Lamsdorff and the Chinese Minister, or be left for discussion at Peking."[1] A month before this official statement of Russia reached the London Government, the latter heard from the Japanese Minister, Baron Hayashi, that Russia and China had already made at St. Petersburg some arrangement regarding Manchuria,[2] evidently referred to by Count Lamsdorff in the quoted passage as "an effective guarantee."

[1] *China, No. 2 (1901).*
[2] *China, No. 2 (1904)*, No. 6.

# CHAPTER X

### A "STARTING-POINT" — THE LAMSDORFF-YANG-YU
### CONVENTION

It was as early as January 12 that the Japanese
Government had made inquiries directly at the
Russian Government regarding the contents of the
Agreement reported to have been made between
Count Lamsdorff and Yang-yu at St. Petersburg.[1]
The report was apparently premature, for its
contents were unknown for more than a month
after, and even on February 18, Dr. Morrison
reported from Peking that, according to a telegram to the Chinese Government from Yang-yu,
it would be several days before Count Lamsdorff
and M. Witte could settle the terms between themselves of the new agreement they wished to propose.[2] The *Times* correspondent, however, was
able to send certain preliminary articles which,
he said, had been verbally communicated by M.
Witte to Yang-yu.[3] On February 27, Sir Ernest

---

[1] *China, No. 2 (1904)*, No. 6.

[2] *The Times*, February 20, 1901, p. 5.

[3] *Ibid.* "The Chinese argue," added Dr. Morrison, "that
Russia, having no interests south of the Great Wall, no missionaries, no trade, and no troops, can reasonably expect in return
benevolent treatment from China in any agreement proposed
outside the Great Wall, especially as Russia is in military occu-

Satow[1] and Dr. Morrison[2] simultaneously reported the contents of the agreement which Yang-yu had been called upon by Count Lamsdorff to sign, and which he had telegraphed to Peking on the 23d. The proposed convention was, according to Dr. Morrison, obviously intended to exist side by side with the Alexieff-Tsêng Agreement concluded in the previous November. The substance of this convention, the authenticity of which the same writer claimed to have been admitted by the Russians in Peking, was as follows : —

1. "The Emperor of Russia, being desirous of manifesting his friendship for China, ignores the outbreak of hostilities in Manchuria, and agrees to restore the whole of that country to China, to be administered in all respects as of old.

2. "By the 6th Article of the Manchurian Railway Agreement, the Railway Company was authorized to guard the line with troops.  The country being at present in disorder, the number of those troops is insufficient for the purpose, and a *corps* must be retained until order is restored and China has executed the last four Articles of the present convention.

3. "In case of emergency the troops retained in Manchuria shall render every possible assistance to China in preserving order.

pation. . . . Russia appears determined to profit by the condition to which China is reduced by the action of the other Powers, just as she profited by obtaining the Primorsk Province after the war of 1860, and Port Arthur and Talien-wan subsequent to the war of 1895."

[1] *China, No. 2 (1904)*, No. 14.  Cf. *ibid.*, Nos. 25 and 42.
[2] *The Times*, February 28, 1901, p. 5.

4. "Chinese troops having been the greatest aggressors in the recent attacks on Russia, China agrees not to organize an army until the railway is completed and opened to traffic. When military forces are organized eventually, their numbers shall be fixed in consultation with Russia. The importation of arms and munitions of war into Manchuria is prohibited.

5. "As a measure for the preservation of Manchuria, China shall dismiss from office all Generals-in-Chief (Tartar Generals) and high officials whose actions conflict with friendly relations, and who are denounced for that reason by Russia. China may organize mounted and foot police in the interior of Manchuria, but their numbers shall be fixed in consultation with Russia.

"Cannon shall be excluded from their armament, and no subjects of another Power shall be employed in the execution of the functions.

6. "In accordance with the understanding formerly accepted by China, no subject of another Power shall be employed to train naval or military forces in the Northern Provinces (i. e., Provinces in North China).

7. "The local authorities nearest to the neutral zone referred to in Article 5 of the Liao-tung Agreement (of March 15/27, 1898) shall make special regulations for the preservation of order in the zone.

"The administrative autonomy of Kin-chow shall be abolished.

8. "Without the consent of Russia, China shall not concede mining, railway, or other privileges to another Power, in the countries adjoining Russia, that is to say, in Manchuria, Mongolia, Tarbagatai, Ili, Kashgar, Yarkand, Khoten, etc. China shall not herself construct a railway in those countries without Russia's consent.

"Outside of Niu-chwang, land shall not be leased to the subjects of another Power.

9. "China is under obligation to pay Russia's war expenses and indemnities to the Powers. The amount of indemnity due to Russia, the dates of payment, and the security, shall be arranged conjointly with the Powers.

10. "The amounts due for damage done to the railway, for the property of the Company's employees which was stolen, and for losses caused by delay of the works, shall be arranged by the company with China.

11. "An understanding may be come to with the Railway Company to set off the whole or part of the above indemnities against privileges of other kinds. This may be arranged by an alteration of the existing Railway Agreement (of August 27 / September 8, 1896), or by the concession of further privileges.

12. "China shall, as previously agreed,[1] grant a concession for the construction of a railway from Manchurian main line, or a branch line, to the Great Wall in the direction of Peking." [2]

There never appeared an authentic text of the convention from either the Russian or the Chinese official sources, but its existence in some drastic form was intimated by the Viceroys Liu and Chang, and by the Court Ministers then at Singan, as well as by the Chinese Emperor himself.[3] Furthermore, it could be plainly inferred that no one but Chinese diplomatic officials could have let out the terms of the proposed convention, or else it would have been impossible for one to believe

[1] See pp. 91–92, above.
[2] *China, No. 2 (1904)*, No. 42. Other versions are similar in substance to this one, which was forwarded by Sir Ernest Satow.
[3] See *China, No. 2 (1904)*, Nos. 16, 17, 32, 35.

that an instrument of so immense a scope and so arbitrary a nature, as had been reported, could have emanated from Russia. If the reported text was in the main authentic, as Sir Ernest Satow believed it was,[1] it is little wonder that Russia exercised a vigorous pressure upon the Peking Government for a speedy signing of the convention before the arrival of effective protests from other Powers, her Minister at Peking stating to Prince Ching and Li Hung-chang that the Agreement concerned only Russia and China, and that the Peking Government should not take any notice of what the foreign Representatives might say about it.[2] The Court appeared seized by a panic, excepting the pro-Russian Li Hung-chang, who pretended that he considered that the proposed convention would not impair the sovereignty of China in Manchuria.[3] The Emperor, declaring that "it was impossible for China alone to incur the displeasure of Russia by remaining firm," appealed, on February 28, to Great Britain, the United States, Germany, and Japan to mediate.[4] The British Government at once instructed Sir Ernest Satow to stay the hand of Li, who was about to sign, till he had received the replies of the four Powers whose mediation had been formally requested by the Emperor, and also to urge the patriotic Yang-tsze Viceroys to memorialize the Throne

[1] *China, No. 2 (1904)*, No. 30.
[2] *Ibid.*, No. 18 (March 1).
[3] *Ibid.*, No. 15 (February 28).
[4] *Ibid.*, No. 16.

against the acceptance of the Russian proposition.[1] The Viceroys, as well as several other subjects of China, had already done so.[2] The British remonstrance to China against entering into separate agreements with individual Powers was repeated on March 20.[3] At the same time Germany suggested, Great Britain and Japan seconding, that China should refer the matter to the conference of the foreign Representatives at Peking, who were, it should be remembered, in the midst of their difficult discussion of the preliminary terms of peace between the Powers and China.[4] It is unnecessary to say that Japan, in concert with Great Britain, strongly urged the Chinese Government not to sign the convention separately with one of the Powers, for such an act was contrary to the principle of solidarity which then united the Powers, and an individual convention with a Power would materially lessen the capacity of China to meet her obligations toward all the Powers.[5]

At this point we have to record a singular conjunction of circumstances which has caused criticisms not altogether favorable to Russia. It has already been shown that she had frequently had recourse to acts which at once placed her somewhat apart from the community of the Powers, and also were liable to be interpreted as being designed to in-

[1] *China, No. 2 (1904)*, No. 21 (March 4).
[2] *Ibid.*, No. 31.                         [3] *Ibid.*, No. 24.
[4] *Ibid.*, Nos. 22 and 23 (March 5).
[5] *Ibid.*, No. 28.

gratiate herself with the afflicted China. Thus Count
Lamsdorff more than once deprecated the contin-
uance of the punitive expeditions which the allied
forces made to one place or another in the Province
of Chi-li.[1] His reasons were so apparently plausible
that, under different circumstances, he might have
been supported by certain other Powers.[2] These
very Powers, however, most keenly resented Russia's detachment from the allies, when she definitely cleared herself from the deliberation of the
Representatives of the Powers at Peking in regard
to the punishment to be inflicted by the Chinese
Government upon certain provincial officials who
had been directly guilty of outrages to foreigners
during the recent trouble. The peace commissioners had almost disposed of the punishment question,
in order next to attack the knotty problem of the
indemnity to be paid by China, but M. de Giers
had been instructed by his Government " not only
to abstain from entering into any discussion as
to the nature or method of execution of the capital sentence, but also to take no part in the further discussions relative to the punishment to be
inflicted on the Chinese dignitaries."[3]  "At the
meeting [of the peace commissioners at Peking]
to-day," wrote Sir Ernest Satow on February 28,

---

[1] *China, No. 6 (1901)*, Nos. 61 (January 30), and 119 (February 20).

[2] Cf., e. g., *ibid.*, No. 62.

[3] From the *Official Messenger* of St. Petersburg of April 5,
1901; *China, No. 2 (1904)*, p. 22.

the day after he reported the draft of the most exhaustive agreement broached by Russia upon China, and the very day when the Chinese Emperor appealed to Great Britain, Germany, the United States, and Japan to intervene, " we presented to our colleagues our list of provincial officials, of whom ten were named as deserving the death penalty and about ninety to be punished in a lesser degree. Objection was made only by the Russian Minister, who stated that he could not accept our proposals unless he received fresh instructions, and that his Government's wish from the beginning had been to substitute a less severe form of punishment for the death penalty. Both my French colleague and I are of opinion that our death penalty list might justly have included far more than what had been demanded, and is exceedingly moderate in its reduced form." [1]  On March 15, that is, about the time when the terms of her proposed agreement were, as will be presently seen, modified by Russia in China's favor, Sir Charles Scott wrote Lord Salisbury that recently Count Lamsdorff had intimated that " he considered the question of the punishment of Chinese officials at an end as far as concerned Russia," and that " he referred to the murders of the missionaries as a subject in which Russia was not interested." [2]

---

[1] *China, No. 6 (1901)*, No. 135.
[2] *Ibid.*, No. 176. It may be remembered that Japan had even a stronger reason than Russia to abstain from all the unpleasant questions connected with the missionaries, but it is need-

Such a remark was regarded as a radical departure from the diplomatic amenities between the Powers. Russia might without offense have pleaded her reasons against the opinion of the majority, and then dissented at the final vote, but it was considered a very different matter for her to declare, in such a way as would openly place the other Powers in a false light in the eyes of the Chinese, that she had nothing to do with the question. The act, it must be said, came with particular ill grace at a time when Russia was believed to be negotiating an agreement with China, separately, and in terms manifestly contrary to the fundamental principles upon which the Powers' diplomacy at Peking was based.[1] A joint vote demanding the punishment of the officials had to be presented to the Chinese commissioners, on April 1, with the signatures of all but M. de Giers.[2]

Directly in connection with this episode may be considered the fact that, at the urgent request of

less to say that, in her joint action with other Powers in the matter of the official punishment and other questions, she regarded missionaries and other foreigners alike as subjects with certain inviolable rights.

[1] Dr. Morrison wrote from Peking on March 3: "To render China more willing speedily to sign the convention, M. de Giers has informed Li Hung-chang that Russia will not participate in the demand for the execution of ten provincial officials guilty of inhuman murders of white men, whose death justice demands. Thus the murdered English men, women, and children may be described as England's contribution toward securing to Russia the advantages derived from this convention." — The London *Times*, March 4, 1901, p. 5.

[2] *China, No. 6 (1901)*, No. 234.

China, Russia had in the mean time somewhat modified the terms of her proposition, about March 19, so as, in brief, to allow China to station troops in Manchuria for the protection of the Russian railways and the prevention of fresh disorders, their numbers and posts to be determined by consulting Russia; and also to prohibit the importation of arms and ammunition only in accordance with the agreement with the Powers (Article 4); to exclude cannon from the armament of the Chinese mounted and foot police forces in Manchuria only until peace is restored (Article 5); to retain the administrative autonomy of Kin-chow (Article 7); and to arrange with the Company the matter of indemnities in accordance with the general method used by the Powers (Article 10). The eighth Article was altered so as to apply the exclusive measure only to Manchuria, and the sixth was entirely expunged.[1] Simultaneously with these modifications in China's favor, Russia seemed to have suddenly increased her pressure upon the helpless Court of China. Count Lamsdorff was reported[2] to have declared to Yang-yu that he would withdraw the draft and break off negotiations if it were not signed within two weeks from March 13. An Imperial Decree, dated March 20, and addressed to Sir Chin-chen Lo-fêng-luh, the Chinese Minister at London, stated: "The Manchurian Agreement has now been amended, but the stipulated time within

---

[1] *China, No. 2 (1904)*, Nos. 28, 29, 42.
[2] *Ibid.*, Nos. 28, 30. Later confirmed by the Chinese officials. See No. 33.

which the Agreement is to be signed will soon expire. As the Marquess of Lansdowne has advised us to wait for his reply [to the Edict of February 28], we have now to command Lo-fêng-luh to ask Lord Lansdowne either (1) to help us out of the difficulty, or (2) to ask Russia to extend the time stipulated for signing the Agreement. Otherwise, we, being placed in great difficulty, will be unable to oppose Russia any further. An immediate reply is expected. Respect this." [1] On the next day came an urgent appeal from Yang-tsze Viceroys and Taotai Sheng, who requested, under instructions from the Chinese Government, that Great Britain, the United States, Germany, and Japan intervene to obtain an extension of time with a view to the modification of the Articles regarding civil administration in the Chinese garrisons in Manchuria, the exclusive trading rights demanded by the Russians, and the proposed railway to the Wall. [2] Six days later, on March 27, the two-week period expired, and the Chinese Court, which still sojourned at Si-ngan in the Shen-si Province, telegraphed to Sir Chin-chen Lo-fêng-luh, as follows: " We have followed the advice of Lord Lansdowne, in not giving our authority to sign the Manchurian Agreement. In your telegrams of the 20th [3] and 23d [4] instant, you have assured us of the moral support of England if we followed her advice. Our Plenipotentiaries, Prince Ching and

[1] *China, No. 2 (1904)*, No. 32.         [2] *Ibid.*, No. 33.
[3] Probably *ibid.*, No. 31.
[4] This telegram has not appeared in the Blue Books.

Viceroy Li, report that Russia will now permanently occupy Manchuria, and that the collective negotiations will have to be suspended. The Court feels great anxiety about this matter. As Manchuria is the cradle of the present dynasty, how could China tolerate a permanent occupation of that region? We now apply for the positive assistance of England in bringing about a satisfactory settlement between China and Russia, in order to avoid a rupture with that Power, which could not fail to be detrimental to the interests of China and the treaty Powers. Please lay the contents of the telegram before Lord Lansdowne and request an immediate reply."[1] It is possible that these messages were simultaneously repeated to some or all of the rest of the four Powers, and, if so, it becomes tenable that, but for the protests of the Powers, Li Hung-chang might have signed the agreement. Nor can it be denied that, even after their final refusal to accept the Russian proposals, the Chinese officials clearly apprehended that, failing the positive support of the Powers, Manchuria would be *permanently* occupied by the northern Power. It is, of course, uncertain, and perhaps also immaterial, whether they had voluntarily reached that conclusion, or whether the Russians had led them to the belief by threats.

Let us now turn to see what explanations Russia had offered, for Japan about January 12[2] and Great Britain on March 4[3] had made inquiries at

---

[1] *China, No. 2 (1904)*, No. 35.    [2] *Ibid.*, No. 6.
[3] *Ibid.*, No. 20.

the Russian Government in respect to the actual
text of the Agreement. Lord Lansdowne repeated
his query on March 9, adding that if the version
reported by Sir Ernest Satow was approximately
accurate, it was " impossible to describe it as a
contract of a temporary and provisional nature,
and our treaty rights were certainly affected by it."
Then, in his oft outspoken vein, the Marquess concluded : " On the other hand, it is surely reasonable
that we should ask his Excellency's [Count Lamsdorff's] help in exposing the trick, and putting the
saddle on the right horse, if, as he suggests, garbled
versions of the Agreement are being circulated by
the Chinese Government in order to create dissen-
sion between the Powers ; and you may state that
to join the Russian Government in exhibiting in its
true light so discreditable a manœuvre would afford
the liveliest satisfaction to His Majesty's Government." [1] Russia, however, would not communicate
the text of the proposed Agreement, and it was
explained later by Count Lamsdorff that there had
been a " programme," the detail of which had at
one time or another been under discussion, but
there had never existed any regular draft Agreement in twelve Articles ; that the Czar had at
no time given him the full powers indispensable
for concluding such an agreement, and that in
her negotiations with China [concerning the pro-
gramme], three different Departments of the Russian Government had been equally engaged. These

[1] *China, No. 2 (1904)*, No. 26.

circumstances, and also " the unwise interference
of the press and public, which seemed to assert a
very dangerous claim to be admitted to a seat and
voice in the councils of the Powers regarding
China," made it very difficult for the Count to be as
frankly communicative as he would otherwise have
wished to have been. Indeed, " it would have been
impossible for him to have discussed the details of
these negotiations with a third Government." [1] To
the Japanese Minister, who had been instructed by
his Government to make the friendly proposal to
Russia that the Representatives of the Powers at
Peking should be given an opportunity to consider
the draft of the Manchurian Agreement before it
was signed, Count Lamsdorff replied in no less interesting manner. He observed, on March 26, that
the Agreement solely concerned two independent
States, and must be concluded without the intervention of any other Powers, and politely but firmly
declined to consider any such proposal as was made
by Japan. The Count added, however, that " he
could give an official assurance to the Japanese
Minister that neither the sovereignty and the integrity of China in Manchuria nor the treaty rights
of any other Power were affected by the proposed
Agreement ; that it was of a provisional nature,
and a necessary preliminary to the Russian troops
evacuating the province. Its early signature was
desired by his Excellency in order that the unjust
suspicions aroused by false reports with regard to

[1] *China, No. 2 (1904)*, No. 39.

it might be removed by its publication." [1] Satisfied neither with this statement nor with China's refusal to sign the Agreement, the Japanese Government is said to have made a second protest at St. Petersburg in a more resolute tone than in the first, on April 5.[2] On the same day, however, appeared in the Russian *Messager Officiel* a long statement recapitulating Russia's relations with China since the beginning of the Boxer affair, and declaring that, owing to the publication in the foreign press of all sorts of false reports of the alleged treaties with China, and to the serious obstacles that had apparently been put in the way of China as regards the conclusion of an agreement with Russia serving as " a starting-point" toward the restoration of Manchuria to China, " it had been found impossible immediately to take the measures contemplated for the gradual evacuation of Manchuria." The negotiations had been dropped. " With regard to the question of the complete and final restitution of this territory to China," concluded the official statement, " it is evident that it can only be accomplished after a normal state of affairs has been reëstablished in the Chinese Empire, and a central Government has been secured in the capital, independent and sufficiently strong to guarantee Russia against the renewal of the disturbances of last year. While maintaining the present temporary form of government with the

---

[1] *China, No. 2 (1904)*, No. 34.
[2] The *Kokumin*, April 6, 1901.

object of insuring order in the neighborhood of
the vast Russian frontier, but remaining unalterably true to their original programme, as repeatedly
formulated, the Imperial Government will quietly
await the future progress of events." [1]

[1] *China, No. 2 (1904)*, No. 37, pp. 17–23.

# CHAPTER XI

## FURTHER DEMANDS

RUSSIA did not wait long before reaching another "starting-point." No sooner did the effort of Viceroy Chang Chih-tung and the late Viceroy Liu Kun-yi to create among the Representatives of some Powers a sentiment in favor of opening all Manchuria to foreign trade, so as to forestall the annexation of the territory by Russia, miscarry,[1] than Sir Ernest Satow reported from " a thoroughly trustworthy source," on August 14, 1901, that Russia was resuming her negotiations with China to bring about the signature of the amended Manchurian Agreement of the preceding March.[2] Lord Lansdowne at once instructed him to inform the Chinese authorities, if his advice was requested, that the proper course for them to pursue would be to call the attention of the Powers to the matter and to communicate the text of the provisions in question, should they prove inconsistent with the treaty obligations of China to other Powers or with the integrity of the Empire; so that the British Government

[1] The *Kokumin*, May 19, 1901.
[2] *China, No. 2 (1904)*, No. 40. In No. 42 (August 21), Sir Ernest gives, in three parallel columns, the original terms proposed by Russia in February, the alterations of March, and the proposals now made in August. The last two are nearly identical.

should be ready to advise whether an infraction of its treaty rights was involved, or whether the provisions were in any other way objectionable.[1] It does not appear that Russia exercised great pressure upon China for the conclusion of the Agreement. Toward the end of the month, M. de Giers was replaced as Russian Minister at Peking by M. Paul Lessar, formerly a railway engineer on the Afghan frontier, and a man of delicate health but brilliant parts. Meanwhile, the peace commissioners of the eleven Powers had at last, on September 17, 1901, succeeded in signing at Peking with the two Chinese Plenipotentiaries the final Protocol between China and the Powers for the resumption of their friendly relations.[2] It seems that, when the affairs in North China were thus finally settled, Russia felt herself freer than she ever had been to deal independently with China concerning the Manchurian question, which the Powers had allowed to remain. Moreover, the Imperial Court was expected shortly to return to the capital, and the Chinese Government began to look anxiously for the withdrawal of foreign troops from the realm. Seizing this opportunity, M. Lessar seems to have mooted, probably on October 5,[3] a new convention of evacuation, whose comparatively mild terms commended themselves powerfully at this moment to the Chinese

---

[1] *China, No. 2 (1904)*, No. 41 (August 16).

[2] See Mayers, pp. 283–318; or the Blue Book, *Treaty Series, No. 17, 1902: Final Protocol between the Foreign Powers and China for the Resumption of Friendly Relations.*

[3] *Tokushu Jōyaku*, p. 266.

commissioners, especially to Li Hung-chang.[1] Considering the feeble attitude of China, it would have been extremely difficult for the interested Powers to protest to her against the acceptance of the Russian demands, had not the Viceroys Liu and Chang, after learning their contents, again strongly reminded the Emperor and the Empress Dowager of the direct peril to the reigning dynasty which might result from acceding to the Russian proposals. In accordance with the wishes of the Court, the dying Li Hung-chang is said to have, on his sick-bed, seen M. Lessar, and appealed to the Russian friendship toward China to modify the terms of the proposed amendment.[2] Li soon passed away, on November 7, leaving the gravest problem of China in a state of extreme uncertainty. As to the contents of the Russian proposition, it is interesting to observe that they were presently revealed from a source whose veracity could hardly be questioned. On December 11, Prince Ching disclosed them to Mr. Conger.[3] They coincided with those that the latter had reported to Secretary Hay on the 3d, namely, that, stated briefly, Russia should evacuate Manchuria, under the usual conditions, in three years; that China should protect the railways and Russian subjects in the territory; that she might station,

[1] See the summary of Li's highly interesting letter of September 30, which has just appeared in the London *Times* for October 12, 1904, p. 6.

[2] *Tokushu Jōyaku*, pp. 266–267; The *Kokumin*, November 2, pp. 23, 30, 190–191.

[3] The U. S. 57th Congress, 2d Session, *House Documents*, vol. i. p. 272.

in places other than lands assigned to the Railway Company, mounted and foot soldiers, whose numbers should, however, be determined by an agreement with Russia, and who should exclude artillery; that troops of no other nationality should be employed in protecting the railways; that the Anglo-Russian Agreement of April, 1899, should be strictly adhered to; that subjects of no other nationality should without Russian consent be allowed to build railways or bridges in Southern Manchuria; and that the Shan-hai-kwan-Niu-chwang-Sin-minting Railways should be returned to China after her payment to Russia of the expenditure incurred by the latter in their occupation.[1] Prince Ching, it appears, presented a counter-proposition to the Russian convention, which, among other things, seems to have requested that the evacuation of Manchuria should be completed within one year, instead of three, as was provided in the original draft. Russia's reply to this arrived in Peking the last of January, 1902, agreeing to reduce the period of evacuation from three to two years.[2] At the same time, however, the Russian Government now strongly supported, in addition to the proposed convention, a separate agreement proposed by the Russo-Chinese Bank. The latter, according to Prince Ching, contained, besides the railway concessions already granted to the Bank,

---

[1] The U. S. 57th Congress, 2d Session, *House Documents*, vol. i. p. 271. Compare a version in *Tokushu Jōyaku*, pp. 266–267.

[2] The U. S. 57th Congress, 2d Session, *House Documents*, vol. i. p. 272.

LI HUNG-CHANG

provision that China should herself undertake all
industrial development in Manchuria, but if she
required financial help from the outside, application
should always first be made to the Russo-Chinese
Bank; only when the latter did not wish to engage
in the work might citizens of other countries be
allowed to undertake it. A clause was also to be
inserted, the practical value of which is not clear,
that citizens of every country should have the same
rights as they then did to trade at the open ports
and in the interior.[1] Prince Ching was obliged to
acknowledge to Mr. Conger, on January 19, 1902,
that, owing to the pressure which Russia increased
simultaneously with the apparent concessions she
had made, she would yield no further, and " he was
convinced that, if China held out longer, they
would never again secure terms so lenient; that
the Russians were in full possession of the territory,
and their treatment of the Chinese was so aggra-
vating that longer occupation was intolerable; that
they must be got out, and that the only way left
for China to accomplish this was to make the best
possible terms. The only terms that Russia would
consent to were the signing of both the Convention
and the Russo-Chinese Bank Agreement." [2]

It is unnecessary to say that against the Russian
demands Great Britain, Japan, and the United
States had separately and more than once entered

[1] The U. S. 57th Congress, 2d Session, *House Documents*,
vol. i. pp. 273–274.

[2] *Ibid.*, pp. 273–274 (Conger to Hay).

firm protests at Peking. The conduct of the first
two Powers, however, is not shown in the published
documents. Secretary Hay reminded the Russian
and Chinese Governments, on February 3, of the
repeated assurances made by the Czar's Foreign
Minister of his devotion to the principle of the
open door in all parts of China, and said : " An
agreement whereby China gives any corporation or
company the exclusive right or privilege of opening mines, establishing railroads, or in any other
way industrially developing Manchuria, can but be
viewed with the greatest concern by the Government
of the United States. It constitutes a monopoly,
which is a distinct breach of the stipulations of
the treaties concluded between China and foreign
Powers, and thereby seriously affects the rights of
American citizens." [1]  To this note, the interesting
reply of Count Lamsdorff, signed by himself, was :
" . . . It [the Russian Government] feels itself
bound . . . to declare that negotiations carried on
between two entirely independent States are not
subject to be submitted to the approval of other
Powers. There is no thought of attacking the principle of the ' open door ' *as that principle is understood by the Imperial Government of Russia,*[2] and
Russia has no intention whatever to change *the
policy followed by her in that respect up to the
present time.* If the Russo-Chinese Bank should

[1] The U. S. 57th Congress, 2d Session, *House Documents*,
vol. i. pp. 926–928.
[2] The italics in the quotation are the author's.

obtain concessions in China, the agreements of a
private character relating to them would not differ
from those heretofore concluded by so many other
foreign corporations.[1] But would it not be very
strange if the ' door' that is ' open' to certain nations should be closed to Russia, whose frontier ad-
joins that of Manchuria, and who has been forced by
recent events to send her troops into that province
to reëstablish order in the plain and common interest of all nations? . . . It is impossible to deny
to an independent State the right to grant to others
such concessions as it is free to dispose of, and I
have every reason to believe that the demands of
the Russo-Chinese Bank do not in the least exceed
those that have been so often formulated by other
foreign companies, and I feel that under the circumstances it would not be easy for the Imperial
Government to deny to the Russian companies that
support which is given by other Governments to
companies and syndicates of their own nationalities. At all events, I beg your Excellency to believe
that there is not, nor can there be, any question of
the contradiction of the assurances which, under the
orders of His Majesty the Emperor, I have had occa-

[1] Observe how powerfully Russia applies this argument. On
February 4, M. Lessar said that Russia was merely asking
privileges in Manchuria similar to those granted to Germany
in Shan-tung. — The U. S. 57th Congress, 2d Session, *House
Documents*, vol. i. p. 274. Russia, if she would, could with a certain amount of impunity inquire of Great Britain and other
Powers how it was that they allowed Germany to acquire her
apparently exclusive rights in Shan-tung, and now objected to
Russia's following her example only on a larger scale.

sion to give heretofore in regard to the principles which invariably direct the policy of Russia."[1] It should be noted here that Count Lamsdorff's statement, while it refers to the Agreement with the Bank, which he supported, contains no reference to the Convention proposed by the Russian Government.

Negotiations lagged, China probably declining to sign under the remonstrances of Great Britain, the United States, and Japan. On March 2, Prince Ching showed Mr. Conger a draft of his new counter-proposals, which Japan was said to have wholly, and Great Britain in the main, approved.[2] These proposals are interesting for their practical identity, save a slight difference,[3] with the final Russo-Chinese Convention of April 8, 1902, which will be fully treated in a subsequent chapter. This fact is a conclusive evidence that after March, Russia suddenly accepted nearly all of the counter-proposals made by China. This abrupt condescension on the part of Russia is supposed to have been partly due to an important event which had recently taken place in the diplomatic world — the conclusion of the Anglo-Japanese Agreement signed at London on January 30, 1902, and simultaneously announced in Parliament and the Imperial Diet of Tokio on February 12.

---

[1] The U. S. 57th Congress, 2d Session, *House Documents*, vol. i. p. 929.

[2] *Ibid.*, pp. 277–279.

[3] I. e., the draft of March limited the period of evacuation to one year, instead of a year and a half, as in the convention of April.

# CHAPTER XII

THE details of the negotiations preliminary to the
consummation of this remarkable stroke of diplomacy have not been made public, but we are in
possession of some salient facts from which succes-
sive steps leading up to the final conclusion may be
inferred with tolerable certainty. It is well known
that Great Britain, which had always occupied a
predominant place in the foreign relations of Japan,
had persistently opposed the latter's ardent wish and
continual struggle to revise the humiliating treaties
which had, about 1858, been imposed by the Powers
upon the weak feudal Government of Yedo. In
1894, however, contrary to her past policy, Great
Britain led other Powers in according to Japan a
cordial recognition of the latter's progress in various lines of her national activity, and assenting to
the revision of her treaties. During the war with
China in 1894–5, the British attitude was one of
friendly neutrality between the two Oriental Empires, but the events after the conclusion of the
war, especially the forced retrocession of the Liao-
tung Peninsula, closely followed by the tightening
hold of the Muscovites upon the Peking Court,

seemed to have aroused the sympathy of Great Britain with Japan, mingled probably with the fear of the loss of some of her own predominant economic interests in China. From this time on, the interests of the two Powers had been seen to coincide in the Far East to an increasing degree, and the relations of their Governments had steadily risen in cordiality.[1] At the rupture of the Boxer insurrection in 1900, the Cabinet of Lord Salisbury manifested so much faith in Japan as to request her immediately to dispatch large forces to the relief of the besieged Legations at Peking, Great Britain going even so far as to engage to undertake the necessary financial responsibilities of the proposed expedition.[2] Both during the campaign and throughout the negotiation for peace, the two Powers, as well as the United States, conducted themselves together, as is apparent from our foregoing discussion, in perfect harmony.[3] The common

[1] The reader will remember the cordial exchange of views between the two Powers when Wei-hai-Wei was leased to Great Britain in 1898. There occurred in the East several affairs of minor importance in which the British and Japanese authorities acted with mutual good-will ; e. g., the arrangement for a British concession at Niu-chwang in 1899. See *China, No. 1 (1900)*, pp. 215–218.

[2] See the *British Parliamentary Papers : China, No. 3 (1900)*, Nos. 146, 121, 129, 134, 141, 155, 169–171, 180–181, 188–189, 191, 193, 203, 210, 216, 238, 241, 212, 217, 224, 236, 246–247, 252, 260, 265–267; *China, No. 1 (1901)*, Nos. 122–124, 42, 4, 18, 23, 29, 32 (July 13, 1900), 41, 52, 57, 38.

[3] Mr. Katō, Foreign Minister at Tokio at the time, remarked later that even in matters about which the two Powers had not exchanged their views, their Representatives at Peking acted in

danger in Manchuria still further cemented their friendship. All this cordial relation, spontaneous as it was, would not, however, account for the formation of a definite alliance between the two Governments. It seems at least probable that the Anglo-German Agreement of October, 1900, as much by the importance of some of its principles as by its very inefficiency, served as a natural step toward a more wholesome alliance.[1] In this new direction, Great Britain is said to have taken the initiative. This supposition will appear not improbable when it is considered that her immense interests in China, which had begun to be eclipsed by other Powers, would be best secured and promoted by the maintenance of the integrity of China and the open door in her market, and that this object could not be better assured than by an alliance with the strongest Eastern Power, whose fast growing interests in the neighboring lands were in a large measure identical with hers. Suggestions for such an agree-

such mutual sympathy that it was suspected that a secret understanding must have existed between them. — *Tokushu Jōyaku*, p. 411.

[1] In this connection it was thought not improbable that Germany herself might have informally suggested the feasibility of a triple alliance between herself and Great Britain and Japan in the same line as the Anglo-German Agreement, which Japan had joined as a signatory. In his speech before the Reichstag, however, Herr von Bülow declared, on March 3, that Germany was not the father of the Anglo-Japanese alliance. At any rate, the German suggestion, if there was one, never materialized, but gave place to another and still more important form of agreement in which the world-politics of the versatile Kaiser played no part.

ment are known to have been made by Great Britain to Japan under the Itō Cabinet in April, 1901, and again under the present Katsura Cabinet in July, but it was not till October of that year that definite negotiations were opened by Japan. The Premier, Viscount Katsura, seems to have ascertained in December that the elder statesmen of the Empire were in hearty accord with the agreement toward which the negotiations had pointed.[1] At this stage of the negotiations, also, there had developed other circumstances under which the "splendid" isolation of Great Britain appeared less tenable than before.

[1] The position which one of the elder statesmen out of office, Marquis Itō, occupied in this diplomatic evolution, has been a subject of much speculation. He was not only on his tour in America and Europe when the Agreement was concluded, but also had made efforts at St. Petersburg to come to an *entente* with Russia. From this, it has even been charged that he was opposed to an Agreement with Great Britain. It now appears, however, that he had discussed the latter question with Premier Katsura before he sailed for Europe, and that he proceeded to St. Petersburg with a full authorization from the Government to exchange views with Count Lamsdorff regarding Korea. In the mean time, the Cabinet continued its negotiations with Great Britain. Each must have kept the other well informed of the progress of the respective negotiations, with this important difference, however, that Marquis Itō apparently entertained the view, which the Cabinet respected without accepting, that a British alliance would be, not less desirable, but more difficult of realization, than a Russian agreement concerning Korea. Unexpectedly to the Marquis, his effort did not materialize as well as he had hoped, while, on the other hand, it seemed as if his significant presence in Russia had hastened the hands of the jealous British Foreign Office, which now put its seal upon the terms as agreed upon with rather unexpected readiness.

COUNT KATSURA
*Premier of Japan*

Half a year after the Anglo-German Agreement was rendered valueless by the declarations of Herr von Bülow, the Czar paid a significant visit, in September, not only to France, but also to Germany. The ebullition of friendly sentiments between the heads of the States was not less effervescent at Danzig than at Dunkirk. The Russo-Chinese Bank presently floated a loan of 80,000,000 marks at Berlin, thus insuring to that extent the interests of the Germans in Russian success in the East. At the same time the situation in Manchuria had been growing more serious than before, while Germany had seemed no longer inclined to join Great Britain in the latter's protests against the menacing conduct of Russia. Grave as was the danger to the political and commercial prestige of Great Britain in the East, her hands were still closely tied by the vexatious South African question. If there ever was need of an agreement with the rising Power of the Orient, it had probably been never more keenly felt by the British Government than in the last part of the year 1901. Side by side with these favorable circumstances for an understanding, the student should not for a moment lose from sight two fundamental conditions which drew together, not only the Governments, but also the people, of Great Britain and Japan with mutual attraction. One was sentimental : each of the two nations found in the other, though in different ways from one another, something of a counterpart of its geographical position, its material needs and aspirations, and

the energy and enterprise of its individual members.
This mutual sympathy was largely intensified by,
not, indeed, so much the identity of their interests
in the East, as the common principles under which
these interests would be best protected — the independence and strength of China and Korea, and the
equal opportunity therein for the economic enterprise of all nations.

The final outcome of the Anglo-Japanese negotiations was a remarkable product, the like of which
is seldom seen in history, especially when it is considered that it united reciprocally two nations widely
apart in race, religion, and history, one of which
had rarely in time of peace entered into a regular
alliance even with a European Power.[1] The most
striking, as well as the most important for our
study, must be regarded the entirely fair and open
principles to which the Agreement gave clear expression. These remarks may not be better sub-
stantiated than by quoting the exact words of the
document itself, and of the dispatch inclosing the
Agreement from Lord Lansdowne to Sir Claude
MacDonald, the British Minister at Tokio, which
read as follows: —

"The Governments of Great Britain and Japan, actuated solely by a desire to maintain the *status quo* and

[1] The writer is indebted to the *Kokumin Shimbun* for many
important suggestions regarding the negotiations between the
two Powers which resulted in the conclusion of the Agreement.
*Tokushu Jōyaku*, pp. 407–411, gives a brief explanatory view of
the conditions under which the Agreement was concluded.

general peace in the extreme East, being moreover specially interested in maintaining the independence and territorial integrity of the Empire of China and the Empire of Korea, and in securing equal opportunities in those countries for the commerce and industry of all nations, hereby agree as follows: —

" ARTICLE I. The High Contracting Parties having mutually recognized the independence of China and Korea, declare themselves to be entirely uninfluenced by any aggressive tendencies in either country.  Having in view, however, their special interests, of which those of Great Britain relate principally to China, while Japan, in addition to the interests which she possesses in China, is interested in a peculiar degree, politically as well as commercially and industrially, in Korea, the High Contracting Parties recognize that it will be admissible for either of them to take such measures as may be indispensable in order to safeguard those interests if threatened either by the aggressive action of any other Power, or by disturbances arising in China or Korea, and necessitating the intervention of either of the High Contracting Parties for the protection of the lives and property of its subjects.

"ARTICLE II. If either Great Britain or Japan, in the defense of their respective interests as above described, should become involved in war with another Power, the other High Contracting Party will maintain a strict neutrality, and use its efforts to prevent other Powers from joining in hostilities against its ally. ,

" ARTICLE III. If in the above event, any other Power or Powers should join in hostilities against that ally, the other High Contracting Party will come to its assistance, and will conduct war in common, and will make peace in mutual agreement with it.

" ARTICLE IV. The High Contracting Parties agree that

neither of them will, without consulting the other, enter into separate arrangements with another Power to the prejudice of the interests above described.

"ARTICLE V. Whenever, in the opinion of either Great Britain or Japan, the above-mentioned interests are in jeopardy, the two Governments will communicate with one another fully and frankly.

"ARTICLE VI. The present Agreement shall come into effect immediately after the date of its signature, and remain in force for five years from that date.

"In case neither of the High Contracting Parties should have notified twelve months before the expiration of the said five years the intention of terminating it, it shall remain binding until the expiration of one year from the day on which either of the High Contracting Parties shall have denounced it. But if, when the date fixed for its expiration arrives, either ally is actually engaged in war, the alliance shall, *ipso facto*, continue until peace is concluded.

"In faith whereof the Undersigned, duly authorized by their respective Governments, have signed this Agreement, and have affixed thereto their seals.

"Done in duplicate at London, the 30th January, 1902.

"LANSDOWNE,
> *His Britannic Majesty's Principal Secretary of State for Foreign Affairs.*

"HAYASHI,
> *Envoy Extraordinary and Minister Plenipotentiary of His Majesty the Emperor of Japan at the Court of St. James.*" [1]

[1] The *British Parliamentary Papers, Treaty Series, No. 3, 1902: Agreement between the United Kingdom and Japan relative to China and Korea, signed at London, January 30, 1902.*

"FOREIGN OFFICE, January 30, 1902.

"SIR CLAUDE MACDONALD [the British Minister at Tokio]:

"I have signed to-day, with the Japanese Minister, an Agreement between Great Britain and Japan, of which a copy is inclosed in this dispatch.

"This Agreement may be regarded as the outcome of the events which have taken place during the past two years in the Far East, and of the part taken by Great Britain and Japan in dealing with them.

"Throughout the troubles and complications which arose in China consequent upon the Boxer outbreak and the attack upon the Peking Legations, the two Powers have been in close and uninterrupted communication, and have been actuated by similar views.

"We have each of us desired that the integrity and independence of the Chinese Empire should be preserved, that there should be no disturbance of the territorial *status quo* either in China or in the adjoining regions, that all nations should, within those regions, as well as within the limits of the Chinese Empire, be afforded equal opportunities for the development of their commerce and industry, and that peace should not only be restored, but should, for the future, be maintained.

"From the frequent exchanges of view which have taken place between the two Governments, and from the discovery that their Far Eastern policy was identical, it has resulted that each side has expressed the desire that their common policy should find expression in an international contract of binding validity.

"We have thought it desirable to record in the Preamble of that instrument the main objects of our common policy in the Far East to which I have already referred, and in the first Article we join in entirely disclaiming any aggressive tendencies either in China or Korea. We have, however, thought it necessary also to place on record the view entertained by both the High Contracting Parties, that should their interests as above described be endangered, it will be admissible for either of them to take such measures as may be indispensable in order to safeguard their interests, and words have been added which will render it clear that such precautionary measures might become necessary and might be legitimately taken, not only in the case of aggressive action or of an actual attack of some other Power, but in the event of disturbances arising of a character to necessitate the intervention of either of the High Contracting Parties for the protection of the lives and property of its subjects.

"The principal obligations undertaken mutually by the High Contracting Parties are those of maintaining a strict neutrality in the event of either of them becoming involved in war, and of coming to one another's assistance in the event of either of them being confronted by the opposition of more than one hostile Power. Under the remaining provisions of the Agreement, the High Contracting Parties undertake that neither of them will, without consultation with the other, enter into separate arrangements with another Power to the prejudice of the interests described in the Agreement, and that whenever those interests are in jeopardy, they will communicate with one another fully and frankly.

"The concluding Article has reference to the duration of the Agreement which, after five years, is terminable by either of the High Contracting Parties at one year's notice.

"His Majesty's Government had been largely influenced in their decision to enter into this important contract by the conviction that it contains no provisions which can be regarded as an indication of aggressive or self-seeking tendencies in the regions to which it applies. It has been concluded purely as a measure of precaution, to be invoked, should occasion arise, in the defence of important British interests. It in no way threatens the present position or the legitimate interests of other Powers. On the contrary, that part of it which renders either of the High Contracting Parties liable to be called upon by the other for assistance can operate only when one of the allies has found himself obliged to go to war in defence of interests which are common to both, when the circumstances in which he has taken this step are such as to establish that the quarrel has not been of his own seeking, and when, being engaged in his own defence, he finds himself threatened, not only by a single Power, but by a hostile coalition.

"His Majesty's Government trust that the Agreement may be found of mutual advantage to the two countries, that it will make for the preservation of peace, and that, should peace be unfortunately broken, it will have the effect of restricting the area of hostilities.

"I am, etc.,<br>"LANSDOWNE." [1]

The singular nature of these documents stands out so clearly on their face that it hardly needs a special reference. Not only has Manchuria at last been clearly interpreted by both Powers as lying within the scope of the Agreement, but it is explicitly admitted therein that Japan possesses extensive interests in the Korean peninsula, which is for that reason included in the sphere within which the contracting parties unequivocally disa-

---

[1] The *British Parliamentary Papers: Japan, No. 1 (1902), Dispatch to His Majesty's Minister at Tokio, forwarding Agreement between Great Britain and Japan, of January 30, 1902.*

vow aggressive tendencies. Nor does this sum up all the difference between this and the Anglo-German Agreement, for, while in the latter the denial of the parties' aggressive designs was limited to the period of the Boxer complication, and, moreover, coupled with a reservation amounting to the recognition of the theory of readjusting the balance between the Powers at the expense of China, the new alliance unconditionally upholds the independence of China and Korea, and any measure, either peaceful or warlike, taken by either party to safeguard its interests, if they are in any way threatened, would by no means alter its devotion to the principles of the territorial integrity of the Chinese and Korean Empires and of the open door in those countries. The alliance exists solely for the purpose of effectively safeguarding the interests already acquired by the two Powers on the common ground, and it is implied in an unmistakable manner that those interests may best be maintained by the total abstention, in any event, from all aggressive or exclusive tendencies in China and Korea, and, what is equally important, that the observation of these principles would forcibly tend to preserve the general peace in the Far East. Owing to the covert violation of these principles by another Power, however, peace has been broken, but the Anglo-Japanese Agreement has not expired. The latter would, however, fall to the ground the moment one of the parties, either as a result of a war or otherwise, should attempt to depart from the principles of the open door and the territorial integrity of the neighboring Empires.

Lord Lansdowne considered the Agreement " a measure of precaution," and hoped that it would " make for the preservation of peace, and that, should peace be unfortunately broken, it would have the effect of restricting the area of hostilities." Presently these hopes were openly seconded, but in reality neutralized, by the Russo-French Declaration of March 17, which stated : —

" The allied Governments of Russia and France have received a copy of the Anglo-Japanese Agreement of the 30th January, 1902, concluded with the object of maintaining the *status quo* and the general peace in the Far East, and preserving the independence of China and Korea, which are to remain open to the commerce and industry of all nations, and have been fully satisfied to find therein affirmed the fundamental principles which they have themselves, on several occasions, declared to form the basis of their policy, and still remain so.

" The two Governments consider that the observance of these principles is at the same time a guarantee of their special interests in the Far East.[1] Nevertheless, being obliged themselves also to take into consideration the case in which either the aggressive action of third Powers, or the recurrence of disturbances in China, jeopardizing the integrity and free development of that Power, might become a menace to their own interests, the two allied Governments reserve to themselves the

[1] Observe the clearness of this statement. This idea is only implied in the Anglo-Japanese Agreement. It is remarkable that an explicit statement of this nature should come, as it did, from the Powers from which it would have been less expected than from their rivals.

right to consult in that contingency as to the means to be adopted for securing those interests." [1]

The St. Petersburg *Messager Officiel* of March 20, published, with the Declaration, the statement that the Russian Government had received the announcement of the Anglo-Japanese Agreement " with the most perfect calm," for Russia likewise insisted on the maintenance and integrity of China and Korea. " Russia," it continued to say, " desires the preservation of the *status quo* and general peace in the Far East, by the construction of the great Siberian Railroad, together with its branch line through Manchuria, toward a port always ice-free. Russia aids in the extension in these regions of the commerce and industry of the whole world. Would it be to her interest to put forward obstacles at the present time ? The intention expressed by Great Britain and Japan to attain those same objects, which have invariably been pursued by the Russian Government, can meet with nothing but sympathy in Russia, in spite of the comments in certain political spheres and in some of the foreign newspapers, which endeavored to present in quite a different light the impassive attitude of the Imperial Government toward a diplomatic act which, in its

---

[1] *China, No. 2 (1904)*, No. 50. The so-called triple alliance of Europe was renewed in May, with a declaration that it, together with the Russo-French alliance, maintained peace. The latter, as is shown here, had extended itself from Europe to the Far East, owing largely to the conclusion of the Anglo-Japanese Agreement. The growing solidarity of the world's international politics may in some degree be discerned here.

eye, does not change in any way the general situation of the political horizon." [1]

It seems to be generally overlooked that, so far as the published documents are concerned, there occurs no statement that the Russo-French alliance extended from Europe to the Far East under precisely the same conditions as those of the Anglo-Japanese Agreement. In other words, although the general principles of the latter are indorsed, one finds nowhere that its terms of war and neutrality and its provisions regarding the duration of the validity of the instrument have also been reproduced by Russia and France in their mutual convention. Regarding the precise conditions of their alliance, therefore, the world is left much in the dark, save what it takes for granted. Nor are the principles of the integrity and the open door of China and Korea so fully and explicitly stated here as in the Agreement of the rival allies, while the reservation at the end of the Declaration does not make it clear that these principles may not be discarded, under certain circumstances, according to the interpretations of the parties themselves of the means to be taken to safeguard their interests.

Turning to the general tenor of the documents, the student will at once observe their marked characteristics. It is at least singular, one would think, that the " most perfect calm " and the " impassive attitude " of the Russian Government should be

---

[1] The *Evening Post*, March 20, 1902 ; *Tokushu Jōyaku*, pp. 415–416.

expressed in so many words. If, again, the allied
Powers were, as they declare, in perfect accord with
the principles of Great Britain and Japan, it is not
intelligible why they should entertain, as it appears,
so deep a suspicion toward the " political spheres "
in which the Russian calmness was said to have been
deliberately misinterpreted, and also toward the
" third Powers " " whose aggressive action " might
" jeopardize the integrity and free development " of
China. This sense of distrust becomes all the more
pronounced when it is contrasted with the assertion
that the agreement between Great Britain and
Japan brought no change on the political horizon
of the East. It was reported about the time when
the Russian Minister and the French *Chargé d' Affaires* at Tokio handed the Declaration to Baron
Komura, that the allied Powers had made their
Declaration because they feared that Great Britain
and Japan might, in virtue of the first Article of
their Agreement, object even to legitimate means
of protecting the French and Russian interests in
the Far East.[1] If the four Powers upheld the same
principles, no such apprehension of two of them
against the other two could be either cordial or even
justifiable. Under these considerations, one can
hardly avoid the conclusion that the allied Governments of Russia and France must have been ani-
mated less by the principles they professed than by
the deep rivalry of their interests with those of the
other allies. For it is at least certain that, ever since

[1] The *Kokumin*, March 23, 1902.

their memorable coalition with Germany in 1895, in the coercion of Japan, Russia and France had acted in mutual good-will, the former being mainly aided by the latter in Manchuria and Korea, and the latter by the former in the southern Chinese provinces,[1] in their diplomatic manœuvres in those ·countries and in their struggles with Japan and Great Britain.[2] If the Agreement and the Declaration are considered the formal expression of the cordial sentiment which had long existed and been growing between the two sets of the Powers, they may be said to have brought no change upon the political horizon ; but it seems impossible to deny that their publication greatly clarified the political atmosphere in the East, and, in spite of the verbal meaning of the declaration, not a little accentuated the widening contrast between the two different policies upheld by the two powerful coalitions. In this sense, the political evolution of the Far East may be said to have now reached an important stage after the European intervention in Japan in 1895.[3]

[1] See, for instance, *Ministère des Affaires Étrangères*, *Documents Diplomatiques: Chine, 1894-8*, No. 19 (p. 12); No. 36 (p. 29); No. 37 (p. 30); No. 61 (pp. 45-46); No. 65 (p. 49).

[2] During the peace negotiations at Peking after the Boxer war, Russia and France coöperated as closely as did Great Britain, Japan, and the United States.

[3] See pp. 77 ff., above.

# CHAPTER XIII

## THE CONVENTION OF EVACUATION

IT will be remembered that we left the Russo-Chinese negotiation regarding Manchuria at the point where Prince Ching, either late in February or early in March, presented a counter-proposal to the Russian demands.[1] It has also been shown that the Anglo-Japanese Agreement closely preceded, and the Franco-Russian Declaration followed, this event. By that time the allied forces had gradually retired from North China, and the Chinese Court, which had fled to Si-ngan, had retraced its steps to Peking, arriving at the palace on January 7, 1902. The political surroundings of the East seemed to have assumed a somewhat more reassuring outlook, except in Manchuria, than they had worn at any time since the siege of the Legations in 1900. The Russian Government seized this opportunity to conclude with China, on April 8, 1902, along the line suggested by the counter-draft of Prince Ching, the now celebrated Convention providing for the evacuation of Manchuria, which went into effect

---

[1] It was said with a great deal of probability that the conclusion of the Anglo-Japanese Agreement had had a reassuring effect upon Prince Ching in his struggle to refuse Russian demands.

simultaneously with its signature. We subjoin this important document,[1] together with the official state-

[1] The following is the French text, which is considered as the standard in the interpretation of the Convention (*China, No. 2 (1904)*, No. 54, inclosure): —

"Sa Majesté l'Empereur et Autocrate de Toutes les Russies et Sa Majesté l'Empereur de Chine, dans le but de rétablir et de consolider les relations de bon voisinage rompues par le soulèvement qui a eu lieu en 1900 dans le Céleste Empire, ont nommé pour leurs Plénipotentiaires, à l'effet d'établir un accord sur certaines questions concernant la Mandchourie: —

"Les susdits Plénipotentiaires, munis de pleins pouvoirs, qui ont été trouvés suffisants, sont convenus des stipulations suivantes: —

"Article 1. Sa Majesté Impériale l'Empereur de Toutes les Russies, désireux de donner une nouvelle preuve de son amour de la paix et de ses sentiments d'amitié envers Sa Majesté l'Empereur de Chine, malgré que ce soit de différents points de la Mandchourie situés sur la frontière que les premières attacques contre la population paisible Russe aient été faites, consent au retablissement de l'autorité du Gouvernement Chinois dans la province précitée, qui reste une partie intégrale de l'Empire de Chine et restitue au Gouvernement Chinois le droit d'y exercer les pouvoirs gouvernementaux et administratifs, comme avant son occupation par les troupes Russes.

"Article 2. En prenant possession des pouvoirs gouvernementaux et administratifs de la Mandchourie, le Gouvernement Chinois confirme, aussi bien par rapport aux termes que par rapport à tous les autres Articles, l'engagement d'observer strictement les stipulations du contract conclu avec la Banque Russo-Chinoise le 27 Août, 1896, et assume, conformément à l'Article 5 du dit contrat, l'obligation de protéger par tous les moyens le chemin de fer et son personnel, et s'oblige également de sauvegarder la sécurité en Mandchourie de tous les sujets Russes en général qui s'y trouvent et des enterprises fondées par eux.

"Le Gouvernement Russe, en vue de cette obligation assumée par le Gouvernement de Sa Majesté l'Empereur de Chine, consent de son côté dans le cas où il n'y aura pas de troubles, et si la manière d'agir des autres Puissances n'y mettra pas obstacle, à

ment with which the former was published in the
St. Petersburg *Messager Officiel* of April 12 : —

retirer graduellement toutes ses troupes de la Mandchourie de
manière à : —

"(a.) Évacuer dans le courant de six mois après la signature
de la Convention les troupes Russes de la partie sud-ouest de la
Province de Moukden jusqu'au fleuve Liao-ho, en remettant
les chemins de fer à la Chine;

"(b.) Évacuer dans le courant des six mois suivants les
troupes Impériales Russes de la partie restante de la Province de
Moukden et de la Province de Kirin; et

"(c.) Retirer dans le courant des six mois suivants le reste des
troupes Impériales Russes qui se trouvent dans la Province de
Hei-Lung-Kiang.

"Article 3. En vue de la nécessité de conjurer à l'avenir la
repetition des troubles de 1900, dans lesquels les troupes Chinoises cantonnées dans les provinces limitrophes à la Russie ont
pris part, le Gouvernement Russe et le Gouvernement Chinois
se chargeront d'ordonner aux autorités militaires Russes et aux
dzian-dziuns de s'entendre en vue de fixer le nombre et de déter-
miner les lieux de cantonnement des troupes Chinoises en Mandchourie tant que les troupes Russes n'auront pas été retirées ;
le Gouvernement Chinois s'engage en outre à ne pas former
d'autres troupes en sus du nombre determiné de cette manière
par les autorités militaires Russes et les dzian-dziuns, et lequel
doit être suffisant pour exterminer les brigands et pacifier le pays.

"Après l'évacuation complète des troupes Russes, le Gouvernement Chinois aura le droit de procéder à l'examen du nombre
des troupes se trouvant en Mandchourie et sujettes à être aug-
mentées ou diminuées, en informant à temps le Gouvernement
Impérial; car il va de soi que le maintien de troupes dans la province précitée en nombre superflu mènerait inévitablement à
l'augmentation des forces militaires Russes dans les districts
voisins, et provoquerait ainsi un accroissement de dépenses militaires, au grand désavantage des deux États.

"Pour le service de police et le maintien de l'ordre intérieur
dans cette région, en dehors du territoire cédé à la Société du
Chemin de Fer Chinois de l'Est, il sera formé, auprès des Gou-
verneurs locaux —, dzian-dziuns, une gendarmerie Chinoise

" The grave internal disorders which suddenly broke out over the whole of China in the year 1900, exposing

à pied et à cheval composée exclusivement de sujets de Sa Majesté l'Empereur de Chine.

"Article 4. Le Gouvernement Russe consent à restituer à leurs propriétaires les lignes ferrées de Shanhaikwan-Yinkow-Sinminting, occupées et protégées par les troupes Russes depuis la fin du mois de Septembre, 1900. En vue de cela, le Gouvernement de Sa Majesté l'Empereur de Chine s'engage:—

"1. Que dans le cas ou il serait nécessaire d'assurer la sécurité des lignes ferrées précitées, le Gouvernement Chinois s'en chargera lui-même et n'invitera aucune autre Puissance à entreprendre ou à participer à la défense, construction, ou exploitation de ces lignes, et ne permettra pas aux Puissances étrangères d'occuper le territoire restitué par la Russie.

"2. Que les lignes ferrées susmentionnées seront achevées et exploitées sur les bases précises tant de l'Arrangement entre la Russie et l'Angleterre en date du 16 Avril, 1899, que du contrat conclu le 28 Septembre, 1898, avec une Compagnie particulière relativement à un emprunt pour la construction des lignes précitées, et, en outre, en observant les obligations assumées par cette Compagnie, c'est-à-dire, de ne pas prendre possession de la ligne Shanhaikwan-Yinkow-Sinminting ni d'en disposer de quelque façon que ce soit.

"3. Que si par la suite il sera procédé à la continuation des lignes ferrées dans le sud de la Mandchourie ou à la construction d'embranchements vers elles, aussi bien qu'à la construction d'un pont à Yinkow ou au transfert du terminus du chemin de fer de Shanhaikwan qui s'y trouve, ce sera fait après une entente préamable entre les Gouvernements de Russie et de Chine.

"4. Vu que les dépenses faites par la Russie pour le rétablissement et l'exploitation des lignes ferrées restituées de Shanhaikwan-Yinkow-Sinminting n'ont pas été comprises dans la somme totale de l'indemnité, elles lui seront remboursées par le Gouvernement Chinois. Les deux Gouvernements s'entendront sur le montant des sommes à rembourser.

"Les dispositions de tous les Traités antérieurs entre la Russie et la Chine, non modifiées par la présente Convention, restent en pleine vigueur.

"La présente Convention aura force légale à dater du jour de

the Imperial Mission and Russian subjects to danger, obliged Russia to take decided measures to protect her Imperial interests. With this object in view, the Imperial Government, as is already known, dispatched a considerable military force to Peking, which had been abandoned by the Emperor and the Government authorities, and introduced a Russian army into the frontier State of Manchuria, to which the disorders in the Province of Pechili had quickly spread, and were manifested by an attack upon the Russian frontier by the native chiefs and army, accompanied by a formal declaration of war on Russia by the local Chinese authorities.

"Nevertheless, the Imperial Government informed the Government of the Emperor that Russia, in undertaking these measures, had no hostile intentions toward China, whose independence and integrity were the foundation of Russian policy in the Far East.

"True to these principles, Russia, as soon as the danger threatening the Imperial Mission and Russian subjects was over, withdrew her forces from Pechili before any of the other Powers, and, at the first indication of peace in Manchuria being restored, declared her readiness to determine, in a private Agreement with China,

la signature de ses exemplaires par les Plénipotentiaires, de l'un et de l'autre Empire.

"L'échange des ratifications aura lieu à Saint-Pétersbourg dans le délai de trois mois à compter du jour de la signature de la Convention.

"En foi de quoi les Plénipotentiaires respectifs des deux Hautes Parties Contractantes ont signé et scellé de leurs sceaux deux exemplaires de la présente Convention, en langues Russe, Chinoise, et Française. Des trois textes, dûment confrontés et trouvés concordants, le texte Français fera foi pour l'interprétation de la présente convention.

"Faite en double expédition à Pékin, le . . . , correspondant au . . . "

the manner and earliest date of her evacuation of that province, with, however, certain guarantees of a temporary nature, which were rendered necessary by the disorderly condition of affairs in the above-mentioned province.

"The conclusion of this Agreement dragged over many months, owing to the difficult position in which the high Chinese dignitaries were placed, being unable, in the absence of the Court, to decide upon action, as becomes the Representatives of a perfectly independent Empire.

"Latterly, however, the pacification of China has progressed with notable success. After the signature of the Protocol of the 25th of August (7th September), 1901, the Imperial Court returned to Peking; the central lawful authority resumed its rights, and in many parts of the Empire the local administrations were reëstablished. At the first reception of the Corps Diplomatique in Peking, the Chinese Empress expressed to the foreign Representatives her gratitude for their coöperation in suppressing the disturbances, and assured them of her unshakable determination to take every measure for the reëstablishment in the country of the normal state of affairs existing before the disturbances arose.

"This, indeed, solved the problem in which Russia was principally interested when the disorders broke out in the neighboring Empire. The Imperial Government, pursuing no selfish aims, insisted that other Powers also should not violate the independence and integrity of China; and that the lawful Government, with which Russia had concluded various agreements, should be reinstated, and thus, when the disorders were over, the friendly relations with China, which had existed from time immemorial, should be continued.

"Taking into consideration that this was the only object with which Russian troops were sent into the Celestial Empire, and that China has given written guarantee

for the maintenance of order in the country, and repaid
Russia with material expenses to which she was put by
her military operations in China, the Imperial Government henceforth sees no necessity for leaving armed forces
within the confines of the neighboring territory. Therefore, by Imperial will, on the 26th March (April 8) was
signed by the Russian Minister at Peking, M. Lessar,
and by the Chinese Plenipotentiaries, the following Agreement as to the conditions of the recall of the Russian
forces from Manchuria.

## "AGREEMENT BETWEEN RUSSIA AND CHINA RESPECT-ING MANCHURIA

"His Majesty the Emperor and Autocrat of All the
Russias, and His Majesty the Emperor of China, with
the object of reëstablishing and confirming the relations
of good neighborhood, which were disturbed by the
rising in the Celestial Empire of the year 1900, have
appointed their Plenipotentiaries to come to an agreement on certain questions relating to Manchuria. These
Plenipotentiaries, furnished with full powers, which were
found to be in order, agreed as follows: —

"ARTICLE 1. His Imperial Majesty the Emperor of
Russia, desirous of giving fresh proof of his peaceable and
friendly disposition toward His Majesty the Emperor of
China, and overlooking the fact that attacks were first
made from frontier posts in Manchuria on peaceable Russian settlements, agrees to the reëstablishment of the authority of the Chinese Government in that region, which
remains an integral part of the Chinese Empire, and
restores to the Chinese Government the right to exercise therein governmental and administrative authority,
as it existed previous to the occupation by Russian troops
of that region.

"ARTICLE 2. In taking possession of the governmental and administrative authority in Manchuria, the Chinese Government confirms, both with regard to the period and with regard to all other Articles, the obligation to observe strictly the stipulations of the contract concluded with the Russo-Chinese Bank on the 27th August, 1896, and in virtue of paragraph 5 of the above-mentioned contract, takes upon itself the obligation to use all means to protect the railway and the persons in its employ, and binds itself also to secure within the boundaries of Manchuria the safety of all Russian subjects in general and the undertakings established by them.                    .

"The Russian Government, in view of these obligations accepted by the Government of His Majesty the Emperor of China, agrees on its side, provided that no disturbances arise and that the action of other Powers should not prevent it, to withdraw gradually all its forces from within the limits of Manchuria in the following manner: —

"(a.) Within six months from the signature of the Agreement to clear the southwestern portion of the Province of Mukden up to the river Liao-ho of Russian troops, and to hand the railways over to China.

"(b.) Within further six months to clear the remainder of the Province of Mukden and the Province of Kirin of Imperial troops.

"(c.) Within the six months following to remove the remaining Imperial Russian troops from the Province of Hei-lung-chang.

"ARTICLE 3. In view of the necessity of preventing in the future any recurrence of the disorders of last year, in which Chinese troops stationed on the Manchurian frontier also took part, the Imperial Russian and Chinese Governments shall undertake to instruct the Russian military authorities and the Tsiang-Tsungs, mutually to come to an agreement respecting the numbers and the disposition of the Chinese forces until the Russian forces shall have been withdrawn. At the same time the Chinese Government binds itself to organize no other forces over and above those decided upon by the Russian military authorities and the Tsiang-Tsungs as sufficient to suppress brigandage and pacify the country.

"After the complete evacuation of Manchuria by Russian troops, the Chinese Government shall have the right to increase or diminish the number of its troops in Manchuria, but of this must duly notify the Russian Government, as it is natural that the maintenance in the above-mentioned district of an over large number of troops must necessarily lead to a reinforcement of the Russian military force in the neighboring districts, and thus would bring about an increase of expenditure on military requirements undesirable for both States.

"For police service and maintenance of internal order in the districts outside those parts allotted to the Eastern Chinese Railway Company, a police guard, under the local Governors ('Tsiang-Tsungs'), consisting of cavalry and infantry, shall be organized exclusively of subjects of His Majesty the Emperor of China.

"ARTICLE 4. The Russian Government agrees to restore to the owners the Railway Shan-hai-kwan-Niu-chwang-Sinminting, which, since the end of September, 1900, has been occupied and guarded by Russian troops. In view of this, the Government of His Majesty the Emperor of China binds itself: —

"1. In case protection of the above-mentioned line should be necessary, that obligation shall fall exclusively on the Chinese Government, which shall not invite other Powers to participate in its protection, construction, or working, nor allow other Powers to occupy the territory evacuated by the Russians.

"2. The completion and working of the above-mentioned line shall be conducted in strict accordance with the Agreement between Russia and England of the 16th April, 1899, and the Agreement with the private Corporation respecting the loan for the construction of the line. And furthermore, the corporation shall observe its obligations not to enter into possession of, or in any way to administer, the Shan-hai-kwan-Niu-chwang-Sinminting line.

"3. Should, in the course of time, extensions of the line in Southern Manchuria, or construction of branch lines in connection with it, or the erection of a bridge in Niu-chwang, or the moving of the terminus there, be undertaken, these questions shall first form the subject of mutual discussion between the Russian and Chinese Governments.

"4. In view of the fact that the expenses incurred by the Russian Government for the repair and working of the Shan-hai-kwan-Niu-chwang-Sinminting line were not included in the sum total of damages, the Chinese Government shall be bound to pay back the sum which, after examination with the Russian Government, shall be found to be due.

"The stipulations of all former Treaties between Russia and China which are not affected by the present Agreement shall remain in force.

"The Agreement shall have legal force from the day of its signature by the Plenipotentiaries of both States.

"The exchange of ratifications shall take place in St. Petersburg within three months from the date of the signature of the Agreement.

"For the confirmation of the above, the Plenipotentiaries of the two Contracting Powers have signed and sealed two copies of the Agreement in the Russian, French, and Chinese languages. Of the three texts which, after comparison, have been found to correspond with each other, that in the French language shall be considered as authoritative for the interpretation of the Agreement.

"Done in Peking in duplicate, the 26th March, 1902.

"At the same time, M. Lessar handed a note to the Chinese Plenipotentiaries, which declares, in the name of the Imperial Government, that the surrender of the civil government of Niu-chwang into the hands of the Chinese administration will take place only upon the withdrawal from that part of foreign forces and landing parties, and the restoration to the Chinese of the town of Tien-tsin, at present under international administration.

"From the above, it is shown that the Imperial Government, in complete adherence to its repeated declarations, commences the gradual evacuation of Manchuria in order to carry it out upon the conditions above enumerated, if no obstacles are placed in the way by the unexpected action of other Powers or of China herself; that the surrender of the civil government of Niu-chwang into the hands of the Chinese administration is to take place according to a written declaration given to the Celestial Government, only when foreign forces and landing parties are withdrawn from the port, and if, at the same time, the question of the restoration of Tien-tsin to the Chinese has been conclusively settled.

"The Chinese Government, on its side, confirms all the obligations it has previously undertaken toward Russia, and particularly the provisions of the 1896 Agreement, which must serve as a basis for the friendly relations of the neighboring Empires. By this defensive Agreement, Russia undertook in 1896 to maintain the principle of the independence and integrity of China, who, on her side, gave Russia the right to construct a line through Manchuria and to enjoy the material privileges which are directly connected with the above undertaking.

"After the instructive events of the last two years, it is possible to hope for the complete pacification of the Far East, and the development of friendly relations with China in the interests of the two Empires. But, undoubtedly, if the Chinese Government, in spite of their positive assurances, should, on any pretext, violate the above conditions, the Imperial Government would no longer consider itself bound by the provisions of the Manchurian Agreement, nor by its declarations on this subject, and would have to decline to take the responsibility for all the consequences which might ensue." [1]

The comparatively mild terms of this Convention may well be pointed out.[2] Except in the negative reservations of Article 4, there is found here no provision for the exclusive control by the Russians of the mining and railway enterprises either in or out of Manchuria. On the contrary, the sovereign rights in Manchuria, including those respecting the disposition of military forces, will in eighteen months be almost completely restored to the Chinese Government, and the entire agreement will become operative from the very day of its signature. The Convention seemed to confirm the avowed intention of Russia to love peace and respect the integrity of China. It is not strange that Prince Ching personally thanked Great Britain, Japan, and the

---

[1] *China, No. 2 (1904)*, No. 51, inclosure.

[2] Glance over the comparative terms, shown in parallel columns, of the Russian demands of February, the amendments of March, 1901, and the present Agreement. *Ibid.*, No. 42, inclosure.

United States for the valuable support they had rendered China in the negotiations which had terminated in the conclusion of this instrument.[1]

If, however, the subsequent conduct of Russia in Manchuria has appeared to contradict the tenor of the Agreement, it is only necessary to point out how elastic and expansive its terms are. Paragraph 5, Article 2, of the Bank Agreement of September 8, 1896, imposing upon the Chinese Government the duty to protect the Manchurian Railway and the persons employed in it, is not only reinforced but also expanded so as to make it incumbent upon China "to secure within the boundaries of Manchuria the safety of all Russian subjects in general and the undertakings established by them." Unless Manchuria is considered a territory distinct from the rest of the Chinese Empire, no Russians or other foreigners have the right to reside in the interior save in the treaty posts. Yet the Chinese Government is held responsible for the security of the Russians and their enterprises in Manchuria, which is regarded virtually as a Russian colony, into which immigrants from Siberia and European Russia have been sent with wonderful rapidity. Nor does this additional obligation on the part of China any longer bind her to a private company called the Russo-Chinese Bank, but henceforth to the Government of the Czar. The discharge of so onerous a duty is made a condition for the Russian evacuation of Manchuria.

[1] See *China, No. 2 (1904)*, No. 55.

It is not generally known that this condition, otherwise so difficult, was practically impossible so long as the presence of the Russian forces kept the Chinese troops greatly reduced in number. The apprehended disorder must come, as it always has done, and as none knew better than the Russians, from the groups of unoccupied men, the so-called mounted bandits (*ma tseh*), who infested the Provinces of Sheng-king and Kirin, where they sided with whatever power suited their fancy and interest, exercised their own law, and in one way or another kept the country in a state of great instability. It should be noted that they were either disbanded soldiers or the possible candidates for the Chinese troops to be levied to safeguard Manchuria — for military life in China seldom attracts peaceful citizens. So long as the presence of the Russian forces rendered the regular service of the outlaws in the Chinese army unnecessary, their means of subsistence would be derived less often from a settled agricultural life than from plundering. Between March, 1902, and August, 1903, a Russian officer successfully enlisted the service of some 450 of these marauders, and employed them in the timber work which the Russians secured in Eastern Manchuria in the name of one of the chiefs of the bandits.[1] Before and after this period, however,

[1] Mr. Eitarō Tsurouka, who has personally visited several of the chiefs of the banditti, gives an extremely interesting account of their origin, their relations to the Chinese authorities and Russian officers, and the history of their affairs down to the end of

the Russian officers continually reported sanguinary
conflicts with the robbers, the fear of whom has
seemed to constitute the main justification for the
steady progress of the Russian measures of tightening a hold upon Manchuria.[1] Side by side with this
grave situation, we should also observe that the
Convention provided that, even after the evacuation, if an evacuation were possible, the numbers
and the stations of the Chinese troops, upon whom
the duty of protecting the rapidly increasing Russian subjects and properties in Manchuria would
devolve, should always be made known to Russia,
so that unnecessarily large forces should not be
stationed. Russia would judge whether the Chinese
forces were excessive, and exert her influence to
keep them in reduced numbers,[2] while, at the same
time, their capacity as well for receiving the banditti

1903. — The *Tō-A Dōbun-kwai Hōkoku*, No. 53 (April, 1904),
pp. 1–14. Cf. *China, No. 2 (1904)*, No. 130, inclosure.

[1] About August, 1901, the British Consul at Niu-chwang, Mr.
A. Hosie, reported that the force then at the disposal of the
Tartar General of the Sheng-king Province was limited by the
Russian authorities to 6500 men, which meant that over 10,000
men possessing firearms had been let loose. The Chinese police
force was insufficient to back the authority of the Governor-
General, and constant military expeditions by the Russians
were consequently rendered necessary. — *China, No. 2 (1904)*,
p. 33. Also see the *British Consular Report* on Niu-chwang for
1901, pp. 3–4.

[2] Early in March, 1903, Prince Ching negotiated with M. Lessar about the number of Chinese troops that should occupy the
country after the withdrawal of the Russians. "The Chinese
Government were proposing to send 18,000 men, whilst the Russian Legation considered that 12,000 men would be sufficient."
— *China, No. 2 (1904)*, No. 84 (Townley to Lansdowne).

into their ranks as for affording protection to the
Russian life and property would, to say the least,
soon reach its limits. Thus the explicit terms of
the Convention were constructed so as to be greatly
neutralized, as it would seem, by what was implied
and could only be inferred by analysis. In the light
of these considerations may be seen the statement
that, " undoubtedly, if the Chinese Government, in
spite of their positive assurances, should, on any
pretext, violate the above conditions [i. e., of the
Convention], the Imperial Government would no
longer consider itself bound by the provisions of
the Manchurian Agreement, nor by its declarations
on this subject, and would have to decline to take
the responsibility for all the consequences which
might ensue," [1] — a reservation which Count Lamsdorff considered " a very necessary one." [2] In the
same light, also, one may read the statement made
by Sir Ernest Satow to Prince Ching, that " the
Convention did not appear to His Majesty's Government to be entirely satisfactory," [3] and also the
pungent remark of Lord Lansdowne to M. de Staal,
that there were several points in the Agreement
which had caused much criticism in England, particularly those provisions which limited China's right
to dispose of her own military forces and to construct railway extensions within her own territory.
" I did not, however," adds the Marquess, " desire

[1] *China, No. 2 (1904)*, p. 38, already quoted in p. 225, above.
[2] *Ibid.*, No. 53 (Lamsdorff's statement to Scott, on April 23).
[3] *Ibid.*, No. 55 (April 15).

to examine these provisions too microscopically, and I shared his [M. de Staal's] hope that the Agreement would be loyally and considerately interpreted on both sides, and that the evacuation of the province would be completed within the appointed time." [1]

The last but not the least difficulty about the Agreement was its absolute silence regarding the so-called " railway guards," organized ostensibly by the Eastern Chinese Railway Company, whose existence would make the promised evacuation almost entirely nominal. It will be remembered that, so far as the published agreements between China and Russia are concerned, one fails to find any conventional ground for the organization of the railway guards, save in Article 8 of the Statutes — not a Russo-Chinese agreement, but purely Russian statutes — published on December 11/13, 1896, which provided : " The preservation of order and decorum on the lands assigned to the railway and its appurtenances should be confined to the *police agents* appointed by the Company. The Company should draw up and establish police regulations." [2] This right of Russia to police the railway lands seems

---

[1] *China, No. 2 (1904)*, No. 52 (Lansdowne to Scott, April 30). This conversation had ensued from M. de Staal's visit to Lord Lansdowne, the purpose of which was, on the part of the Russian Ambassador, to explain to the British Foreign Minister the unreasonableness of the popular allegation that Russia had, in concluding the Agreement of April 8, surrendered to the diplomatic pressure exerted by Great Britain.

[2] *Russia, No. 2 (1904)*, p. 6. Already quoted in p. 98, above.

to have been tacitly perpetuated by the present Convention of 1902,[1] and, from this, it may perhaps be assumed that the Chinese Government had some time before April 8, 1902, agreed to the statutory rule of Russia which has just been quoted. However that may be, a permission to establish a police force could scarcely justify the organization of railway guards selected from the regular troops and receiving a higher pay than the latter. Moreover, it still remains to be officially declared that the numbers of the guards would not be determined by Russia at will and without consulting China. These guards seem to have numbered only 2000 or 3000 before the Manchurian campaign of 1900, but in October of that year Mr. Charles Hardinge, the British *Chargé d'Affaires* at St. Petersburg, wrote to Lord Salisbury: "I learn that active recruiting for this force is now in progress, and its numbers are to be raised to 12,000 men under command of officers in the regular army. Intrenched camps are also being constructed at all the strategic positions along the line." [2] Then, on the eve of the termination of the first period of evacuation in 1902, it was reported by Consul Hosie: "I am credibly informed that the number of the military guard of the Russian railways in Manchuria has been fixed at 30,000 men." [3] Latterly, the name has

---

[1] Cf. the last clause of Article 3.

[2] *China, No. 5 (1901)*, No. 23.

[3] *China, No. 2 (1904)*, No. 63, September 9, 1902 (Hosie to Satow).

been changed to the " frontier guards," which, after the beginning of the present war, were said to have been made up of fifty-five mounted squadrons, fifty-five foot companies, and six batteries of artillery, aggregating 25,000 men, instead of 30,000, and guarding the railways in sections of thirty-three miles.[1] There is no intention here to maintain the accuracy of these reports, or to decide whether the numbers are adequate for the purpose in view, but one would be tempted to think that the Russian Government made a regrettable omission in the new Manchurian Agreement, when it made no reference to the forces which were justified by no open contract with China, and, theoretically speaking, were not incapable of an indefinite expansion.

[1] Telegraph from Miandonha [?], May 18, 1904. In the *Evening Post* of a few days later.

# CHAPTER XIV

## THE EVACUATION

UNSATISFACTORY as the Manchurian Agreement of April 8, 1902, appeared to Great Britain and Japan, they refrained from entering any protest against its conclusion. They probably preferred the imperfect obligation the Convention imposed upon the contracting parties to an indefinite prolongation of the dangerous conditions which had prevailed. What remained for them and for China was to watch the conduct of Russia in Manchuria and test her veracity according to their own interpretations of the Agreement. In the mean time, the questions which had existed between China and the Powers were being one after another disposed of; the distribution of the indemnities was finally agreed upon on June 14, the Provisional Government of Tien-tsin by the Powers came to an end on August 15, and the rendition of the city to the Chinese authorities was accomplished. The date set for the evacuation of the southwest of the Sheng-king Province up to the Liao River, October 8, drew on, and the evacuation took place. The Tartar General Tsêng-chi had received an Imperial mandate to take over from the hands of the Russians the specified territory and its railways, even before the middle of September,[1] and, on October 28, Prince Ching was able to state to Sir Ernest Satow: "Their Excellencies the Minister Superintendent of Northern Ports and the Military Governor of Mukden have now severally reported by telegram that all the railways outside the Great Wall have been handed back, and that the southwest portion of the Mukden (Sheng-king) Province as far as the Liao River has been completely evacuated by Russian troops."[2] But what was evacuation? Some troops may have been sent to European Russia, others to different stations in Siberia, including the strategically important Nikolsk, near the eastern border of Manchuria, and still others to Mongolia, where Russian forces were reported to have suddenly increased, until in December they were said to have numbered about 27,000.[3] No small number were also transferred to Port Arthur[4] and Vladivostok.[5] It was, however, alleged by several observers that the main part of the so-called evacuation meant nothing more than the transferring of Russian troops from Chinese towns and settlements to the rapidly developing Russian settlements and quarters within Manchuria. It was

---

[1] *China, No. 2 (1904)*, No. 65, inclosure 2.

[2] *Ibid.*, No. 66, inclosure.

[3] The *Tō-A Dōbun-kwai Hōkoku*, No. 38 (January, 1903), pp. 105–106.

[4] E. g., 400 men from (probably) Shan-hai-kwan, June 24. — *China, No. 2 (1904)*, No. 58, inclosure. Also some from Liao-yang, in August. — *Ibid.*, No. 61, inclosure.

[5] E. g., from Kin-chou-Fu early in September. — *Ibid.*, No. 62, inclosure.

reported from various sources [1] that along the 2326
versts of the railroads there were about eighty so-
called depots, each two to five square miles in extent, which had been marked out as the sites of new
Russian settlements, and in many cases as stations
of the railway guards. The most important line,
connecting Port Arthur with Harbin, was studded
with such depots at every fifteen or twenty miles.
In many of these depots were to be seen extensive barracks built of brick, one at Liao-yang, for
example, being capable of holding 3000 men,
and another at Mukden, in the building of which
bricks of the wall of the Chinese Temple of Earth
were surreptitiously utilized,[2] accommodating 6000.
Besides the barracks, permanent blockhouses were
met with every three or four miles. The guards
of the railways, whose numbers were just at this
time fixed at 30,000,[3] were recruited from the regular troops, from whom they were distinguished by
green shoulder-straps and collar-patches, and also by
higher pay, and the regular troops themselves could
be contained in large numbers in the depots and
barracks and blockhouses when the evacuation was
completed.[4] At the same time, the Russians seemed

[1] Cf. Dr. Morrison's articles in *The Times*, January 3 (p. 8)
and 14 (p. 5), 1903.

[2] *China, No. 2 (1904)*, No. 56, inclosure (Hosie to Satow).

[3] *Ibid.*, No. 63, inclosure (Hosie to Satow, September 9).

[4] Cf. *ibid.*, No. 61, inclosure (Hosie to Satow, August 21),
which says : "I have the honor to report that a considerable
town, to consist of some 300 cottages, of which about 100 have
already been built, is in course of construction on both sides of

to have destroyed nearly all the forts and confis-
cated the guns of the Chinese, whose defense had
thus been reduced almost to nil. The military
power of the Tartar Generals at the capitals of the
three Manchurian Provinces was held under a strict
surveillance of the Russian officers, who also readily
controlled highroads and rivers. It was, moreover,
uncertain how much of this control and supervision by the Russians would be relaxed after the
promised evacuation, or how much it would then
be replaced by the powerful position the Russians
would hold in their own quarters in Manchuria.
The conclusion seemed inevitable to some people
that by the so-called evacuation, if it should ever
take place in the face of the enormous obstacles

the Russian railway to the immediate northwest of the city of
Liao-yang Chou. These cottages, which when completed will
occupy a large piece of land bought from the Chinese proprietors by the Railway Company, are intended for the residence of
railway employees and of the artisans who will be engaged at the
cleaning and repairing shops to be established at this important
depot.

"While this foreign town is growing outside, the Chinese Government buildings inside the city of Liao-yang are being rapidly
evacuated, in many cases the only vestige of the Russian occupation being a solitary sentry keeping guard over the property.
Russian troops are also being withdrawn from Liao-yang and
conveyed by rail to Port Arthur."

A more direct testimony came from the Russian diplomats,
probably M. Lessar himself, who, even so late as at the beginning of September, 1903, or a month before the end of the stipulated period for the complete evacuation of Manchuria, intimated to Prince Ching that the reason for the delay of the actual
evacuation was "that the barracks for the railway guards were
not ready."— *China, No. 2 (1904)*, No. 156.

which the Agreement did not seek to remove,
Russia would gain a much stronger hold upon the
Manchurian territory than during the preceding
period of open military occupation.[1] It was also
pointed out that the forts, docks, and other military and naval establishments at Port Arthur, costing millions of rubles, were not compatible with the
short term of the lease of the port, and their practical value would be seriously impaired by a true
evacuation of the rest of Manchuria.

So far as the immediate interests of foreign
nations, aside from the general principle of the integrity of the Chinese Empire, were concerned,
nothing was more to be desired than a speedy
evacuation of the treaty port of Niu-chwang, where
the Russians had maintained a provisional government since August 5, 1900.[2] At the conclusion of
the Agreement of April, 1901, M. Lessar delivered
a *note verbale* to the Chinese Government, stating

[1] The *Novoe Vremya* itself declared toward the end of the
year 1902 that, contrary to the popular notion that Russia was
evacuating Manchuria, she was just beginning to consolidate her
influence in that region.

As regards the number of the Russian troops left in Manchuria after the first period of evacuation, we have the following
authoritative statement by Count Cassini, Russian Ambassador
to the United States: "Faithfully adhering to the terms of her
treaty with China respecting Manchuria, she [Russia] had withdrawn the major portion of her troops from that province until
*between 60,000 and 70,000* only remained." — The *North American Review* for May, 1904, pp. 682–683. It is not clear whether
this number included the Russian soldiers stationed outside of
the Chinese quarters.

[2] See pp. 144–145, above.

that Niu-chwang would be restored as soon as the Powers terminated their administration of Tientsin, and that, if the latter event did not take place before October 8, then Niu-chwang would be surrendered to China in the first or second month after that date.[1] The rendition of Tien-tsin was accomplished by the Powers on August 15, but the restoration of Niu-chwang not only did not follow it, but seemed to be indefinitely delayed for the trivial reasons presented one after another by the Russian authorities: that, for instance, one or two foreign gunboats were present in the harbor;[2] that the Chinese had refused to agree to the constitution of a sanitary board;[3] and that the Chinese Tao-tai detailed to receive back the civil government of the port had not arrived from Mukden, where, it has been discovered, he had been detained by the Russians much against his will.[4] Up to the present time, the maritime customs dues at this important trade port have been paid to the Russo-Chinese Bank, and, for a large sum thus received, the Bank is said to have paid to the Chinese authorities neither the amount nor the interest.[5]

[1] *China, No. 2 (1904)*, pp. 38 and 42.
[2] *Ibid.*, Nos. 72, 74, 75, 111, 112.
[3] *Ibid.*, Nos. 131, 132.
[4] *Ibid.*, Nos. 70, 122, 130, 131.
[5] The *Kokumin*, May 30, 1904; a Peking correspondence. Also see *China, No. 2 (1904)*, Nos. 44, 46–48, 69, 73, 96, 99, 102, 105, 124.

# CHAPTER XV

## DEMANDS IN SEVEN ARTICLES

THE most important section of Manchuria, strategically, namely, that part of the Province of Sheng-
king which lies east of the Liao River and the entire
Province of Kirin, was to be evacuated, according
to the Agreement, before April 8, 1903. As that
date drew near, and long afterward, the disposition of the Russian forces appeared incompatible
with even the nominal withdrawal which characterized the first period of evacuation. It is true that
in the Sheng-king Province, except the regions
bordering on the Yalu River on the Korean frontier, the Russian troops began to withdraw soon
after the end of the first period, but only " to the
railway line." [1] The important border regions, especially Fêng-hwang-Chêng and An-tung, however,
remained in Russian occupation, the former still
holding 700 cavalry in June.[2] From March, there
had been mysterious movements of small detachments of troops toward this frontier,[3] of which
Count Lamsdorff and M. Witte alike professed

[1] *China, No. 2 (1904)*, No. 57, inclosure (Hosie to Satow.
November 7, 1902). Also No. 106 (Townley to Lansdowne, May
5, 1903).

[2] *Ibid.*, No. 128 (Hosie, June 22, 1903).

[3] *Ibid.*, No. 116 (April 8).

a complete ignorance,[1] but concerning which M. Plançon, the Russian *Chargé d'Affaires* at Peking, had made an explanation which seemed utterly unintelligible, that the Russian troops had been moved in order to counteract a threatened Japanese movement. It soon appeared, however, that the Russians had begun to cut timber on both sides of the Yalu River,[2] and, with the consent of Admiral Alexieff, had hired the services of some Russian soldiers,[3] some of whom had gone to Yong-am-po on the Korean side of the Yalu.[4] The detachments outside of Fêng-hwang-Chêng, amounting at first to only five men at Ta-tung-kao and twenty at Yong-am-po, would have been small enough to be ignored, had it not been for the significant fact that the occupation of Yong-am-po, which will be discussed later on,[5] constituted a menace to the integrity of the Korean Empire similar to one which threatened China when Russia leased Port Arthur; for a railway concession granted in the Russo-Chinese Agreement of March 27, 1898,[6] would bring this port into connection with the entire railroad and military system of Manchuria and the great Russian Empire. Further west, at Liao-yang, except the nominal withdrawal reported in the pre-

---

[1] *China, No. 2 (1904)*, No. 75 (April 15); 113 (May 14).

[2] For the Manchurian side, see p. 227, above. The timber concession on the Korean side will be taken up in a later section.

[3] *China, No. 2 (1904)*, Nos. 75, 115, 128.

[4] *Ibid.*, Nos. 115, 129.

[5] Pp. 289 ff., 318 ff., below.

[6] Article 8. See pp. 130–131, above.

vious August,[1] there was no indication of its evacuation,[2] and at Mukden, the capital of Sheng-king, 3200 soldiers, who constituted the major part of the forces, were reported to have evacuated,[3] but the remainder, after proceeding to the train, suddenly returned and took up their old quarters,[4] some or all of them wearing civilian dress.[5] It is unknown whither the 3200 men had gone, but the Russian Consul merely moved to the railway outside the town.[6] To the north, it was evident in May that the Province of Kirin had hardly begun to be evacuated even in the nominal sense, as in parts of the Sheng-king Province.[7] So late as in September, the Russian authorities at Peking talked to Prince Ching of leaving 6000 or 7000 troops in the Kirin and Hei-lung Provinces for another year.[8]

Long before September, however, it had become apparent that the delay in the second part of the Manchurian evacuation was due to no casual event. The appointed time-limit, the 8th of April, had hardly been twenty days past, with no signs indicative of a possible speedy withdrawal, when new demands in seven articles of an highly exclusive

---

[1] See p. 235, note 4, above.

[2] *China, No. 2 (1904)*, No. 130, inclosure (May 4, 1903).

[3] *Ibid.*, No. 71 (April 14).

[4] *Ibid.*, No. 122.

[5] *Ibid.*, No. 130, inclosure (May 4).

[6] *Ibid.*

[7] *Ibid.*, No. 137, inclosure (Consul Fulford at Niu-chwang, May 19).

[8] *Ibid.*, No. 156 (Satow to Lansdowne, September 10).

nature, which the Russian *Chargé d' Affaires* had lodged at the Foreign Office of Peking,[1] leaked out,[2] were confirmed by Prince Ching,[3] and spread broadcast over the astonished world. Further evacuation was probably implied, if not declared, to be dependent upon the acceptance of these demands,[4] the most authentic version [5] of which is here subjoined : —

"1. No portion of territory restored to China by Russia, especially at Niu-chwang and in the valley of Liaoho, shall be leased or sold to any other Power under any circumstances ; if such sale or lease to another Power be concluded, Russia will take decisive steps in order to safeguard her own interests, as she considers such sale or lease to be a menace to her.

"2. The system of government actually existing throughout Mongolia shall not be altered, as such alteration will tend to produce a regrettable state of affairs, such as the uprising of the people and the disturbances along the Russian frontier; the utmost precaution shall be taken in that direction.

---

[1] The author has been informed from a reliable source that the *Chargé's* note containing those demands was dated April 5, 1903.

[2] Again the revelation must have emanated from the Chinese official circle. M. Lessar is said to have, about June 4, bitterly complained at the Peking Foreign Office of their breach of faith, and requested that there should be appointed two special Chinese negotiators, who should be entirely responsible for the secrecy of the matter.

[3] *China, No. 2 (1904)*, No. 81 (Townley to Lansdowne, April 24).

[4] *Ibid.*, No. 127.

[5] *Ibid.*, No. 94. Also see Nos. 77, 78, 81, 82, 86.

"3. China shall engage herself not to open, of her own accord, new ports or towns in Manchuria, without giving previous notice to the Russian Government, nor shall she permit foreign consuls to reside in those towns or ports.

"4. The authority of foreigners who may be engaged by China for the administration of any affairs whatever, shall not be permitted to extend over any affairs in Northern Provinces (including Chili), where Russia has the predominant interests.

"In case China desires to engage foreigners for the administration of affairs in Northern Provinces, special offices shall be established for the control of Russians: for instance, no authority over the mining affairs of Mongolia and Manchuria shall be given to foreigners who may be engaged by China for the administration of mining affairs ; such authority shall be left entirely in the hands of Russian experts.

"5. As long as there exists a telegraph line at Niu-chwang and Port Arthur, the Niu-chwang-Peking line shall be maintained, as the telegraph line at Niu-chwang and Port Arthur and throughout Sheng-king Province is under Russian control, and its connection with her line on the Chinese telegraph poles at Niu-chwang, Port Arthur, and Peking is of the utmost importance.

"6. After restoring Niu-chwang to the Chinese local authorities, the customs receipts there shall, as at present, be deposited with the Russo-Chinese Bank.

"7. After the evacuation of Manchuria, the rights which have been acquired in Manchuria by Russian subjects and foreign companies during Russian occupation shall remain unaffected ; moreover, as Russia is duty-bound to insure the life of the people residing in all the regions traversed by the railway, it is necessary, in order to provide against the spread of epidemic diseases in the

Northern Provinces by the transportation of passengers and goods by railway train, to establish at Niu-chwang a quarantine office after the restoration of the place to China; the Russian civil administrators will consider the best means to attain that end. Russians only shall be employed at the posts of Commissioner of Customs and Customs Physician, and they shall be placed under the control of the Inspector-General of the Imperial Maritime Customs. These officials shall perform their duties conscientiously, shall protect the interests of the Imperial maritime customs, and shall exhaust their efforts in preventing the spread of those diseases into the Russian territories. A permanent Sanitary Board, presided over by the Customs Tao-tai, shall be established. The foreign Consuls, Commissioner of Customs, Customs Physician, and Agent of the Chinese Eastern Railway Company shall be Councilors of the Board. As regards the establishment of the Board and the management of its affairs, the Customs Tao-tai shall consult with the Russian Consul, and the Customs Tao-tai shall devise the best means to obtain funds necessary for the purpose."

These demands, as will be seen, comprised, besides the non-alienation of Manchuria to any other Power, and the *status quo* in Mongolia, drastic measures of closing the former territory against the economic enterprise of all nations but the Russians; and, in that respect, were supplementary to the Agreement concluded a year before, which studiously omitted clauses prejudicial to the principle of the open door. From the standpoint of this last principle, therefore, no demands could be more objectionable than those now presented by M. Plançon.

The Empress Dowager of China was said to have sneered at. the report, and to have remarked that, if she had been disposed to grant such demands, she would never have requested the Powers to withdraw as soon as possible their forces from North China.[1] Prince Ching not only considered the Russian terms quite unacceptable, but failed to see any reason or right on the part of Russia to impose fresh conditions which infringed China's sovereign rights. He accordingly refused to entertain these conditions, perhaps on April 23.[2] The Japanese Government had already entered a firm protest,[3] and was followed by that of the British Government, which considered the demands as violating the most-favored-nation clause, and otherwise highly inadmissible.[4] Before the British protest reached him, Mr. Townley, the British *Chargé*, had assured Prince Ching that the latter would receive from Great Britain similar support in resisting the Russian demands to that which was given him during the negotiation of the Manchurian Convention.[5] Soon afterward, the United States Government also instructed Mr. Conger to urge on the Peking Foreign Office the advisability of refusing the first and second of the conditions laid down by Russia, and, moreover, made direct inquiries at the Russian Government in a friendly spirit, pointing out that the

[1] The *Kokumin*.
[2] *China, No. 2 (1904)*, Nos. 78, 81, 127.
[3] Perhaps on April 21.
[4] *China, No. 2 (1904)*, Nos. 79 and 80 (April 23).
[5] *Ibid.*, Nos. 81, 82 (April 24).

reported demands were not in accordance with the proposed stipulations contained in the new draft treaty between the United States and China, a copy of which was communicated to Count Lamsdorff.[1] This latter act of Secretary Hay was promptly followed by Great Britain, whose Government instructed its Ambassador at St. Petersburg to address the Foreign Minister in language similar to that used by the American Representative.[2] It may be safely inferred that the Japanese Government also took a similar step. There thus resulted a natural coöperation between the three Powers, whose straightforward policy was clearly expressed by Lord Lansdowne as follows : " To open China impartially to the commerce of the whole world, to maintain her independence and integrity, and to insist upon the fulfillment of treaty and other obligations by the Chinese Government which they have contracted towards us." [3]

According to the instructions he had received from his Government, Mr. MacCormick, the United States Ambassador, had an interview with Count Lamsdorff in the evening of April 28. The Count at once denied in the most positive manner that such

[1] *China, No. 2 (1904)*, Nos. 83, 85 (April 26 and 27). Cf. No. 82.

[2] *Ibid.*, No. 89 (April 28). It does not appear that this instruction was carried out, for when Count Lamsdorff gave to the American Ambassador a positive denial of the truth of the current reports, the British Ambassador deemed it unnecessary to repeat the inquiry. See *ibid.*, No. 91 (April 29).

[3] *Ibid.*, No. 90, Lansdowne to Herbert (April 28).

demands as were rumored had been made by the
Russian Government. He expressed surprise that
they should have been credited in any quarter, and
that a friendly government like that of the United
States should be the only one to question him as to
whether Russia could have made demands some of
which were on the face of them ridiculous, as, for
instance, those for the right of using China's telegraph poles and for the restriction of foreign trade
in Manchuria. It may be questioned whether Count
Lamsdorff has ever made to a strong Power another
denial in as positive language, which was, one
will soon observe, as quickly falsified by subsequent
events, as this remarkable disclaimer of April 28,
1903. He went on to say that he could give the
United States Government the most positive assurances that Russia would faithfully adhere to its
pledges regarding Manchuria, and to her assurances
to respect the rights of other Powers. Moreover,
American capital and commerce were what Russia
most desired to attract in order to develop Manchuria. The Count also intimated that any delay in
the evacuation was due to the natural necessity of
obtaining assurances that China was fulfilling her
part of the agreement. This could be better ascertained by the Russian Minister, M. Lessar, who
had been absent from Peking on sick leave, but
was about to return to his post, than by an acting
*Chargé d'Affaires*.[1] A careful reading of this dis-

[1] Namely, M. Plançon. The same M. Plançon stated the
next day to Prince Ching that the delay in the evacuation was

claimer will show that it denied that the reported demands had been made by Russia, but it did not establish that no demands whatsoever had been made by her. This consideration would seem to make it truly remarkable that Mr. MacCormick should have been, as he was, entirely satisfied with the result of the interview, and should have had no further remark to make. He could perhaps have inquired whether M. Plançon had acted without authorization, what were the conditions he had proposed, and by what means M. Lessar was expected to obtain the assurances from China that her obligations would be fulfilled.[1]

The positive statements of Count Lamsdorff were partly reinforced and partly neutralized by the clever remarks made on April 29 by Count Cassini, the Russian Ambassador at Washington, which appeared in the New York *Tribune* of May 1. He considered it unfortunate that Mr. Conger should have been misinformed, by unreliable parties, of Russia's intentions in Manchuria, of which they were grossly ignorant, — a matter which was regretted, he was sure, no less by the American Government than by Russia. He, however, not only intimated that some sort of negotiation was in progress between Russia and China regarding Man-

due to the military party in Russia. — *China, No. 2 (1904)*, No. 95. The statements of the two diplomats are not necessarily contradictory to each other.

[1] For the interview between MacCormick and Lamsdorff, see *ibid.*, Nos. 91, 92, 103.

churia, but was bold enough to say that the United
States would assist Russia in quieting the uneasy
sentiment caused by false reports.   He said : —

"Because of the singularity of the interest held by the
United States in Manchuria — for all the world realizes
that yours is a trade, not a territorial one — it lies within
the power of your Government to exert a powerful influence in the preservation of peace there.   Russia's desire
is also for peace, not disturbances, in Manchuria, and
it is to this end that negotiations are now proceeding in
Peking in the effort to establish a condition of evacuation, and to safeguard Manchuria against a recurrence of
the troubles of 1900.

"Striking evidence of the direct effect in this country
caused by unrest in China was seen in 1900, when, I am
told, many cotton mills in the United States were forced
to shut down until conditions in China were again normal.
This fact and the evidence the United States has already
given of its desire to make for peace are sufficient assurance that the Washington Government will lend its strong
moral support to calm excitement wherever it has been
aroused by the incorrect reports from Peking."

According to Count Cassini, it was " because of
the long standing and genuine friendliness which,
without exception, had characterized the relations
of these two great countries, as well as in recognition of the frankness with which the American
Secretary of State had dealt with my Government
in all diplomatic matters," that the latter took
pleasure in assuring the United States regarding
negotiations pending with another Power, " even
though in so doing all diplomatic precedent was

broken." "I am not aware," he said, "that any other Powers have received from the Foreign Office [of St. Petersburg] such a statement as was handed your Ambassador." In referring to Mr. MacCormick's interview, however, it will be seen that Count Lamsdorff made no direct reference to the negotiations at Peking, still less to their contents, and the assurances he gave had before and have since been frequently and in similar terms repeated to other Powers by Russia.

By far the most illuminating part of M. Cassini's conversation was its practical confirmation of the truth of one of the reported demands of Russia which were considered the most objectionable, and which Count Lamsdorff specifically denied, characterizing them " as on the face of them ridiculous," namely, that no new ports should be opened in Manchuria for the world's trade. " Of the opening of new treaty ports in Manchuria," said M. Cassini, " it is impossible for me to speak at present, but it is the earnest conviction of those best acquainted with the state of affairs there that such a move will not be to the best interest of the territory. Were the question solely a commercial one, it would be different. But open a treaty port in Manchuria, and close upon the heels of commerce will follow political complications of all kinds, which will increase the threats to peace." In this statement Count Cassini not only virtually contradicted Count Lamsdorff, but also, as we shall soon see, was subsequently contradicted by the latter.

A careful reader of these words uttered by one of Russia's greatest diplomatic agents abroad will feel satisfied that, despite Count Lamsdorff's elastic statement to the contrary, Russia was actually proposing some terms to China, and that one of those terms probably was that Manchuria should have no more treaty ports. When diplomacy relies, even to a slight extent, upon subterfuges, it risks a certain lack of consistent unity among its exponents, and the rule could hardly have for exceptions even such highly trained diplomats as Lamsdorff and Cassini.

Count Lamsdorff's disclaimer was uttered on April 28, and Count Cassini's statement was dated April 29 and appeared in the press on May 1. In the mean time, the Foreign Office of Peking had refused the Russian conditions in an official note. Yet, on April 29, M. Plançon suggested that each condition might be answered separately, and the suggestion was verbally refused by Prince Ching. Thereupon the Russian *Chargé* presented a note intimating that his Government wished to be assured on the first three of the original demands, namely, whether a territorial cession to another power in the Liao Valley was contemplated by China; whether there was an intention to assimilate the administration of Mongolia to that of China proper; and whether China would permit the appointment of foreign Consuls in Manchuria in other places than Niu-chwang. In reply, Prince Ching stated, naturally, that there had never been any question of ceding territory in the Liao Valley

to a foreign Power; that the question of altering
the administrative system of Mongolia had been
discussed, but it had been disapproved by the
Throne, and was not under consideration for the
present; and that, in regard to the appointment of
new Consuls in Manchuria, it depended upon the
opening of new ports, which would be decided only
by the extent of the commercial development of
Manchuria.[1] On the next day, or, as the late Sir
M. Herbert rather inaccurately wrote to Lord Lansdowne, "two days after the Russian Government
had categorically denied that the demands had been
made," M. Plançon reiterated to Prince Ching, not
three, but all, of the seven conditions, and, consequently, the Chinese treaty commissioners at Shanghai were instructed, for the present, to refuse to
their American colleagues the opening of treaty
ports in Manchuria, which the latter had been demanding. The United States Government, however, taking little heed of M. Cassini's argument,
instructed its commissioners at Shanghai, on the
strength of Count Lamsdorff's denial, to insist upon
the opening of new Manchurian ports.[2] Against
this demand, M. Plançon seems to have renewed
his pressure upon the Chinese Government several
times during May,[3] saying that he had received no
instructions from St. Petersburg to revoke his opposition.[4] At last, Secretary Hay instructed Mr.

[1] *China*, *No. 2 (1904)*, No. 95.　　　[2] *Ibid.*, No. 98.
[3] *Ibid.*, Nos. 110 (May 8); 114 (May 19); 117 (May 23).
[4] *Ibid.*, No. 114 (May 19).

Conger to suggest to M. Lessar, on the latter's arrival at Peking, that a simultaneous communication should be made by them to the Peking Foreign Office to the effect that the Russian Government had, as Count Lamsdorff had said, no objection to the opening of the treaty ports.[1] The Russian Minister returned to Peking toward the end of May, and telegraphed to his Government the suggestion made by the American Government.[2] He, as well as M. Cassini, renewed the assurance that Russia was not opposed to the opening of the ports, and Mr. MacCormick, who returned on leave to Washington, confirmed the assurance.[3] Secretary Hay now hoped that the only possible opposition to be met would come from none but the Chinese Government, and requested the support in the matter[4] of the British and Japanese Ministers at Peking, which was willingly given. So late as on June 5, however, M. Cassini addressed a note to Mr. Hay, inquiring what was the meaning attached by the United States Government to the term "treaty port," and what action it wished Russia to take. Mr. Hay could only refer, in answer to the first query, to the correspondence which passed between the Russian and the United States Governments in 1899,[5] and request, in reply to the

---

[1] *China, No. 2 (1904)*, No. 117.
[2] *Ibid.*, No. 119.
[3] *Ibid.*, Nos. 119, 120.
[4] *Ibid.*, No. 120 (June 4).
[5] See Chapter V., above.

second, that Russia should inform China that it was untrue that the former was, as had been stated by China, preventing the opening of the treaty ports.[1] Secretary Hay was so urgent about this matter that he considered it indifferent whether the opening was granted in a treaty or, as a compromise, by a special Imperial edict.[2] M. Lessar had the first interview after his return with Prince Ching on June 10,[3] and, according to the Japanese press, renewed the original seven conditions,[4] including the refusal of ports. The Prince was believed to have refused to discuss any of the conditions except those regarding the establishment of a sanitary board and the payment of customs duties into the Russo-Chinese Bank at Niu-chwang, which might be reconsidered. The Prince was then granted another five days' sick leave, returned to the summer palace, and declined to see any foreign Minister.[5] Rumors were then afloat which would have one believe that the Prince, in spite of the earnest protests of the British and Japanese Representatives, was gradually yielding to Russian influence. It is at least significant that at this critical point he informed Mr. Townley, the British *Chargé d' Affaires*, on June 19, that an agreement would soon be arrived at with Russia whereby

[1] *China, No. 2 (1904)*, No. 121.
[2] *Ibid.*, Nos. 117, 121.
[3] *Ibid.*, No. 123.
[4] Cf. *ibid.*, No. 125.
[5] *Ibid.*, No. 123, and the Japanese press.

M. LESSAR
*Russian Minister at Peking*

Manchuria would be preserved to China without any loss of sovereign rights. He added that China would open treaty ports in Manchuria, if she saw fit, after the Russian evacuation.[1] The significance of these remarks could easily be read between the lines. Not only was the Russian evacuation uncertain, but also it was no less patent to Russia than to China that, in the marts, the opening of which was under discussion, namely, Mukden and perhaps Harbin, as well as An-tung and Tatung-kao near the Korean boundary, the immediate trade prospects were not considered so great as the political danger which their opening might to some degree avert. Had the evacuation been certain, and had the commercial consideration been the sole question involved, it would have been unnecessary either to hasten their opening or even to select those very places. Nor would MM. Cassini, Lessar, and Plançon have been so strongly opposed to the proposition. Seen in the light of these considerations, Prince Ching's new position appeared plainly to indicate the gaining of Russian influence upon the helpless Foreign Office of Peking.

Nor for two years and a half since the first agreement was reported to have been concluded between Admiral Alexieff and Tartar General Tsêng-chi, had the Manchuria question vexed the world. If the question had concerned none but Russia and China, and the former had been slow to promise and loyal to her pledges and the latter strong

[1] *China, No. 2 (1904)*, No. 126.

enough to guard her own interest, the uncertain
conditions in Manchuria would not have constituted,
as they did, a grave and continual menace to the
general peace of the Far East.  Unfortunately, the
Russian pledges, on the one hand, were attended by
serious conditions, some of which it seemed impossible to fulfill and others contrary to the recognized
principles of international intercourse to which
Russia had professed constant devotion, and, on the
other, China had again and again shown herself
impotent to resist what she would otherwise reject.
Above all, Great Britain and the United States were,
both from interest and from principle, firmly committed in the East to a policy which was in constant
danger of being undermined by the conduct of
Russia.  For Japan, however, the Manchurian question possessed an even graver significance, for, with
the fall of the Three Eastern Provinces into the
Russian hands, the independence of Korea, as well
as the security of Japan herself, would be threatened,
while a consequent closure of Manchuria against
Japan's economic activity would seriously maim her
growth and life as a nation.  It was now considered,
therefore, that the irritating situation should no
longer be allowed to continue, and that the time
had at last come when Japan should with determination deal *directly* with Russia, in order to effect
once for all an arrangement satisfactory and beneficial to all the parties concerned and to the world at
large.

# CHAPTER XVI

MANCHURIA, however, constituted only one half — perhaps the less important half — of the great Eastern problem which perplexed the world and imperiled the future life of Japan. In the other half, namely, Korea, Japan was confronted by a situation similar and closely allied to that in Manchuria, and more directly menacing to herself. Let us briefly describe the evolution of the complex Korean question which ensued upon the Chinese-Japanese war of 1894–5.

The war had arisen from the conflicting wishes of the belligerent Powers regarding Korea, China asserting suzerain rights over the Peninsular Kingdom, and the interests of Japan making its effective independence imperative. Unfortunately, Korea's lack of material strength rendered her real independence impossible, and her strength could be secured, from the Japanese point of view, only by a thoroughgoing reform of her administrative, financial, and economic system, which had sunk into a state of unspeakable corruption and decay. By her victory, the colossal task devolved upon Japan of reforming the national institutions of a people whose political training in the past seemed to have made them particu-

larly impervious to such an effort. Perhaps no work
more delicate and more liable to blunder and misunderstanding could befall a nation than that of
setting another nation's house in order who would
not feel its necessity. In this difficult enterprise,
the Japanese showed themselves as inexperienced as
the Koreans were reluctant and resentful. Three
million *yen* were furnished by Japan to Korea in
the interest of various reforms, as also were numerous councilors, including such able men as Shūi-
chirō Saitō and the late Tōru Hoshi. Some of the
others, however, were either inferior in attainments
or impatient of slow processes. The entire movement was intrusted to the direction of the new
Japanese Minister, Count K. Inoüé, a generous,
brilliant, and bold statesman. He presented to the
Korean sovereign a plan of reform, which included
the proposal to remove from her share of political
control the versatile Queen, whose family of the
Min had grown powerful by means of the abuses
which the Count wished to eradicate. In this attempt, in which he was largely successful, of draw-
ing a line of demarcation between the Court and
the Government, he inevitably incurred the deep
ire of the family whose influence had been predominant both at the capital and in the country. Other
measures of his reform further antagonized the official nobility of the Kingdom.[1] The influence of
the Count, however, was so great, and the training
of Korean troops by Japanese officers seemed so

[1] Cf. *Dōbun-kwai*, No. 49, p. 7.

successful, that even the domineering Queen was obliged to await a more favorable moment to regain her lost prestige.

At that time Russia was represented at Seul by M. Waeber, who had been in Korea for more than ten years, and whose personality and diplomatic arts had won him warm friends in the Court, particularly the Queen and her party. At one time, before the late war, when the ascendency of the Chinese Resident, Yuan Shi-kai, had created disaffection among certain Koreans, M. Waeber was said to have succeeded in quietly allying himself with those people and promoting Russian influence over them.[1] It was now again found possible for him and his talented wife to recommend themselves to the large body of men and women whose feeling the Japanese had in one way or another alienated, and slowly but surely to undermine the latter's influence in Seul.[2] The successful coercion of Japan by the three Powers after the treaty of Shimonoseki must also have gone far toward reducing the prestige of Japan in the eye of the Koreans, who are singularly susceptible to the influence of events of this nature.

As soon as Count Inoüé left Seul, the Queen again came to the front. On July 7, 1895, she suddenly accused of treason the most influential member of the Cabinet and chief of the pro-Japanese party, Pak Yong-hio, who again had to flee to Japan, where he had recently spent ten years of a

[1] *Tokushu Jōyaku*, pp. 731–732.     [2] *Ibid.*, p. 740.

refugee's life.[1] Count Inoüé returned to Seul, and
again the Queen held her breath. A Cabinet was
organized of partisans of reform. The Count was,
however, relieved of his post late in July, and in
September was succeeded as the Japanese Minister by Viscount Lieutenant-General Gorō Miura, a
man of undoubted sincerity, but utterly without
diplomatic training. No sooner had Inoüé left
Korea than the Queen reasserted herself, increased
the personnel of her household, and restored many
of her old extravagances so lately removed by the
reformer. She had been further embittered by
the sharp rivalry shown against her and the Min by
the King's father, Tai-wen-kun, and his party. The
Queen finally planned a *coup d'état*, early in October, with a view to disbanding the soldiers trained
by Japanese officers and replacing the progressive
Cabinet members with her friends. A crisis was
imminent, and it was at this juncture that some
of the Japanese in Seul betrayed themselves into
a crime which caused a bitter disappointment and
lasting disgrace to the Government and the nation
at home. Perceiving that a passive attitude would
result in a great calamity, certain Koreans and
Japanese rose early on October 8, to bring Tai-wen-
kun out of his secluded residence. Accompanied by
two battalions of trained soldiers, the veteran statesman rode toward the King's palace, where he was
to present a plan of reform, but was opposed by the

---

[1] G. Takeda, *Kinji Kyokutō Gwaikō Shi* (recent history of
diplomacy in the Far East, Tokio, 1904), pp. 22–23.

guard, who fired at his escort. In the midst of the mêlée which ensued, some of the bravoes rushed into the Inner Palace and murdered the Queen.[1] The deed was no less crushing a blow to the Japanese nation than it was to the bereaved King of Korea, for the former's ardent desire always to adhere to the fairest principles of international conduct was, for once, frustrated by the rash act of a handful of their brethren at Seul. The pernicious influence of the Queen passed away, and the power of the reform Cabinet was for the moment assured, but only at the expense of a revolting crime which the Japanese will never cease to lament. It is probable that the murder of the ·Queen, as apart from the rise of Tai-wen-kun, was premeditated, and also that Minister Miura had been prevailed upon to connive at the guilt. The Japanese Government at once recalled and tried him and forty-seven other suspected persons, and prohibited Japanese from visiting Korea without special permission.

Mr. (now Baron) Komura, who presently succeeded to the Ministry at Seul, seemed to reverse the policy of his predecessors and abstain from active interference. The Korean Cabinet also appeared powerless to check the Russian party, whose power was growing apace. Prominent politicians out of office frequently conferred at the Russian

---

[1] G. Takeda, pp. 25–30; Y. Hamada, *Nichi-Ro Gwaikō Jū-nen Shi* (ten years of Japanese-Russian diplomacy, Tokio, 1904), p. 47. Also see the *Korea Review*, July (pp. 331–336) and August (pp. 369–371), 1904.

Legation, where some of them were even said to
have taken refuge from the law.  There a leader of
this party (who till May of the present year represented Korea at St. Petersburg) matured a plan to
overthrow the Cabinet, or, in case of failure, to ab-
duct the King and the Crown Prince to Vladivostok.
The plan, however, was discovered on November
28,[1] only to be followed by another, which proved
successful.  In January, 1896, there took place a
slight uprising in Northern Korea, at the instiga-
tion, it was said, of pro-Russian leaders.  When the
major portion of the army had been sent out of
the capital to suppress the alleged rebellion, 127
Russian marines with a cannon suddenly landed at
Chemulpo on February 10, and immediately entered
Seul.  The next day, before dawn, the King, with
the seal of the state, as well as the Crown Prince
and Princess and some court ladies, fled in disguise
to the Russian Legation, where the King remained
for a twelvemonth, till February 20 of the following year.  At his arrival at the Legation, an edict
was issued proclaiming the Cabinet Ministers guilty
of treason, and ordering their decapitation.  Another edict canceling the order appeared too late,
for the Prime Minister and two other Ministers had
been murdered on the streets in broad daylight,
and their heads exposed by the wayside, while
three others had fled to Japan for life.[2]  The mur-

---

[1] G. Takeda, pp. 30–32.

[2] *Ibid.*, pp. 33–34; *Tokushu Jōyaku*, pp. 740–741.  See
also the *Korea Review*, August, 1904, pp. 377–378.

ders of February, 1896, would have come down to history as more atrocious than the crime of October 8, 1895, had it not been for the fact that the latter involved the life of a queen.

The King being virtually in the custody of the Russians, their ascendency resulted as a matter of course. They secured, among other things, an immense timber concession on the northern frontier and on Uinung Island,[1] and a mining concession along the Tumên River.[2] The Korean forces trained by Japanese officers were abolished in May,[3] and the Japanese soldiers stationed at the ports and Seul also were reduced in number.[4]

The Government at Tokio even appeared, for a time at least, to forsake its historic policy of safeguarding Korea's independence by its sole aid, but to seek Russia's coöperation toward the same end. With this object in view, Japan seized the occasion of the coronation of the Czar to send Field Marshal Marquis Aritomo Yamagata[5] as special envoy to St. Petersburg, with a commission to negotiate with the Russian Government an agreement regarding the relative position of the two Powers in Korea. The result was the following

[1] The contract dated August 28, 1896 (o. s.). — *Tokushu Jōyaku*, pp. 781–791.

[2] The contract of April 22, 1896. — *Ibid.*, pp. 772–775.

[3] G. Takeda, p. 45.

[4] *Tokushu Jōyaku*, pp. 740–741.

[5] It is said that Marquis Itō himself had a mind to represent Japan at the coronation, but the mission was finally intrusted to the Field Marshal. It will be remembered that China sent Li Hung-chang for this occasion.

Yamagata-Lobanoff Protocol, signed on June 9, 1896: —

"ARTICLE I. The Japanese and Russian Governments should, with the object of remedying the financial embarrassments of Korea, counsel the Korean Government to suppress all unnecessary expenses and to establish an equilibrium between expenditure and revenue. If, as a result of the reforms which should be considered indispensable, it should become necessary to have recourse to foreign debts, the two Governments should, of a common accord, render their support to Korea.

"ARTICLE II. The Japanese and Russian Governments should try to abandon to Korea, in so far as the financial and economic situation of that country should permit, the creation and the maintenance of an armed force and of a police organized of native subjects, in proportions sufficient to maintain internal order, without foreign aid.

"ARTICLE III. With a view to facilitating communications with Korea, the Japanese Government shall continue to administer the telegraphic lines which are actually in its possession.

"It is reserved to Russia to establish a telegraphic line from Seul to her frontier.

"These various lines should be purchased by the Korean Government, as soon as it finds means so to do.

"ARTICLE IV. In case the principles above expounded require a more precise and more detailed definition, or if in the future other points should arise about which it should be necessary to consult, the Representatives of the two Governments should be instructed to discuss them amicably." [1]

[1] Tokushu Jōyaku, pp. 742–744; the Kaitei Jōyaku Isan, pp. 601–602; the Treaties and Conventions between the Empire of Japan and other Powers, p. 393.

A few days earlier, on May 14, there was concluded at Seul between M. Komura and M. Waeber,
the Japanese and Russian Ministers, a Memorandum
dealing with matters of more immediate interest
to the two Powers.[1] M. Waeber agreed to advise
the Korean King to return from the Russian Legation to his palace, as soon as there was no more
apprehension for his safety, M. Komura pledging
in return to keep the Japanese political bravoes
(*sō-shi*) in Seul under a strict surveillance (Article
I.). It was declared that the present Cabinet members[2] of Korea were noted for generous and mild
principles, and had been appointed to their posts
by the King of his own accord. The Japanese and
Russian Representatives should always make it their
aim to advise the King to govern his people in
generous spirit (Article II.). The remainder of the
Memorandum is more worthy of record : —

"ARTICLE III. The Representative of Russia quite
agrees with the Representative of Japan that, at the
present state of affairs in Korea, it may be necessary to
have the Japanese guards stationed at some places for
the protection of the Japanese telegraph line between
Fusan and Seul, and that these guards, now consisting of
three companies of soldiers, should be withdrawn as soon
as possible and replaced by gendarmes, who will be stationed as follows: fifty men at Tai-ku, fifty men at Ka-
heung, and ten men each at ten intermediate posts between Fusan and Seul. This distribution may be liable

[1] See the same references as are given in the preceding note,
pp. 740–742, 596–600, and 391, respectively.
[2] Some of them were strongly pro-Russian.

to some changes, but the total number of gendarme force shall never exceed 200 men, who will afterwards be gradually withdrawn from those places in which peace and order have been restored by the Korean Government.[1]

"ARTICLE IV. For the protection of the Japanese settlements at Seul and the open ports against the possible attacks by the Korean populace, two companies of Japanese troops may be stationed at Seul, one company at Fusan and one at Gensan, each company not to exceed 200 men. These troops shall be quartered near the settlements, and should be withdrawn as soon as no apprehensions of such attacks could be entertained.

"For the protection of the Russian Legation and Consulates, the Russian Government may also keep guards not exceeding in number the Japanese troops at these places, which will be withdrawn as soon as tranquillity in the interior is completely restored."[2]

A casual reading of these agreements will show how far the Japanese Government had receded from the position she originally took in regard to Korea. Ever since Japan concluded her treaty with Korea in 1876,[3] which for the first time established the international position of the latter State as a sovereign Power, Japan's policy had been to uphold the independence and the opening of the Peninsu-

[1] These gendarmes had never been withdrawn before the present war broke out. The Koreans frequently tried to cut the telegraph line.

[2] Japanese soldiers in Korea before the present war were stationed to the fullest extent stipulated in this Article. Owing to the small number of the Russian residents in Korea, the Russian Government never stationed as many soldiers in Korea as did the Japanese.

[3] *Tokushu Jōyaku*, pp. 714–717.

lar Kingdom. From the strict terms of this policy, Japan has allowed herself to depart twice, — in her agreements, first, with China in 1885, and, again, with Russia in 1896, — not by forsaking its principles, but in each case by entering, in the pursuit of the policy, into an impossible association with an aggressive Power. In each of the two instances the attempt failed within a decade, and resulted in hostilities. In 1885, Japan and China simultaneously withdrew their forces from Korea, and thereby cleared the ground for the renewed conflict of their opposing interests, which were artificially placed on a par with one another. In 1896, Japan admitted Russia's right to build a telegraph line in North Korea which should correspond to the Japanese line in the south, and to station in Korea a number of troops equal to that of the Japanese soldiers. Despite the millenniums of her historic relations with Korea, and the actual preponderance of her interests therein, and after her successful liberation of the Kingdom from Chinese suzerainty by a costly war, Japan now admitted into the Peninsular politics on an equal footing with herself a Power which owed its bright success to a mere diplomacy of less than two years' standing, and whose policy seemed to be guided by principles entirely at variance with the independence and strength of Korea.

At the coronation of the Czar, Korea was represented by an influential, pro-Russian member of the Min family. It was then rumored that he concluded

with the Russian Government a secret agreement
by which Korea undertook to employ Russian military instructors and financial councilors. However
that may be, the Russian Representatives at Seul
are said to have since appealed more than once to
the " secret agreement " in their attempts to force
the engagement of Russian service upon the Korean
Government.[1] If these reports were true, no better proof of the light estimate with which Russia
from the first regarded the Yamagata-Lobanoff
Protocol could be found than her alleged agreement with Min Yong-hwan, for the latter was a direct reversal of the first two Articles of the former.
Russia may be credited with having succeeded, by
her separate and mutually contradictory arrangements with Min, Yamagata, and Li Hung-chang,[2] in
simultaneously bringing the three Eastern Powers
to terms.

Whatever the truth of the reported Russo-
Korean Agreement, Russia did no sooner sign her
Japanese Protocol of June 9, than she began to
violate its terms. In the same month, it was resolved that Korean troops should henceforth be
instructed under the Russian system of military
education, and accordingly, in October, three army
officers, a medical officer, and ten soldiers from
Russia arrived at Seul. In April, 1897, M. Waeber
was urging upon the Seul Government the employment of 160 officers and soldiers, and, despite the
reluctance of Korea and inquiries from Japan,

[1] G. Takeda, pp. 50–51.          [2] See pp. 87 ff., above.

three Russian officers and ten soldiers entered the capital in July, whose service for three years was finally, on September 6, imposed upon the Korean Government by M. A. de Speyer, the new Russian Minister. Thus the royal guard and five battalions of the Korean infantry, numbering about 3000, came under Russian instruction.[1] A month later, M. Speyer requested that the control of all the receipts from the taxes and customs be placed in the hands of one M. Kir Alexieff. At that time, however, a British subject, Mr. MacLeavy Brown, had not served his term as Financial Adviser and General Director of Customs of Korea. Failing the assent of the Finance Department, M. Speyer pressed upon the Foreign Department, which yielded at last. The British Consul, Mr. Jordan, protested in vain, for, on October 26, the Korean King issued an edict releasing Mr. Brown from his duties. A Russo-Korean Bank was soon organized to transact the financial and economical affairs of Korea. On December 27, seven British men-of-war visited Chemulpo, and Mr. Jordan went thither, returning to Seul accompanied by a naval officer and ten marines. Mr. Brown was consequently restored to his office, and M. Alexieff had to content himself with a subordinate position under him.[2]

It was a misfortune to Russia that her able representative at Seul, M. Waeber, who had been in Korea since 1884, had been transferred to Mexico, and was replaced by M. Speyer. The former dip-

[1] G. Takeda, pp. 45–47.          [2] *Ibid.*, pp. 48–50.

lomat's pleasing manners were succeeded by the latter's overbearing conduct, which appeared gradually to alienate from Russian influence many a former friend of M. Waeber. The anti-Russian sentiment grew finally so strong that a large number of intelligent Koreans organized the Korean Independence Society, whose object was declared to be to restore the military, financial, and political control of the Kingdom to the hands of the Koreans. The impatient M. Speyer was reported to have written a note to the Korean Government, on March 7, 1898, asking for a reply within twenty-four hours to the query whether Korea was really in want of the service of the Russian experts, whose position had become rather precarious. The astounded Government replied politely but firmly in the negative. Other events occurred which further evinced the arbitrary attitude of M. Speyer. With an equally astonishing decision, he ordered, on March 17, all the financial and military councilors to be recalled to Russia. The Russo-Korean Bank was also disorganized. M. Speyer himself leaving Korea in April, his post was occupied by the amiable M. Matunine.[1] About this time, a new Russo-Japanese Protocol was signed at Tokio between Baron Rosen, the Russian Minister to Japan, and Baron Nishi, the Foreign Minister of the Japanese Government.

It is evident that the relaxation of Russia's diplomacy in Korea was in no small measure due to

[1] G. Takeda, pp. 53–54, and Jumpei Shinobu, *Kan Hantō* (the Korean peninsula), pp. 505–512.

the swift movement of events, as well as her own all-engrossing activity, in China. The Nishi-Rosen Protocol of April 25, 1898, concluded as it was at this unfavorable moment for Russia, was far more in Japan's favor than the agreements of 1896. It not only gave an explicit recognition of the independence of Korea, but also incorporated in the second Article the best principles of the previous agreement, and, in addition, fully recognized the special economic interests of Japan in the Peninsula. The entire Protocol deserves quotation : —

"ARTICLE I. The Imperial Governments of Japan and Russia definitely recognize the independence and the perfect sovereignty of Korea, and mutually engage to abstain from all direct interference in the internal affairs of that country.

"ARTICLE II. Desirous of removing all possible causes of misunderstanding in the future, the Imperial Governments of Japan and Russia mutually engage, in case Korea should have recourse to the counsel and assistance of either Japan or Russia, not to take any measure regarding the nomination of military instructors and financial advisers, without having previously arrived at a mutual accord on the subject.

"ARTICLE III. In view of the great development of the commercial and industrial enterprises of Japan in Korea, as also of the considerable number of the Japanese subjects residing in that country, the Russian Imperial Government shall not obstruct the development of the commercial and industrial relations between Japan and Korea." [1]

[1] *Tokushu Jōyaku*, pp. 744–745; the *Kaitei Jōyaku Isan*, p. 603; the *Treaties and Conventions*, p. 394 (French text).

Each one of these three Articles should be carefully noted, for five years later, in 1903, they, together with the last Article of the Yamagata-Lobanoff Protocol of June 9, 1896, became a conventional ground for Japan's direct negotiations with Russia which preceded the present war. Particular attention is called to the third Article, wherein Russia recognized for the first time the peculiar interest of the Japanese nation in the economic development of Korea.

Less artificial as the Protocol was in comparison with the former agreements, it was, however, hardly adequate as an instrument to reconcile the conflicting interests of Russia and Japan. Fresh complications could well be expected from the second Article, for it, on the other hand, barred the reformatory attempts of a Power whose interests demanded the independence and strength of Korea, and, on the other, cleared the ground for the renewed activity of another Power which had little intention to abstain from undermining the vital interests of Japan. Under these precarious circumstances was opened the second period of the Russo-Japanese relations in Korea.

# CHAPTER XVII

## DIPLOMATIC STRUGGLE IN KOREA, II

FROM 1899, both Japan and Russia were represented at Seul by new Ministers, Mr. G. Hayashi and M. Paul Pavloff. The latter had been the *Chargé* at Peking, where he had recently made a brilliant success in securing for Russia a lease of Port Arthur and Talien-wan, and the right to connect these ports by rail with the great Siberian line. The contrast of character between the bold and ambitious Pavloff and the slow, tenacious Hayashi was an interesting index to the dramatic struggle which ensued in Korea between the rival Powers. For five years after the arrival of the diplomats, the desires of Russia and Japan seemed to clash, not only in Seul, but also in all directions within the Peninsula. Nearly every move made by either Power was countervailed by the other, Russia in most cases being the prime mover and Japan closely disputing the action of her rival. The feeble Government of Korea was sorely vexed between the vigorous demands and protests of the contending Powers, while the flexible will of the Emperor[1] and

[1] The sovereign of Korea, formerly King (*wang*), assumed the title Emperor (*Hwang-ti*), on October 12, 1897, for, in the Chinese language, the *wang* may be a tributary prince, but the *ti* is the master of an independent state.

the discord and venality of his servants aggravated the endless confusion of the situation. Let us now briefly observe how this keen rivalry manifested itself in the south, at the capital, and in the north of Korea.

In South Korea, nothing better could be desired by Russia than a lease of Masampo, a harbor unsurpassed for its naval facilities and most admirably situated as a connecting-point between Vladivostok and Port Arthur. An opportunity came in May, 1899, when Masampo, together with two other ports, was opened for foreign trade, for the foreigner is at liberty to purchase land within the three-mile radius of an open port. In the same month, M. Pavloff with the Military *Attaché* visited Masampo on his way home on a furlough, and was met there by Admiral Makaroff, commander of the Eastern squadron of the Russian navy, and, after making an extended survey of the coast and the harbor, selected the most strategic site on the foreshore, which he earmarked by setting up posts at its limits. This large lot, M. Pavloff notified the local authorities, would presently be purchased by a private Russian steamship company as the site for a dock and coaling-sheds. It was not till July that M. Stein, interpreter at the Russian Legation, went to the port with a view to effecting the purchase of the selected lot, which, to his chagrin, had already been bought by certain Japanese subjects from its legitimate owners. In vain the Russian *Chargé* demanded the Seul Government to cancel

**M. PAVLOFF**

*Late Russian Minister at Seul*

the contract and resell the land to the Russian company, for, as the Government repeatedly explained, the authorities had no right to interfere with the alienation of private land by its owners within the three-mile radius of any treaty port. As unavailing was the request of the *Chargé* upon Mr. Hayashi to induce the buyers to relinquish even a portion of the purchased lot. Then the local authorities at Masampo were approached by the Russian Representatives, and consequently the deed of purchase was for a long time withheld by them, though it was at length given to the new owners. On September 14, M. Stein, now the *Chargé*, notified the Korean Government that, under the instructions of the Russian Foreign Minister, he would be obliged to take liberty of action in order to protect Russian interest, if the Japanese contract was not canceled ; on October 4, again, he threatened that a forcible seizure of land would result from the non-compliance of the Korean Government. The replies of the latter were unalterably firm in refusing to annul a lawful transaction.[1] In the mean time, Russian diplomatic agents, naval officers, and engineers from Seul and Vladivostok were frequently visiting Masampo, and buying from the natives tracts of indifferent value.[2] In March, 1900, M. Pavloff returned from his furlough, and demanded the signature of the Masampo lease-con-

[1] *Tokushu Jōyaku*, pp. 747–751. See also *The Times*, August 30, 1899.
[2] The *Kokumin*, October 10, 1899.

tract in quite indefinite terms which he had previously framed. On March 16, Rear Admiral Hilidebrand came to Chemulpo with several war-vessels, and proceeded to Seul, where he was magnificently received by M. Pavloff and had an audience with the Emperor. Two days later, the lease agreement was signed [1] by the Korean Foreign Minister and M. Pavloff, which, however, was of little practical use so long as the most important tract had been bought by the Japanese. On the same day, the Minister secured from the Korean Government a pledge not to alienate any part of the Kojedo Island near Masampo and its surrounding territories, Russia herself engaging not to seek such alienation on her part.[2]

No sooner did Russia appear to content herself with these valueless formal pledges from Korea than she again sought to acquire land round Masampo. At the close of March, M. Pavloff had almost succeeded in securing the purchase of Nampo outside the three-mile limit of Masampo, but the reminder of Mr. Hayashi, expressed through the Foreign Office of Seul, that the foreigner was not entitled to own land beyond the fixed radius of a treaty port, produced its desired effect. Nampo was forsaken, and another lot inside the three-mile boundary was purchased by the Russians.[3] In May, M. Pavloff wished to lease Tja-pok on the inner shore of Masampo, but, finding again that a Japan-

---

[1] *Tokushu Jōyaku*, pp. 751–752.    [2] *Ibid.*, pp. 752–753.
[3] The *Kokumin*, April 1, and 3, 1900.

ese subject had already leased it, finally acquired the lease of Pankumi upon the outer shore, for the purpose of erecting a hospital, warehouses, and a recreation ground, for the use of the Russian navy.[1] This concession, however, has not been extensively utilized by the Russians, owing probably to the inferior site of Pankumi.[2] Mr. Hayashi met the Russian concession by acquiring, between May and October 29, 1901, about forty acres of land within the treaty limits of Masampo as a settlement for Japanese citizens.[3]

It is needless to add that the firm attitude of the Korean Government, which alone saved Masampo from the fate of Port Arthur, was in the main due to the persistent representations and support rendered to Korea by Mr. Hayashi against Russian encroachment. For if the control of Masampo was a matter of supreme importance for the Russian navy, Japan, on her part, could not for a moment tolerate the presence, in the harbor so near to herself, of a Power whose vast dominion was extending eastward with tremendous pressure. Russia's ill success at Masampo, however, was not to mark the end of her activity on the southern coast of Korea, which contains a few other harbors only second in importance to Masampo. In one of these, Chin-

---

[1] The *Kokumin*, May 25, 1900, and May 21, 1901.

[2] *Tokushu Jōyaku*, p. 751.

[3] The *Kokumin*, May 21 and November 1, 1901. The final agreement between Hayashi and the Korean Foreign Minister was signed on May 17, 1902, and published in the *Kwampō*.

hai Bay, M. Pavloff made, about March, 1901, an unauthorized demand for a lease, which again was refused.[1] From that time till the opening of the Russo-Japanese negotiations in 1903, the Russian Representative did not think the time opportune to prefer further demands on this coast.

Turning now to the diplomacy at the Korean capital, we observe that its first aim seems to have been to repeat the old policy of replacing Mr. Mac-Leavy Brown, a British subject, as the Director-General of Korean Customs, with M. Kir Alexieff, and also to put Korea under financial obligation to Russia by means of a loan. In March, 1901, Mr. Brown was suddenly ordered by the Korean Government, which acted obviously at the instance of the Russian Representative, to vacate his residence and surrender his post. The British *Chargé*, Mr. Gubbins, had barely succeeded in prevailing upon the Korean Government to revoke the latter half of the order, when in May another order was issued calling for the delivery, not only of Mr. Brown's official residence, but also of the customs office building — an order equivalent to a dismissal from office. From this predicament Mr. Brown was narrowly rescued by an earnest representation made on May 5 by Mr. Hayashi to the Korean Emperor.[2] By this time, the affair had been complicated by an agreement of a 5,000,000 *yen* loan, which had been signed on April 19, between the Korean Govern-

[1] The *Kokumin*, March 20, 1901, and August 7, 1902.
[2] *Ibid.*, May 5 and 10, 1901.

ment and the French agent, M. Cazalis, of the Yunnan Syndicate.[1] It is hardly necessary to give the detail of this abortive agreement, for it was never ratified by the Emperor, but fell through from the inability of the Syndicate to fulfill its terms.[2] It is only necessary to say that if the loan had materialized, a large control over the coinage, mining, and general finances of Korea would have passed into the hands of the French subjects and perhaps also of the Russo-Chinese Bank. This Bank, in the latter half of 1902, seems to have offered a fresh loan through its agents at Seul, Gunzburg and Company, under the condition that the firm should obtain a permanent monopoly of ginseng, which had then been in the hands of the Japanese, and also the right of working certain mines.[3] This proposition also miscarried, evidently owing to the protest from the Japanese Minister, who discovered in it a violation of the first Article of the Yamagata-Lobanoff Protocol of June 9, 1896. A Belgian loan, which was rumored early in 1903, seems to have shared the same fate with all the loans previously suggested.[4]

In this connection, it should be noted, in justice to all the parties concerned, that toward the latter half of 1900 there was a movement in Japan to suggest a loan to the Korean Government, but that the

[1] The *Kokumin*, April 23, 24, May 3, June 9, 1901.

[2] *Ibid.*, May 18, 1901; January 19, February 1, correspondence dated April 2, 1902.

[3] *Ibid.*, October 22, November 17, 1902.

[4] *Ibid.*, January 27, 1903.

Premier, Marquis Yamagata, declined to counte-
nance the scheme.[1] He probably did not wish his
nation to become a party to a violation of an agreement it made with Russia in 1896.

In 1902–3, the interest of Russia was represented
at Seul, not only by her regular Representative, but
also by Baron Gunzburg, who served as an agent
for many an economic enterprise in Korea proposed
by the Russians, by an Alsatian lady, Mlle. Sonntag, a relative of Mme. Waeber and an influential member of the court circle, and, temporarily,
by M. Waeber himself,[2] who had come to Seul as
special envoy of the Czar to attend the fortieth an-
niversary of the accession of the Korean Sovereign
to the throne.[3] These persons were further supported by a few Koreans who had lived in Siberia
and adopted Russian citizenship, and whose rapid
promotion in office had excited jealousy among the
nobility in Seul.[4] Among the latter, also, there were
Russian sympathizers of the greatest political influence. Taking advantage of the continual discord
among the politicians in Seul, which at that time

[1] From a statement made by an intimate friend of Marquis
Itō, who, in October, 1900, succeeded Yamagata in the premier-
ship. See the *Kokumin*, November 10, 1903.

[2] From 1900 till May, 1903.

[3] A Government can seldom afford so many foreign councilors
and commissioners as were found in Korea. Besides these
and several other Russians, there were in Seul, Mr. Masuo Katō,
a Japanese adviser, Mr. Sands, the once influential American
adviser, several French engineers, and a Belgian councilor to
the ministry of internal affairs.

[4] The *Kokumin*, Seul correspondence, dated August 7, 1902.

manifested itself in the rancorous hatred between
the supporters of the Crown Prince and those of
Lady Öm, who aspired to the position of the Queen,
the Russians succeeded in enlisting the good-will
of the leaders of both parties, Yi Yong-ik and Yi-
Keun-thaik. Once a lad of mean birth in the
north,[1] Yi Yong-ik, by his unscrupulous methods,
had amassed a large fortune and risen to the Ministry of the Imperial Household, until, in November,
1902, he found himself the object of a sharp opposition by Yi Keun-thaik and a large section of the
gentry of Seul. He at once took refuge in the Russian Legation, and was then taken on board the
" Korietz " to Port Arthur, where he used his seal
of the Imperial Estates Board and transacted his
official business as before.[2] On January 13, 1903,
he returned to Seul, and used his influence to further the already started obstruction to the bank-
notes issued by the Korean branch of the First Bank
of Japan. These notes had first appeared in May,
1902, and, beside the deplorable monetary system
of Korea, met so great a demand from the commercial world that, by the end of the year, the amount
issued had risen nearly to 1,000,000 *yen* against a
reserve only a little below that sum.[3] Suddenly, at
the instance of the Russians who wished to issue
similar notes from the Russo-Chinese Bank, the

[1] The *Kokumin*, Seul correspondence, dated June 3, 1899;
November 30, 1902.

[2] *Ibid.*, Seul correspondence, dated December 23, 1902.

[3] See p. 23, above.

Korean Government had prohibited the circulation of the Japanese notes in December, 1902. The credit of the notes and the benefit of their use had been so obvious, however, that, in spite of the Government order, the Director-General of the Customs had still received payments in them, and the Chinese Minister had advised his countrymen to continue their use. The veto had then been removed, only to be renewed at the return of Yi Yong-ik from Port Arthur. He had entertained the desire, which has been found utterly impracticable, of himself establishing a central bank and issuing paper notes.[1] He employed all the means at his disposal to resist the opposition of the Japanese Representative, who was now supported by his British colleague, Mr. Jordan. The bank-notes were not reinstated till February 13, 1903, when a compromise was at last reached with the Korean Government.[2] It is impossible to establish the complicity of the Russian diplomats in Yi Yong-ik's obstruction, which thus ended in failure, beyond the fact that the Korean politician had been in close touch with the Muscovites. From the historical point of view, Russia could hardly have interfered with the issue of the Japanese bank-notes without transgressing the third Article of the Nishi-Rosen Protocol of April 25, 1898.

Thus far we have related the comparative failure of Russia's diplomacy in South Korea and at the

[1] The *Kokumin*, telegrams, March 11, 26, 27, April 11, 1903.
[2] *Ibid.*, correspondence, February 2, 5, 9, 16, 18, March 4, 1903.

capital. In the north, however, which was conterminous with her dominion and with Manchuria, Russia achieved a greater success. On March 29, 1899,[1] M. Pavloff succeeded, after his earlier and much larger demands had failed, in leasing for twelve years, for the use of Count H. Keyserling, a Russian subject, three whaling stations[2] on the northeastern coast, each 700 by 350 feet in extent. This concession was offset by one secured by a Japanese citizen, on February 14, 1900,[3] which conferred upon him the right of whaling for three years, subject to renewal, along the Korean coast, excepting the waters for the distance of three *li* adjoining the three provinces on which the Keyserling concessions were situated and the Province of Chul-la.

Further north, upon the frontier, the long boundary line naturally divides itself into two parts, namely, the Tumên River, separating Korea from Primorsk of Siberia and the Kirin Province of Manchuria, and the Yalu River, which borders upon the strategically most important Province of Shengking of South Manchuria. Along the former stream, Russia acquired by a treaty of 1884[4] the opening

---

[1] The contract is found in *Tokushu Jōyaku*, pp. 800–806. Also see the U. S. 56th Congress, 1st Session, *House Documents*, vol. i. pp. 484–488.

[2] (1) Along the coast near Cape Tikhmeneff, Ulsan Bay, Kiong-sang Province; (2) on the island of Ching-po, Hamkiung Province; and (3) at Chang-shing, Kang-wan Province.

[3] *Tokushu Jōyaku*, pp. 799–800.

[4] *Ibid.*, pp. 731–732 (August 8, 1884, o. s.).

of the port of Kiong-hung to the Russian land
trade, and a free navigation of the Tumên. A
dozen years later,[1] when the Sovereign sojourned
at the Russian Legation, the Muscovites concluded
an agreement with the Seul Government whereby
they were granted the privilege of mining gold and
other minerals for fifteen years, and coal for twenty
years, in two districts near Kiong-hung, as well as
the right to construct a railway or carriage-road
from the mines to the shore. It has often been reported that the poverty-stricken people as well as
the venal officers along the river have continually
mortgaged their property to the Russians, who thus
have acquired extensive tracts of land, circulated
Russian coins among the natives, and otherwise im-
planted their influence far and wide. Then early
in 1902, M. Pavloff sought to make a step in advance in this direction, when, without permission
from Korea, a telegraph line was extended from
Possiet to Kiong-hung across the Tumên River.
He desired that the Seul Government should recognize the accomplished fact, and Rear Admiral
Skrydloff, commanding the Pacific squadron of the
Russian navy, visited the capital on February 17,
and intimated his hope that the question would be
amicably settled. The Foreign Minister, Pak Che-
sun, however, successfully ordered on February 22
that the telegraph line so surreptitiously built be
removed. In the mean while, it was discovered that
the St. Petersburg Government had had nothing to

[1] *Tokushu Jōyaku,* pp. 772-775, April 22, 1896.

do with the building of the line which had recently
been removed. M. Pavloff, however, succeeded in
securing the dismissal of Pak from his post. He also
persisted in demanding the right of the Russians to
reconstruct the line across the Tumên River. He
was as much justified in preferring such a demand,
as was the Korean Government in refusing to accede to it. The latter was probably apprehensive
that its concession to Russia would be followed by
similar demands from other Powers. At present,
the Korean telegraph line reaches from Seul to
Kion-song, some forty miles from Kiong-hung.[1]

On the Yalu River, also, M. Pavloff desired a telegraphic connection with Wiju from Port Arthur
and from Harbin, which, after a failure in May,
1902, was at last granted in April, 1903.[2]

More important, however, is the question of the
Seul-Wiju Railway, which had been the bone of contention between Japan and the allied Powers of
Russia and France, until the outbreak of the present
war suddenly changed the situation in favor of the
former. By the temporary articles of August 20,
1894,[3] Korea had granted a prior right to the Japanese Government or companies to construct railways
between Seul and Fusan. The actual undertaking,
however, was so delayed, that, on March 29, 1896,[4]

---

[1] The *Kokumin*, Seul correspondence, dated April 8, 1902.

[2] *Ibid.*, telegram, May 8, correspondence, May 11, 1902 ; telegram, March 28, and correspondence, April 16, 1903.

[3] *Tokushu Jōyaku*, p. 722.

[4] *Ibid.*, pp. 761–764.

Mr. James R. Morse, an American citizen, succeeded
in acquiring the Seul-Chemulpo concession, and began to build the line. In October, 1898, Mr. Morse
sold the concession to certain Japanese capitalists,
and the line, which was the first railway owned
abroad by Japanese subjects, has been in running
order since July, 1900. The contract for the other
line — Fusan-Seul — was not made by the Japanese
till September 8, 1898.[1] Prior to this, on July 3,
1896,[2] a French company had acquired a grant to
connect Seul with Wiju on the Yalu by rail. Finding, however, little prospect of starting the work

---

[1] *Tokushu Jōyaku*, pp. 765–768. This contract includes
certain interesting provisions, which the reader may compare
with those of the Manchurian railways. There occur two exclusive measures, that none but Koreans and Japanese may hold
shares of the railway capital (Article 15), and that no other foreigners shall reside within lands assigned for the depots (Article 5). The work should be begun within three years after the
signature of the contract, and be completed within ten years
hence (Article 10). After fifteen years of operation, the Korean
Government might purchase the entire line, and, if unable to do
so, the purchase would be postponed by periods of ten years
(Article 12). As soon as the Korean finances should admit, the
railway might be made a common work between the Koreans
and Japanese (Article 13). The laborers and the timber employed in the construction should as far as possible be obtained
in Korea (Article 6). The lands assigned for the line and its
depots shall belong to the company only so long as it operates
the road, and the Korean Government should furnish no other
lands to the company (Articles 3 and 8). It should be added
that the Japanese Government guaranteed a six per cent. interest for the capital of the company.

For further details of the Seul-Chemulpo and Fusan-Seul
Railways, see p. 24, and notes, above.

[2] For the contract, see *Tokushu Jōyaku*, pp. 770–772.

within the specified period of three years, the company tried to sell the concession, first to the Russian Government and then to Japan, but neither was prepared to accept the proposed terms. About 1900, Yi Yong-ik instituted in the Imperial Household Department the Northwestern Railway Bureau, over which he presided, with the express purpose of building the line with Korean capital. The French Minister at Seul, however, had a short time before obtained exclusive right to furnish material and engineers for the building of the line, so that Korean money and French skill were to be enlisted for the service.[1] After a long delay, President Yi held a great undertaking ceremony on May 8, 1902, but it was patent to every one that no Korean capital was forthcoming. As was expected, not a mile of rail having been laid, the work was suspended in June, and indefinitely postponed.[2] Considering, however, that a Seul-Wiju line would naturally pass through the gold mines of Yun-san and Yin-san and the coal region of Ping-yang, and the great agricultural province of Hwang-hai, as well as such commercial centres as Kai-song, Ping-yang, Hwang-ju, and An-ju, the advantages of controlling this line appeared too great for the competing foreigners to leave its construction to the care of the impecunious Korean Government. Particularly jealous were the Russians of the line passing into the hands

---

[1] *Tokushu Jōyaku*, pp. 768–770; the *Kokumin*, September 7, 1901.

[2] The *Kokumin*, July 4, 1902.

of their political rivals, for then — if, furthermore, a railway connection were effected by the same rivals between Wiju and Niu-chwang — the deep-laid design of Russia to make Dalny the great trading port for Manchuria and North China would be seriously upset by the railway reaching directly from the producing centres of these regions and Korea to the port of Fusan, whence a ready communication oversea might well radiate toward Japan, Europe, and America. It was natural, therefore, for M. Stein, Russian *Chargé d'Affaires*, again to recommend, as he did on February 15, 1903, the honest Baron Gunzburg to the Korean Government, and to demand of the latter on behalf of the Baron the right of laying the Seul-Wiju Railway. The Government, however, declined[1] to entertain the application, as it was its intention to complete the line on its own resources, and not to concede it to any foreign Power.[2] Later, another attempt was made in August by the Seul Government to reopen the work of construction, for which a French syndicate represented by M. Rondon was to supply all machinery,[3] but, again, the lack of funds frustrated the attempt.

[1] It is said that the Russian Representative obtained a promise from the Korean Government to grant to no other foreigners the right of either the construction or the mortgage of this railway. — The *Kokumin*, December 10, 1903. It now matters little whether this report was true or not, since the Korean Government abrogated on May 18, 1904, all the agreements it had concluded with the Russians.

[2] The *Kokumin*, February 18, 1903; the *Dōbun-kwai*, No. 41, pp. 91–93.

[3] The *Kokumin*, August 4, 1903.

Since that time, no important development of this question had transpired before the beginning of hostilities between Russia and Japan.

We have so far seen enough of Korean diplomacy to comprehend something of the Russian method of furthering her influence over Korea, and of the manner in which Japan struggled to safeguard her fast increasing interests [1] in the peninsula and to maintain the terms of the Russian agreements of 1896 and 1898. We have, however, reserved up to this point the latest and most important question of the timber concession upon the northern frontier. In no other matter had the characteristic method of Russian diplomacy excited more apprehension in Korea and Japan, for nothing could better illustrate the close connection, in the Muscovite policy, of Manchuria and North Korea — a connection which appeared to threaten at once the integrity of the two adjoining Empires and the safety of Japan — than the Yong-am-po incident which arose in April, 1903, in relation to the timber concession. The contract [2] for this concession dated so far back as August 28, 1896, when the Korean King was a guest at the Russian Legation. It had secured for a Russian merchant at Vladivostok the right to organize a Korean lumber company (Article 1), having a monopoly for twenty years of the forestry enterprise round the Mu-san region upon the Tumên River and also on the Uinung Island in Japan Sea (Article 2). The work, in order to be valid,

[1] See, e. g., pp. 10–30.     [2] *Tokushu Jōyaku*, pp. 781–791.

had to be begun within one year after the signature
of the agreement (Article 15). Only when work in
these two regions should have been under way, the
company might, within five years [1] from the same
date, start a similar exploitation along the Yalu
River (Article 2).[2] Accordingly, the Russian syndicate undertook to fell trees at Mu-san in 1897 and
again in 1898,[3] though never on a large scale.[4]
On the Uinung Island, however, where good timber
had nearly been exhausted after many years of cutting by the Japanese, the Russians had at no time
made a serious attempt to exploit it. Under these
circumstances, the right of the Russians to exploit
forests upon the Yalu so late as 1903 was at least
not clear.[5] Nevertheless, the extensive public works
at Port Arthur and Dalny and on the railways
had created so great a demand for timber, that
the Chinese woodmen were cutting trees along the
foot of the Long White Mountains and sending
them downstream to An-tung, where alone the
traffic annually aggregated the sum of 1,500,000

[1] It is said that the time-limit was extended, on January 1,
1901, for twenty years. See *Tokushu Jōyaku*, p. 783.

[2] The company agreed to pay to the Korean Imperial House,
through the Russo-Chinese Bank, a royalty amounting to one
fourth of the annual profit. The company was to furnish all the
capital, and was exempt from all kinds of taxes and dues (Articles 10, 11, 14).

[3] The *Kokumin*, correspondence, April 18, 1903; *Tokushu
Jōyaku*, pp. 781–782.

[4] Toward the end of May, 1903, simultaneously with their
activity on the Yalu, the Russian soldiers began again to cut trees
at Mu-san.

[5] Cf. Article 2 of the contract.

*taels.*[1] The Russians now seemed to have planned to exploit both sides of the Yalu, and they would not have caused trouble, had they employed legitimate means to accomplish their ends. On the Manchurian side, finding that a foreigner could not get a timber concession from the Chinese authorities, they used the name of a leader of the mounted bandits whom a Russian military officer had befriended, and, after securing a concession, employed those bandits in felling trees.[2] In regard to the Korean side of the river, after nearly seven years' inactivity since the grant of the concession, M. Stein, Russian *Chargé* at Seul, suddenly notified the Korean Government, on April 13, 1903, that Baron Gunzburg would henceforth represent at Seul the interest of the timber syndicate, which would now commence its work upon the Yalu.[3] Early in May, forty-seven Russian soldiers in civilian dress, presently increased to sixty, besides a larger number

[1] The *Kokumin*, correspondence, July 27, 1903. Lower down the stream, at Tatung-kao, the amount sometimes reached the annual value of 7,000,000 *taels*.

[2] See an address by Eitaro Tsuruoka, who has recently traveled in Manchuria and is acquainted with several of the leaders of the bandits. The *Dōbun-kwai*, No. 53 (April, 1904), pp. 1–14.

[3] The *Kokumin*, April 23, 1903. The capital of the syndicate was reported to be 5,000,000 rubles, of which 2,000,000 were said to have been furnished by the Russian Government. — *Ibid.*, correspondence, June 19, 1903. This rumor was not authenticated. It is safe to say, however, that Baron Gunzburg's connection with the syndicate was largely nominal. The present writer is not in a position to explain the relation of the notorious M. Bezobrazoff to the timber work on the Yalu.

of Chinese and Koreans under Russian employ, were reported to have come to Yong-am-po,[1] a point near the mouth of the river and rather remote from the places[2] where actual cutting was in progress, and had begun to construct what was claimed to be timber-warehouses, but later proved to be, besides some godowns, a blacksmith plant and a six-foot mound.[3] At the same time, there was taking place a mysterious mobilization of troops from Liao-yang and Port Arthur towards Fêng-hwang-Chêng and An-tung on the other side of the Yalu.[4] The Korean frontier officers reported that a panic had been created among the inhabitants, and that the Korean-Manchurian commerce had stopped.[5] Presently, the Russian soldiers at Yong-am-po were reported to have been increased, first by 100, and then by 200, who purchased from the natives, under the name of a Korean citizen and against the wishes of the local authorities, fifteen houses and some twelve acres of land.[6] When the Korean Government had, on May

[1] The *Kokumin*, telegram, May 8 and 9, 1903.

[2] Principally Mt. Paik-ma.

[3] The *Kokumin*, telegram, June 11, correspondence, June 19, 1903. When Japanese soldiers reached Yong-am-po soon after the beginning of the present war, they found there a large warehouse, and fifteen large brick and twenty or more smaller buildings. Rails had been laid between the sea and the warehouse, which was also connected with the Yalu by a new canal. A fort had also been left standing, but the guns had been taken away.

[4] *Ibid.*, telegram, May 8 and 9, 1900. Cf. the *British Parliamentary Papers : China, No. 2 (1904)*, Nos. 115, 116, 128, 129, 131, 134.

[5] The *Kokumin*, telegram, May 9, 1903.

[6] *Ibid.*, telegram, May 22 and 25, 1903.

15, demanded of M. Stein to order the evacuation of the Russians,[1] M. Pavloff, who had recently returned from his trip to Russia, requested, on the contrary, that the Korean Government should protect the Russian subjects at Yong-am-po.[2] A desultory discussion then ensued between M. Pavloff and the Korean Government, while further increases of the Russian forces at An-tung beyond the river were reducing the frontier regions generally into a state of anarchy.[3] About the middle of June, the Russians forcibly seized rafts belonging to some Koreans and Chinese that came down the stream, and shot two Chinese who resisted.[4] A Japanese-Chinese syndicate, also, which had secured a timber concession in this region in March from the Korean Government, reported that its rafts had been seized, and its work had consequently been suspended.[5] Prior to this, four Russian war-vessels under command of Admiral Starck came to Chemulpo in the night of June 5,[6] and stayed there till the 11th. No matter whether there was any significance in this act, it is sufficient to record that it took place at this critical moment. Not the least serious feature of the affair was the disagreement of opinion about it inside the Korean Government. When, on June 11, the Council of State passed a resolution that the

[1] The *Kokumin*, telegram, May 16.
[2] *Ibid.*, correspondence, May 20.
[3] *Ibid.*, telegram, June 13.
[4] *Ibid.*, telegram, June 17.
[5] *Ibid.*, June 16.
[6] *Ibid.*, telegram, June 6.

conduct of the Russians upon the frontier was contrary to the treaty arrangements between the two Powers, the Foreign Office, on the 14th, sought to refute the ground in an elaborate note.[1] The gravity of the situation as evinced in all these facts need hardly be pointed out. Whatever the intentions of the Russian Government or even of its Representative at Seul, the action of the Muscovites at Yong-am-po was precisely of a nature to remind one of their previous fortification of Port Arthur, which had eventually prepared their entry into the whole of Manchuria. The fact that the occupation of Yong-am-po took place simultaneously with the suspension of the evacuation of Manchuria and with the active military connection between its army centres and the Korean frontier, gave the present affair an exceedingly ominous appearance. And yet, in the face of these perilous circumstances, the Korean Government showed itself so impotent and so little alive to the situation as to be divided against itself on a minor point of the law of the case. In such a state of things, the usual method of Japan to resist Russia through Korea would be utterly futile.

It is unnecessary to recall that any attempt upon the integrity of Korea was in violation of the fundamental principle which formed the first Article of the Nishi-Rosen Protocol of April 25, 1898,[2] as well as against the spirit of this and the two

[1] The *Kokumin*, correspondence, June 19.
[2] See p. 271, above.

other Russo-Japanese agreements regarding Korea. These agreements seemed to Japan to have in one way or another been palpably violated by the Russians in many of their actions in Korea, to which the Yong-am-po affair was a climax. Under circumstances so continually irritating to the peace of the East and so threatening to her own vital interests, the Government of Japan now felt justified, when the climax was reached, in opening *direct* negotiations with Russia, in order to arrive at such a definite understanding of the relative position of the Powers in Korea, as would insure the mutual benefit of the three nations concerned.

# CHAPTER XVIII

## THE RUSSO–JAPANESE NEGOTIATIONS, I

It was in view of these dangerously unstable circumstances in Manchuria and Korea that, on June 23, 1903, the four principal members of the Japanese Cabinet [1] and five Privy Councilors [2] met before the Throne, and decided on the principles upon which negotiations with Russia should be opened.[3] Having thus formulated the policy to be pursued, Baron Komura telegraphed to the Japanese Minister at St. Petersburg, Mr. Kurino, on July 28, as follows [4] : —

[1] Viscount Katsura, Premier ; Baron Komura, Foreign Minister ; and Messrs. Terauchi and Yamamoto, Ministers, respectively, of the Army and Navy.

[2] Marquises Itō and Yamagata, and Counts Matsukata, Inoüé and Ōyama.

[3] The Japanese dailies.

[4] The *Nichi-Ro Kōshō ni kwan su ru Ōfuku* (diplomatic correspondence respecting the negotiations between Japan and Russia), dispatch No. 1. This correspondence (hereafter abbreviated as *N.–R.*) was presented by the Japanese Government to the Houses of the Imperial Diet, respectively, on March 23 and 26, and published in the *Kwampō* (Official Gazette) of March 24 and 27, 1904. It contains fifty-one dispatches, all telegraphic, covering the period of more than six months between the opening of the negotiations and the severance of all diplomatic relations between the two Powers, namely, between July 28, 1903, and February 6, 1904.

An authoritative English translation of this correspondence

BARON KOMURA
*Japanese Foreign Minister*

"The Imperial Government [of Japan] have observed with close attention the development of affairs in Manchuria, and its present situation causes them to view it with grave concern.

"So long as it was hoped that Russia would carry out, on the one hand, the engagement that she made with China, and, on the other, the assurances she had given to other Powers, regarding the subject of the evacuation of Manchuria, the Imperial Government maintained an attitude of watchful reserve. But the recent conduct of Russia has been, at Peking, to propose new demands, and, in Manchuria, to tighten her hold upon it, until the Imperial Government is led to believe that Russia must have abandoned the intention of retiring from Manchuria. At the same time, her increased activity upon the Korean frontier is such as to raise doubts as to the limits of her ambition.

"The unconditioned and permanent occupation of Manchuria by Russia would create a state of things prejudicial to the security and interest of Japan. The principle of equal opportunity would thereby be annulled, and the territorial integrity of China impaired. There is, however, a still more serious consideration for the Japanese Government. That is to say, if Russia was established on the flank of Korea, it would be a constant menace to the separate existence of that Empire, or at least would make Russia the dominant Power in Korea. Korea is an important outpost in Japan's line of defense, and Japan consequently considers her independence absolutely es-

has been issued from Washington, probably by members of the Japanese Legation there. In the quotations from the correspondence that appear in these pages, the language of the translation — accurate as it is — has been largely changed, in order to make it coincide as closely as possible with the literal meaning of the original.

sential to her own repose and safety. Moreover, the political as well as commercial and industrial interests and influence which Japan possesses in Korea are paramount over those of other Powers, These interests and influence, Japan, having regard to her own security, cannot consent to surrender to, or share with, another Power.

"The Imperial Government, after the most serious consideration, have resolved to consult the Russian Government, in a spirit of conciliation and frankness, with a view to the conclusion of an understanding designed to compose questions which are at this time the cause of their anxiety. In the estimation of the Imperial Government, the moment is opportune for making the attempt to bring about the desired adjustment, and it is believed that, failing this opportunity, there would be no room for another understanding.

"The Imperial Government, reposing confidence in your judgment and discretion, have decided to place the delicate negotiations in your hands.

"It being the wish of the Imperial Government to place their present invitation to the Russian Government entirely on an official footing, you are accordingly instructed to open the question by presenting to Count Lamsdorff, Minister of Foreign Affairs of Russia, a *note verbale* to the following effect: —

"'The Japanese Government desire to remove from the relations of the two Empires every cause of future misunderstanding, and believe that the Russian Government share the same desire. The Japanese Government would therefore be glad to enter with the Imperial Russian Government upon an examination of the condition of affairs in the regions of the extreme East, where their interests meet, with a view to defining their respective special interests in those regions.

"'If this suggestion fortunately meets with the approval,

in principle, of the Russian Government, the Japanese
Government will be prepared to present to the Russian
Government their views as to the nature and scope of
the proposed understanding.'

"In presenting the foregoing note to the Russian Foreign Minister, you will be careful to make him understand that our purposes are entirely friendly, but that we
attach great importance to the subject.

"You will present the note to Count Lamsdorff as soon
as possible, and keep me fully informed regarding the
steps taken by you under this instruction ; and immediately upon the receipt of an affirmative reply from the
Russian Government, the substance of our proposals will
be telegraphed to you."

To this request of Japan, Count Lamsdorff expressed a perfect agreement,[1] for, as he had very
often said to Mr. Kurino, " an understanding between the two countries was not only desirable, but
was the best policy." " Should Russia and Japan
enter into a full understanding," said he, " no one
would in future attempt to sow the seeds of discord between the two countries." [2] The assent of
the Foreign Minister was later sustained by the
Czar.[3]

Thus the way was opened for an amicable in-
terchange of the views of the two Powers. This
auspicious beginning of the negotiations stands
in striking contrast to their disastrous end. The

[1] N.-R., No. 2.

[2] It is singular that even Count Lamsdorff should thus participate in the characteristic plaint of the Russians that they are
an object of unjust machinations of other nations.

[3] N.-R., No. 3, received at Tokio on August 6.

discrepancy was perhaps in no small measure due to a political situation at St. Petersburg which was completely beyond the control of Count Lamsdorff, and probably also of the Czar. It should be remembered that Baron Komura, like Marquis Itō, was of the opinion that the conclusion of a satisfactory agreement with Russia was not only desirable, but also possible. The same belief was strongly shared by Mr. Kurino. It is also difficult to suppose that Count Lamsdorff entered upon the negotiations with a deliberate intention to introduce into them insurmountable difficulties, as he was presently obliged to do, so as to bring them to a complete deadlock. On the contrary, his remarks quoted in the preceding paragraph seem to indicate that he and Mr. Kurino had frequently talked of the wisdom of coming to a perfect adjustment of the interests of the two Powers in the East, and that he was gratified that the opportunity was offered by the Japanese Government to give effect to what he had long considered " the best policy." About this time, however, it had begun to be surmised abroad that the peace party, with which the Count and M. Witte were said to be in sympathy, had been largely overshadowed by the less intelligent warlike fact. ~ It was unknown what were the results of the observations of General Kuropatkin, the then Minister of War, who had made a tour of the East between the end of April and the end of July. Nor was it possible to discover what took place in the great conference held at Port Arthur early in July, in which the General, as well as Admiral Alexieff, MM. Lessar, Pavloff, Rosen, and Pokotiloff, took part. However that may be, it could hardly be denied that henceforth the Eastern affairs passed under the sway of a less thoughtful body of men at St. Petersburg, and of that executive officer of great talent, but strategist and diplomat of unknown value, Admiral Alexieff, at Port Arthur. M. Witte was relieved of his Ministry of Finance, and transferred to the presidency of the council of ministers, which was known to be of small real authority. On August 13, an Imperial *ukase* was published in the Russian *Official Messenger*, stating that, " in view of the complex problems of administration of the eastern confines of the Empire, we [the Czar Nicolas] found it necessary to create a power capable of assuring the peaceful development of the country and satisfying urgent local needs." For this purpose, a special vice-regency called the Far East was created out of the Amur and Kwantung territories, and Admiral Alexieff was appointed Viceroy of the Far East. He was vested with supreme power in the civil administration of the territories, with the command of the naval forces in the Pacific and of all the troops quartered in the country under his jurisdiction, and with the management of the diplomatic relations of these regions with the neighboring States. The Viceroy was released from the jurisdiction of the Ministers at St. Petersburg, and the only control to be exercised over him by the central power was through a special committee of men [1] nominated by the Czar and presided over by himself.[2] Statutes concerning this special committee of the Far East — which has in itself no executive power — were promulgated on September 30.[3] When we consider the probable state of Russian politics at the time, the significance of thus elevating Alexieff and clothing him with enormous powers could hardly be concealed. Henceforth the control of the Eastern diplomacy of Russia seemed to have rested more with the Viceroy at Port Arthur than with the Foreign Minister at St. Petersburg.[4]

Admiral Alexieff was appointed Viceroy on August 13. On the preceding day,[5] the first Japanese note was handed to Count Lamsdorff by Mr. Kurino, who had held it for about a week pending the

[1] These men were, according to Article 2 of the Statutes of September 30, "the Ministers of the Interior, of Finance, of Foreign Affairs, and of War, the head of the Ministry of Marine, and such persons as His Majesty the Emperor may find it expedient to summon, either to sit permanently on the committee, or to take part temporarily at its meetings. The Viceroy of the Far East, being, by his duties, a member of the committee, shall be present at the meetings when he is in St. Petersburg."

[2] The *British Parliamentary Papers: China, No. 2 (1904)*, No. 144.

[3] *Ibid.*, No. 155.

[4] After the opening of hostilities in February of the present year, the Russian Foreign Office made a statement of Russia's case, in which it was said that, when the Japanese Government proposed in August, 1903, to open the negotiations, "Russia consented, and Viceroy Alexieff was charged to draw up a project for a new understanding with Japan in coöperation with the Russian Minister at Tokio. . . ." See p. 327, note 9, below.

[5] *N.-R.*, No. 6.

ADMIRAL ALEXIEFF

*Viceroy of the Far East*

Czar's assent to Japan's proposition of July 28, already quoted. In this note, delivered on August 12, Baron Komura wrote as follows : —

"In reference to my telegram of the 28th July, the Imperial Government, after giving most serious consideration to the condition of affairs in those regions where the interests of the two Powers meet, have decided to propose the following articles as the basis of an understanding between Japan and Russia : —

" 1.  'A mutual engagement to respect the independence and territorial integrity of the Chinese and Korean Empires, and to maintain the principle of equal opportunity for the commerce and industry of all nations in those countries.

" 2.  'A reciprocal recognition of Japan's preponderating interests in Korea and Russia's special interests in railway enterprises in Manchuria, and of the right of Japan to take in Korea, and of Russia to take in Manchuria, such measures as may be necessary for the protection of their respective interests as above defined, subject, however, to the provisions of Article 1 of this Agreement.

" 3.  'A reciprocal undertaking on the part of Russia and Japan not to impede the development of those industrial and commercial activities, respectively, of Japan in Korea and of Russia in Manchuria, which are not inconsistent with the stipulations of Article 1 of this Agreement.

" 'An additional engagement on the part of Russia not to impede the eventual extension of the Korean Railway into Southern Manchuria so as to connect with the Eastern Chinese and Shan-hai-kwan-Niu-chwang lines.

" 4.  'A reciprocal engagement that, in case it should be found necessary to send troops by Japan to Korea, or by

Russia to Manchuria, for the purpose either of protecting the interests mentioned in Article 2 of this Agreement, or of suppressing insurrection or disorder liable to create international complications, the troops so sent are in no case to exceed the actual number required, and are to be forthwith recalled as soon as their missions are accomplished.

"5. 'The recognition on the part of Russia of the exclusive right of Japan to give advice and assistance in the interest of reform and good government in Korea, including necessary military assistance.

"6. 'This Agreement to supersede all previous arrangements between Japan and Russia respecting Korea.'

"In handing the foregoing project to Count Lamsdorff," wrote Baron Komura to Mr. Kurino in the same dispatch which contained the proposed Articles, "you will say that it is presented for the consideration of the Russian Government in the firm belief that it may be found adequate to serve as a basis upon which to construct a satisfactory arrangement between the two Governments, and you will assure Count Lamsdorff that any amendment or suggestion he may find it necessary to offer will receive the immediate and friendly consideration of the Imperial Government. It will not be necessary for you to say much in elucidation of the separate items of the project, as they are largely self-explanatory ; but you might point out that the project taken as a whole will be found to be little more than a logical extension and amplification of the principles already recognized by, or of conditions embodied in the previous engagements [1] concluded between, the two Governments." [2]

[1] Evidently the reference is to the three Russo-Japanese agreements concerning Korea concluded in 1896 and 1898.

[2] *N.–R.*, No. 3, originally dated Tokio, August 6.

These articles are memorable, as their more essential features were never altered in the later notes from Japan, as the persistent rejection by Russia of the principles embodied in these articles inevitably ended in hostilities, and, the most important of all, as much of the future of the East would seem to depend upon whether these principles should win or fail through the war. The principles were as obvious as the note was " largely self-explanatory." At their basis was the desire for a general, lasting peace of the Far East, or, in other words, an effective elimination of unnatural, irritating circumstances, so that the East may develop its enormous material and moral resources, and thereby establish with the West an intimate and mutually beneficial relationship. Upon this fundamental desire were built two great principles, which had long been the mottoes of Eastern diplomacy; namely, the territorial integrity of, and the " open door " in, China and Korea. These principles, which Russia had frequently avowed on her own initiative, Japan now requested her to uphold mutually with herself. Side by side with these considerations, the vested interests and the peculiar position, respectively, of Russia in Manchuria and Japan in Korea, were to be reciprocally recognized by the two Powers, in such a way, however, as not to infringe the two great principles already named. Observe that the Russian interests in Manchuria were not less respected than the Japanese interests in Korea, nor was the Russian occupation of Manchuria more guarded against

than the Japanese annexation of Korea. The only
ground in the note for a possible misinterpretation
was the Article which provided for Japan's sole
right to advise and aid Korea for the cause of the
good government and reform of the latter. Experience had shown that the independence and progress
of Korea, upon which one half of Japan's own
future rested, would be possible only by the internal
reform and development of the Peninsular Empire,
and that, unfortunately, the task of reform could
not safely be left either with the indolent Korea
or with another Power, be it China or Russia, whose
ultimate object would be best served were Korea to
remain feeble. The reform of Korea may truly be
called the penalty of Japan's geographical position,
and the latter's success in the fulfillment of this
most delicate mission must depend on her sense
of just proportion and utmost self-control. And
nothing seems to kindle the Japanese nation with
a higher ambition than their profound determination to perform what they deem their historic mission
in the fairest spirit of human progress. Only along
these lines, moreover, by a peculiar coincidence of
circumstances, the securest interests of Japan as a
nation seem to lie. For it appears to be her singular fortune that her interests become every year
more closely tied with the best tried principles of
progress. Upon fairness her life depends, and upon
it the natural growth of the millions of the East
would seem to rest. It appeared, therefore, evident
to the Japanese statesmen that in no other manner

than along the course suggested by their propositions to Russia could the welfare of all the interested parties be assured, and the future repose and
progress of the East guaranteed. On the other
hand, however, nothing could be more distasteful
to the party presumably in control of the Eastern
policy of Russia at the time than the reciprocal understanding proposed by Mr. Kurino in his note of
August 12.

Before replying to this note, Count Lamsdorff
suddenly demanded, on August 23, that negotiations should be conducted at Tokio instead of at St.
Petersburg, as had been desired by Japan.[1] This
move of Russia was closely parallel to the policy
she once pursued in China regarding the lease of
Port Arthur, when she declined to negotiate at the
Russian Capital.[2] A discussion at St. Petersburg
might save it from many of the vexatious delays
which would naturally attend its being held at an
Eastern capital, away from the Foreign Office of
the Power whose interest counseled procrastination.
Of the several reasons presented by Russia for her
proposition, one was that the local knowledge of
Viceroy Alexieff had constantly to be consulted.
Japan pointed out that the proposed Agreement
concerned matters of principle, and not of local
detail.[3] Her repeated request, however, to negotiate

[1] *N.–R.*, No. 7.
[2] The *British Parliamentary Papers: China, No. 1 (1898)*,
Nos. 100 and 109.
[3] *N.–R.*, Nos. 8, 11.

at St. Petersburg was firmly refused by Russia, as was also Japan's suggestion that her note be made the basis of the discussion.[1] Negotiations were therefore transferred to Tokio, and the Japanese note and the Russian counter-note — the latter not then received — were together to serve as the base of the *pourparlers*.[2] This question, which marked the beginning of many long delays to follow, itself consumed two weeks before any real progress of the negotiations could be made.

After a delay of nearly eight weeks, Russia, on October 3, sent her counter-note, which, as will be seen from the following telegram of the 5th, from Baron Komura to Mr. Kurino, revealed the utter irreconcilability of the wishes of the two Powers : —

"Baron Rosen [Russian Minister at Tokio] came back from Port Arthur on the 3d instant. He called on me the same day, and handed me the following as the Russian counter-proposals, which, he said, had been sanctioned by His Majesty the Emperor of Russia, upon the joint representations of Admiral Alexieff and himself: —

"1. 'Mutual engagement to respect the independence and territorial integrity of the Korean Empire.

"2. 'Recognition by Russia of Japan's preponderating interests in Korea, and of the right of Japan to give advice and assistance to Korea tending to improve the civil administration of the Empire without infringing the stipulations of Article 1.

"3. 'Engagement on the part of Russia not to impede the commercial and industrial undertakings of Japan in Korea, nor to oppose any measures taken for the pur-

[1] *N.-R.*, Nos. 10, 11.    [2] *Ibid.*, No. 14, September 7.

pose of protecting them, so long as such measures do not infringe the stipulations of Article 1.

" 4. ' Recognition of the right of Japan to send, for the same purpose, troops to Korea, with the knowledge of Russia, but their number not to exceed that actually required, and with the engagement on the part of Japan to recall such troops as soon as their mission is accomplished.

" 5. ' Mutual engagement not to use any part of the territory of Korea for strategical purposes, nor to undertake on the coasts of Korea any military works capable of menacing the freedom of navigation in the Straits of Korea.

" 6. ' Mutual engagement to consider that part of the territory of Korea lying to the north of the thirty-ninth parallel as a neutral zone into which neither of the contracting parties shall introduce troops.

" 7. ' Recognition by Japan of Manchuria and its littoral as in all respects outside her sphere of interest.

" 8. ' This Agreement to supersede all previous agreements between Russia and Japan regarding Korea.' " [1]

In comparing this counter-note with the original note of Japan, it will at once be seen that Russia seriously reduced Japan's demands concerning Korea by excluding her right of rendering advice and assistance to Korea in the latter's military affairs, and also by quietly suppressing the important clause providing for mutual recognition of the principle of the equal economic opportunity for all nations in Korea. Moreover, Russia imposed upon Japan the following new conditions regarding Korea: not to use any part of the territory for stra-

[1] *N.-R.*, No. 17.

tegical purposes; not to fortify the southern coast; and to consider the territory north of the thirty-ninth parallel, covering nearly one third of the area of the Empire, as neutral[1] between the two Powers. As regards Manchuria, Russia silently discarded the two fundamental principles proposed by Japan and often avowed by Russia herself, namely, China's sovereignty over it and the equal economic opportunity for all nations therein. On the contrary, Russia requested Japan to declare Manchuria and its littoral as outside of her sphere of interest. If the Power which exchanged necessaries of life with Manchuria in fast growing quantities, controlled more than ninety per cent. of the exports at Niu-chwang, and numbered tens of thousands of its subjects residing in the Three Provinces, should be required by Russia to declare itself uninterested in Manchuria, the exclusive designs of Russia upon the territory would seem to need no stronger proof. The general tenor of the note of October 3 was, thus, to exclude Manchuria from discussion, and, furthermore, to restrict Japan's influence in Korea. Russia

[1] The Russian Government explained later, in the note delivered on January 6, 1904, that the creation of a neutral zone was "for the very purpose which the Imperial Japanese Government had likewise in view, namely, 'to eliminate everything that might lead to misunderstandings in the future;' a similar zone, for example, existed between the Russian and British possessions in Central Asia."— *N.-R.*, No. 38.

It is easy to see, however, that *neutralization* is merely *common appropriation* in a negative form, and might, like cases of the latter, as in Primorsk and Sakhalien, result in *absorption* by one of the two Powers between which the territory was neutralized.

explained that the question of Manchuria rested between herself and China, and that she had no reason to make any arrangement about it with a third Power. To this, Japan replied that she had asked from Russia no concession of any kind in Manchuria, but merely requested her to recognize anew the principles which she had voluntarily and repeatedly professed. Such a recognition, Japan contended, was of vital interest to her, inasmuch as the Russian occupation of Manchuria would continually threaten the independence of Korea.[1] It was evident from Russia's counter-note that there lay an impassable gulf between the propositions of the two Powers, not only in the actual terms under discussion, but also in the principles involved in them, for, to all appearance, nothing could prove more clearly that Russia was bent upon absorbing and closing up all Manchuria, as well as marking out Northern Korea as an eventual sphere of her influence, and that she was unwilling to recognize the profound and increasing common interest of Japan and Manchuria, and the vital importance to the former of the independence, strength, and development of Korea.

The date fixed in the Convention in April, 1902, for the final evacuation of Manchuria arrived on October 8, 1903 — five days after the Russian counter-note was received by Japan, but the day came and passed with no sign of the evacuation. On the contrary, the Russian Minister at Peking was engaged, regardless of the negotiations at

[1] *N.-R.*, No. 20.

Tokio between his Government and the Japanese, in urging Prince Ching to change the terms of the Convention. Those who had been impressed by the manner and contents of the Russian reply to the Japanese note did not fail to observe in M. Lessar's conduct at Peking another proof of the slight weight which the Russians attached to the overtures of Japan at least concerning Manchuria. For, if Russia succeeded in securing China's consent to her new demands regarding Manchuria, which in every way transgressed the principles contained in the Japanese note, the Manchurian negotiations between Russia and Japan would become unnecessary. The Russian course of action at Tokio and Peking was thus consistent in ignoring Japan's vital interests in Manchuria, and, therefore, was regarded as consistently insulting to Japan. The secret of the situation seemed to be, as has been already suggested, that the centre of gravity of Russian diplomacy in the East had largely shifted from St. Petersburg to Port Arthur — from Count Lamsdorff to the inflexible Admiral Alexieff. Ever since the latter had convened, at Port Arthur, early in July, a large council of the diplomatic, military and naval, and financial agents of Russia in the Eastern Asiatic countries, as well as General Kuropatkin, who was then traveling in the Orient, it had appeared that the Viceroy of the Far East,[1] and

---

[1] Before August 13, when he was appointed Viceroy of the Far East, Alexieff was as yet Governor-General of the Kwantung region.

not the Foreign Office at the Russian Capital, was the guiding spirit of the Czar's policy in Korea, China, and Japan. Hereafter, Count Lamsdorff could perhaps moderate the terms, and transmit to Japan the revised contents, of the Viceroy's unconciliatory views, but had otherwise lost the control of the situation. The reason why Alexieff had risen to such a great influence may not be known until the relations he had with M. Bezobrazoff, the late von Plehve, and other influential politicians at St. Petersburg of that day, become more clearly understood than they are to-day. As to the probable views of the Viceroy regarding the situation in the East, it is not hard to infer them from the diplomatic history in China, Korea, and Japan, during the half year ending with February, 1904.

Let us make a brief review of the· diplomatic manœuvres of the Russian Representative at Peking regarding Manchuria, which proceeded much as if his Government were not engaged in negotiations with Japan in respect to the same territory. The secret Manchurian agreement which was reported to have been concluded on July 20 [1] was probably unfounded, and its detail may otherwise be safely left unnoticed. The nature of the Russian policy regarding Manchuria could, however, be inferred· from the remarkable exchange of views which took place at London in July between Lord Lansdowne and the Russian Ambassador, Count Benckendorff. In this interview on July 11, the latter said, in

[1] The Japanese dailies.

effect: " Whatever may be the result of the negotiations which are pending between Russia and
China, . . . the Imperial Government [of Russia]
has no intention of opposing the gradual opening
of China, as *commercial relations develop*,[1] of some
towns in Manchuria to foreign commerce, *excluding, however, the right to establish ' Settlements.'*
This declaration does not apply to Harbin. The
town in question being within the limits of the concessions for the Eastern Chinese Railway, *is not
unrestrictedly subject to the Chinese Government;*[1]
the establishment there of foreign consulates must
therefore depend upon the consent of the Russian
Government." [2] The three conditions here printed
in italics would seem not only contradictory to the
declaration made by Count Lamsdorff to Mr. Mac-
Cormick on April 28,[3] but also almost tantamount
to opposing the opening of any new treaty port in
Manchuria. For it was well understood that the
desire on the part of some Powers for the speedy
opening of some new ports in Manchuria was largely
calculated to prevent the aggressive and exclusive
proceedings of Russia in that territory. If, as Count
Benckendorff suggested, the development of trade
relations was the sole reason for " gradually " opening some towns, if foreign settlements should be
excluded from the new ports, and if Harbin, and
logically all the towns situated at the " depots " of

---

[1] The italics in the quotation are the author's.
[2] *China, No. 2 (1904)*, No. 133 (Lansdowne to Scott).
[3] See pp. 246–248, above.

the railway, could not be opened without Russian consent, Manchuria, excepting the regions touching the few towns which had already been opened, would remain open to the growing influence of Russia, but practically sealed to the rest of the world.[1] This inference was presently demonstrated by the new demands made at the Peking Foreign Office by M. Lessar on September 6. These demands, presented, as they were, in the midst of the Russo-Japanese negotiations at Tokio and on the eve of the close of the period of Manchurian evacu-

[1] It is highly interesting that at this moment, when the Russian Government was, on the one hand, negotiating with Japan, and, on the other, proposing new demands upon China, the Russian Ambassador at London intimated the desire of his Government to come to an agreement with Great Britain regarding their interest in China. It appears that Russia wished Great Britain to declare Manchuria as outside of her sphere of interest, in return for a similar declaration by Russia regarding the Yangtsze valley. Lord Lansdowne's reply was characteristic. "I repeated," he wrote to Sir C. Scott, "that we should be glad to arrive at one [i. e., an agreement with Russia], but that it must, of course, include the Manchurian question. We could, however, of course not come to terms unless we were fully informed as to the intentions of the Russian Government [in Manchuria]. Count Benckendorff again asked me whether, if we were satisfied upon this point, we should be likely to *assist* in bringing about an arrangement between the Russian and Chinese Governments. I said that we should certainly make no secret of our concurrence, if we were thoroughly satisfied. Meanwhile, however, I was afraid that our attitude must remain observant and critical." — *China, No. 2 (1904)*, No. 142 (August 12). Cf. No. 139.

The Russian Government could not have forgotten that Great Britain had agreed with Japan, on January 30, 1902, that neither of the two Powers should come to a separate understanding with another Power regarding China or Korea without a full and frank discussion between themselves.

ation, deserve a special notice. Briefly stated, M. Lessar requested : (1) that China should not alienate, in any manner, any port, of whatever size, of Manchuria to any other Power ; (2) that Russia should be allowed to construct wharves on the Sungari River, to connect them by telegraph, and to station Russian troops to protect the telegraph lines and the ships plying the river ; (3) that Russia should be allowed to establish post stations along the road from Tsitishar to Blagovestchensk ; (4) that no greater duties should be imposed on goods brought into Manchuria by rail than those now imposed on goods transported by road or river ; (5) that after the withdrawal of the Russian troops, the branches of the Russo-Chinese Bank should be protected by Chinese troops, but at the cost of the Bank ; and (6) that a Russian doctor should be appointed member of the Sanitary Board at Niu-chwang.  On these conditions, the Russian forces would evacuate Niu-chwang and the rest of the Sheng-king Province on October 8, the Kirin Province after four months, and the Hei-lung Province at the end of one year.[1] Of these, the first demand was interpreted to imply the prevention of the establishment of new foreign settlements and concessions in any part of Manchuria.  As to the meaning of stationing troops along the Sungari and building a post road from Tsitsihar to Blagovestchensk, it is instructive to observe that Prince Ching opined that, if China conceded these demands and Russia then nominally withdrew, the

[1] *China, No. 2 (1904)*, Nos. 147, 148, 149, 156.

latter would still be in virtual possession of the
territory.[1] The British and Japanese Ministers at
Peking naturally warned China not to accept the
Russian propositions.[2] The Foreign Office, after
some hesitation,[3] finally refused all of the demands
in a written note, on September 24.[4] This refusal,
however, by no means terminated the Manchurian
negotiations at Peking.  As the Chinese Government
showed inclinations, vacillating as they were, to
sympathize with Japan in her efforts to maintain
the sovereign rights of China in Manchuria, M.
Lessar is said to have resorted to occasional threats
that, if a war should occur between Russia and
Japan and the latter be defeated, China would re-
pent her sorry plight only too late, for then Manchuria would not be hers.  Particularly vigorous
was his obstruction of the effort of the United
States Commissioners at Shanghai to secure the
opening of new ports in Manchuria to foreign
trade.[5]  In spite of all this, however, on October 8
— the very day once fixed for the final evacuation
of Manchuria — the American-Chinese treaty was
signed, opening Mukden and An-tung as treaty
ports.  The next day saw the conclusion of the
Japanese-Chinese treaty, bearing the date of October 8, which also provided for the opening of

[1] *China, No. 2 (1904)*, No. 150.
[2] *Ibid.*, Nos. 149, 151, 153, 160.
[3] *Ibid.*, Nos. 147 and 156.
[4] *Ibid.*, Nos. 150 and 160.
[5] See pp. 252 ff., above.

Mukden and Tatung-kao. It was perhaps nothing more than a singular coincidence of circumstances that Mukden should be, as it was, occupied by Russian soldiers shortly after its opening had been secured by the United States and Japan. Early in the morning of October 28, 780 Russian soldiers with eight cannon suddenly, without warning, rushed through the city gate and took possession of the *Yamên* of the Tartar General, Tsêng-chi, holding him in custody and reducing the military forces under his control.[1] A generally accepted ground for this precipitous act was naught more than that a subordinate Taotai under the jurisdiction of the Tartar General had undertaken to punish some recalcitrant bandits who had been under Russian employ. The *Journal de Saint Pétersbourg* explained, however, that the seizure of Mukden was owing " to the apathy of the Chinese authorities, to the non-execution of the promises made on their part, and to the agitation which prevailed in the district." [1] Mukden being the sepulchral city of the reigning dynasty of China, its sudden occupation by the Russians appeared to have aroused a bitter resentment among the educated classes throughout the Empire.

Turning to the Korean frontier, the conduct of the Russians at Yong-am-po [2] on the left side of the Yalu, near its mouth, had now assumed an unmistakably political character. Early in July a telegraphic connection had been made without permission with

[1] *China, No. 2 (1904)*, No. 159.     [2] See pp. 289 ff., above.

An-tung, a strategic centre in Eastern Manchuria. At the instance of the Japanese Minister, the Korean Government succeeded in enforcing the removal of the line.[1] Late in the same month, the Commissioner of Forestry of Korea and Baron Gunzburg visited Yong-am-po, and drafted an agreement leasing the port to the Timber Company, nominally represented by the Baron. The contract bore neither a definite period of time for the lease nor fixed area of the leased territory, in the Korean text of the agreement, but, according to the Russian document, the lease is said to have extended over twenty years and covered a space equivalent to 204 acres. The company also was granted, in the Korean text, judiciary rights over the residents within the leased area.[2] At the same time, extensive works had been started by the Russians at Yong-am-po, including the erection of large brick buildings and the laying out of roads, streets, and light railways, to be later increased by what was conceded to be a fort; while, beyond the river, the military forces at An-tung and other centres had been in the process of augmentation.[3] The situation had now become so grave that Mr. Hayashi, Japanese Minister at Seul, was obliged to enter sharp protests at the Korean Foreign Office against the conclusion of the lease agreement,[4] and to urge

[1] The *Kokumin*, Seul telegrams, July 6, 10, 17 (1903).
[2] *Ibid.*, July 23, 27 ; August 2, 8, 18.
[3] *Ibid.*, July 27, etc.
[4] *Ibid.*, August 12, 14, 23 (cf. July 17, etc.).

again the opening of Wiju, and now also of Yong-am-po, to foreign trade. Both the British and American Representatives also pressed the Seul Government to open these ports.[1] The Russian Minister, M. Pavloff, however, was as strenuously opposed to the opening of these ports as Mr. Hayashi was to the conclusion of the lease agreement. The conditions were almost identical with those in 1898 under which Great Britain urged the opening of Talien-wan, so as to counteract the Russian aggression upon it and Port Arthur, and also with those in Manchuria, in this same year, where the American and Japanese Governments demanded the opening of new ports in order to prevent the exclusion of foreign trade and industry from Manchuria under Russian rule. The struggle between the open and the exclusive policy, however, continued much longer in Korea than in China, owing largely to the extremely unstable political conditions at Seul, which enabled the Russian diplomats oftener and longer to influence the Korean court.[2] As regards the lease of Yong-am-po, the Korean Government was now so alive to the serious nature of the agreement that

[1] The *Kokumin*, August 10, September 2, etc.

[2] The opening of Wiju was once granted by the Foreign Office, but the Emperor refused to sanction it. — *Ibid.*, November 21. This is another illustration of the peculiar circumstances at Seul, that there exist two political centres, the Government and the Court. (The opening of neither Wiju nor Yong-am-po had been effected before the outbreak of the present war.)

it proposed to modify its terms late in August.[1]
M. Pavloff, however, persistently urged the Korean
Government to ratify the original agreement. On
August 27, for instance, he and Baron Gunzburg
remained at the Foreign Office from one to six
o'clock in the afternoon, requesting the immediate
conclusion of the contract, until the Foreign Minister escaped out of the door and tendered his
resignation.[2] At the same time, the conduct of the
Russians on the frontier grew even more menacing
than before. The cutting of timber was started at
different points, where many Koreans were forced
into unpaid service, and the bandits in Russian
employ created disorder among peaceful citizens.[3]
Moreover, according to the reports of Korean officials, the Russians had occupied at Yong-am-po —
now named Nicolas — a ground far more extensive
than the lease-area stipulated in the yet unratified
agreement.[4] All this while, the Russians at the
Capital exercised a powerful influence over both Yi
Keun-thaik and Yi Yong-ik, two of the most noted
politicians at Seul, and over the strong party upholding the interests of Lady Öm.[5] It was through

[1] The *Kokumin*, August 29.

[2] *Ibid.*, August 27, 29.

[3] *Ibid.*, September 29.

[4] About 2¾ by 5¾ miles. — *Ibid.*, November 1. Late in December, a report reached the Korean Government from the frontier
that the Russians had forbidden all but their countrymen to
enter into the Russian territory at Yong-am-po. — *Ibid.*, December 23.

[5] Many stories have been told of M. Pavloff's influence over

these pro-Russian people that the unique idea of declaring the neutrality of Korea before the outbreak of any war — an idea which had more than once been unsuccessfully proposed[1] — was again brought forward, and finally, early in 1904, carried into effect in an awkward manner.[2]

Russian activity in Korea and Manchuria, which has been briefly described, may be said to constitute

the venal politicians of Seul. Of these, two are given below, which are not verifiable, but certainly interesting.

Yi Keun-thaik is said to have told the Emperor, late in December, 1903, that the following assurance had been given by the Russian Representative: if the Korean refusal to open Wiju and Yong-am-po to foreign trade should result in the mobilization of Japanese forces, Russia would also dispatch troops against them; in 1894, Korea erred when she relied on China, but Russia was not a China, and might implicitly be relied upon. — The *Kokumin*, telegram, December 25.

One day, it is said, M. Pavloff remarked in the presence of the Korean Emperor and his attendants: "The Koreans often rely upon Japan, or else are afraid of her, but where in the world is Japan?" Then he scanned a map through a pocket magnifier, and said: "Oh, I find a tiny country called Japan in a corner of the Pacific Ocean. My Russian Empire is the greatest country on the globe, spreading over two continents. If Korea relies upon our Empire, she will be as safe as in navigating a sea in a colossal vessel. Should Japan object to it, our Russia would only have to do thus." Here, placing a few matches on his palm, he blew them off. — The *Kyōiku Jiron*.

[1] In the latter half of 1900, for example.

[2] Korean neutrality is said to have been telegraphed to the Korean Representatives abroad through the French channel. It was not until some time after the other Powers had received the declaration that it reached Japan. Russia, it will be remembered, told the world that Japan infringed the neutrality of Korea when the former's warships had an encounter with the "Variag" and "Koietz" at Chemulpo. See pp. 355 ff., below.

the reverse side of the diplomacy of the Czar's Government at Tokio. The actual control of the Eastern situation having probably passed from the central power to Port Arthur, it was now founded, perhaps not upon greater practical wisdom than before, but apparently upon a uniform basis. For the conclusion is forced upon the student that Viceroy Alexieff's policy must have been, on the one hand, to deal with Japan's overtures lightly and leisurely, but, on the other, to hasten the establishment of Russian control in Manchuria and upon the Korean frontier, so that Japan might in time be compelled to bow to the situation and accept terms dictated by Russia. The proof of this policy had already seemed abundantly sufficient by the time when the Russian counter-note reached Baron Komura on October 3. It is impossible to tell whether, in framing such a policy, the Viceroy had taken into consideration the fact that the entire nation of Japan felt as one man that they had come to the greatest crisis known in their long history.

# CHAPTER XIX

## THE RUSSO-JAPANESE NEGOTIATIONS, II

The Russian counter-note having been received on October 3, Baron Komura began to confer with Baron Rosen upon the basis of both the Japanese note and the Russian reply.[1] Meanwhile, the Japanese statesmen again held deliberations on the 10th and 24th of October,[2] and agreed upon the " irreducible minimum," which was accordingly communicated to the Russian Minister on the 30th in the form of the following note : —

"1. Mutual engagement to respect the independence and territorial integrity of the Chinese and Korean Empires.

"2. Recognition by Russia of Japan's preponderating interests in Korea, and of the right of Japan to give to Korea advice and assistance, including military assistance, tending to improve the administration of the Korean Empire.

"3. Engagement on the part of Russia not to impede the development of the commercial and industrial activities of Japan in Korea, nor to oppose any measures taken for the purpose of protecting those interests.

"4. Recognition by Russia of the right of Japan to send troops to Korea for the purpose mentioned in the preceding Article, or for the purpose of suppressing in-

[1] *N.-R.*, Nos. 18, 19, 20, 21.    [2] The Japanese dailies.

surrection or disorder calculated to create international complications.

"5. Engagement on the part of Japan not to undertake on the coasts of Korea any military works capable of menacing the freedom of navigation in the Korean Straits.

"6. Mutual engagement to establish a neutral zone on the Korean-Manchurian frontier extending fifty kilometres on each side, into which zone neither of the contracting parties shall introduce troops without the consent of the other.

"7. Recognition by Japan that Manchuria is outside her sphere of special interest, and recognition by Russia that Korea is outside her sphere of special interest.

"8. Recognition by Japan of Russia's special interests in Manchuria, and of the right of Russia to take such measures as may be necessary for the protection of those interests.

"9. Engagement on the part of Japan not to interfere with the commercial and residential rights and immunities belonging to Russia in virtue of her treaty engagements with Korea, and engagement on the part of Russia not to interfere with the commercial and residential rights and immunities belonging to Japan in virtue of her treaty engagements with China.

"10. Mutual engagement not to impede the connection of the Korean Railway and the Eastern Chinese Railway when those railways shall have been eventually extended to the Yalu.

"11. This Agreement to supplant all previous Agreements between Japan and Russia respecting Korea." [1]

It will be seen from this note that Japan made several important concessions. These naturally fall

[1] N.-R., No. 22.

under three classes : concessions made to an expressed wish of Russia; those in which desires of
Russia were changed from a one-sided into a reciprocal form; and those made voluntarily on the
part of Japan. To the first class belongs the free
passage of the Korean Straits (Article 5), while the
neutralization of territory on both sides of the
northern frontier (Article 6), and the mutual declaration that Korea was beyond the sphere of the
" special " interests of Russia, and Manchuria of Japan (Article 7), may be said to fall under the second
class. Purely voluntary concessions may be said to
consist of the tenth Article regarding the Eastern
Chinese and Korean Railways meeting on the Yalu,
and a part of the eighth Article, in which the
" special " interests — not necessarily in the railway
work alone, as in the first Japanese note — of Russia in Manchuria were unequivocally recognized.
Other Articles are largely identical with those of the
first note, except the new ninth Article, which embodied the matter-of-fact principle that the treaty
rights of Russia in Korea, and of Japan in Manchuria, should be mutually respected. Taken as a
whole — with the only exception regarding the preponderating interests of Japan in Korea, and the
natural wishes of Japan arising from this peculiar
situation, the former of which had been wholly,[1]
and the latter partially,[2] recognized by Russia —

[1] In Article 3 of the Nishi-Rosen Procotol of 1898, and in
Article 2 of the Russian counter-note of October 3.
[2] See the same Article of the counter-note.

the prevailing characteristic of the second Japanese note may be said to be its reciprocal nature. The special interests of Russia[1] in Manchuria counterbalanced the preponderant interests of Japan in Korea,[2] and each other's right to take necessary measures to protect those interests was recognized.[3] At the same time, Manchuria was declared as far beyond the sphere of Japanese special interests as was Korea of the Russian,[4] while, on the other hand, the treaty rights of Russia in Korea, and of Japan in Manchuria, were to be respected as a matter of course.[5] If Russia was requested not to impede the economic activity of the Japanese in Korea,[6] Japan also agreed not to fortify the Korean coast.[7] The case of the neutral zone[8] need not be repeated. In spite, however, of the reciprocal nature of the note, it is unnecessary to say, so long as the control of the Eastern policy of Russia remained in the same hands as before, she could hardly be expected to acquiesce in the Japanese proposals.[9]

[1] Article 8.    [2] Article 2.    [3] Articles 4 and 8.
[4] Article 7.    [5] Article 9.
[6] Article 3, made necessary from the past experience in Korea.
[7] Article 5.    [8] Article 6.
[9] Observe the following passage from the explanatory note issued by the Foreign Office at St. Petersburg on February 9, 1904: —

"Last year, the Tokio Cabinet, under the pretext of establishing the balance of power and a more settled order of things on the shores of the Pacific, submitted to the Imperial Government a proposal for a revision of the existing treaties *with Korea*. Russia consented, and Viceroy Alexieff was charged to draw up a

As has been said, the second note was handed by Baron Komura to Baron Rosen on October 30. To this note, after a repeated application from Japan for a speedy answer,[1] Russia replied only on December 11, or more than forty days after the receipt of the Japanese note. This second reply of Russia [2] was as much a reduction of her former con-

project for a new understanding with Japan in coöperation with the Russian Minister at Tokio, who was intrusted with the nego-tiations with the Japanese Government. Although the exchange of views with the Tokio Cabinet on this subject was of a friendly character, Japanese social circles and the local and foreign press attempted in every way to produce a warlike ferment among the Japanese, and to drive the Government into an armed conflict with Russia. Under the influence thereof, the *Tokio Cabinet began to formulate greater and greater demands in the negotiations,* at the same time taking most extensive measures to make the country ready for war." (The italics are the author's.)

[1] *N.-R.*, Nos. 26, 27, 28, 29, 30, 32, 33.

[2] The second reply was as follows: —

"1. Mutual engagement to respect the independence and ter-ritorial integrity of the Korean Empire.

"2. Recognition by Russia of Japan's preponderating interest in Korea, and of the right of Japan to assist Korea with advice tending to improve her civil administration.

"3. Engagement on the part of Russia not to oppose the de-velopment of the industrial and commercial activities of Japan in Korea, nor the adoption of measures for the protection of those interests.

"4. Recognition by Russia of the right of Japan to send troops to Korea for the purpose mentioned in the preceding Article, or for the purpose of suppressing insurrections or dis-orders liable to create international complications.

"5. Mutual engagement not to make use of any part of the Korean territory for strategical purposes, and not to undertake on the Korean coast any military works capable of menacing the freedom of navigation in the Korean Straits.

"6. Mutual engagement to consider the territory of Korea to

cessions as was the second note of Japan an increase
upon hers; for Russia was now entirely silent on
the subject of Manchuria, and, regarding Korea,
repeated the restrictions proposed in September, as
if the second Japanese note had never reached her,
besides refusing to recognize Japan's right to give
Korea anything beyond mere advice for the reform
of her civil administration. In short, the second
counter-note was equivalent to the first *minus* the
clauses regarding Manchuria and Japan's right to
assist Korea in the latter's reform. The possibility
of a reconciliation of the views of the two Powers
now appeared remoter than before. If the exact
contents of the reply had been publicly shown to
the Japanese people, it would have been extremely
difficult for the Katsura Cabinet to control their
resentment against what would have been regarded
under the circumstances as a deliberate insult to
their country.

After another meeting of the Cabinet members
and Councilors on the 16th, Baron Komura made
one more attempt to appeal to the friendly sentiment
of the Russian Government. The nature of the
third Japanese overture will be seen from the fol-

the north of the thirty-ninth parallel as a neutral zone, within
the limits of which neither of the contracting parties shall introduce troops.

"7. Mutual engagement not to impede the connection of the
Korean and Eastern Chinese Railways, when those railways
shall have been extended to the Yalu.

"8. Abrogation of all previous agreements between Russia
and Japan respecting Korea." — *N.-R.*, No. 34.

lowing dispatch, telegraphed by the Baron to Mr. Kurino on the 21st : —

"In my interview with the Russian Minister on December 21, I pointed out that, between our original proposals and the new Russian counter-proposals, there was a fundamental difference concerning the geographical sphere of the understanding. After fully explaining how the Imperial Government had come to consider it desirable, in the general interest, to include in the proposed understanding all the regions in the Extreme East where the interests of the two Empires met, I expressed the hope that the Russian Government would reconsider their position regarding that branch of the question. I also informed him, in detail, of the amendments which the Imperial Government considered it necessary to introduce into Russia's new counter-proposals. Accordingly, in order to remove every possibility of misunderstanding on the part of Russia respecting the attitude of the Imperial Government, you are instructed to deliver to Count Lamsdorff a *note verbale* to the following effect : —

"'The Imperial Government have examined with great care the new Russian counter-proposals of the 11th instant. They regret that the Russian Government did not agree to extend the compass of the suggested understanding over the territory whose inclusion was deemed essential by Japan.

"'The Imperial Government, in their original proposition to the Russian Government in August last, endeavored to make it entirely clear that they desired, with a view to remove from the Japanese-Russian relations every cause for future misunderstanding, to bring within the purview of the proposed arrangement all those regions in the Extreme East where the interests of the two

MR. KURINO
*Late Japanese Minister at St. Petersburg*

Empires met. They cannot believe that a full realization
of that desire could be expected if a large and important
section of those regions was wholly excluded from the
understanding. Accordingly, the Imperial Government
feel constrained to ask the Russian Government to reconsider their position on the subject, and they hope that
the Russian Government will be able to see their way
to arrive at a satisfactory solution of the question.

"'The Imperial Government also find it necessary to
ask for the following amendments to the new Russian
counter-proposals: —

"'*a*. ARTICLE II. to read: Recognition by Russia of
Japan's preponderating interests in Korea, and of the
right of Japan to give Korea advice and assistance tending to improve the administration of the Korean Empire;

"'*b*. ARTICLE V. to read: Mutual engagement not to
undertake on the Korean coast any military works capable of menacing the freedom of navigation in the Korean
Straits; and

"'*c*. ARTICLE VI. to be suppressed.

"'Not only as the main points of these amendments
cannot be said to be in excess of the modifications which
were agreed to *ad referendum* at Tokio, but also as the
Imperial Government considered those changes indispensable, it is believed that they will receive the ready
agreement of the Russian Government.'

"In presenting the foregoing note to Count Lamsdorff,
you will say that I have spoken to Minister Rosen in a
similar sense, and you will also express the desire for a
prompt reply." [1]

Mr. Kurino carried out his instructions on December 23, and telegraphed on the same day to
Baron Komura: " . . . He [Count Lamsdorff]

[1] *N.-R.*, No. 35.

told me he had received a telegram from Minister Rosen, stating that the latter had had an interview with Baron Komura, and that particulars would follow; but such particulars had not yet been received by him [the Count.] [1] When I handed him the *note verbale*, he received it, and said that he would do his best to send the Russian answer at the earliest possible date; but added that he would have to communicate with Viceroy Alexieff. In conclusion I stated to the Count that, under existing circumstances, it might cause serious difficulties, even complications, if we failed to come to an *entente*, and I hoped he would exercise his best influence so as to enable us to reach the desired end." [2]

When Minister Kurino saw Count Lamsdorff on January 1, 1904, the latter, as he had been persistently doing during the past few days, remarked that he saw no reason why an *entente* could not be arrived at, for Minister Rosen would soon be instructed to proceed with the negotiations in a friendly and conciliatory spirit.[3] Other statements of the same pacific nature were frequently made, not only by the Count, but also by the Czar, and were circulated through the press and foreign telegraphic service. When, however, the reply of Russia [4]

[1] Is it probable that Baron Rosen consulted Viceroy Alexieff by telegraph before he did Count Lamsdorff?

[2] *N.-R.*, No. 36.

[3] *Ibid.*, No. 38.

[4] The Russian counter-note was as follows: —

"Having no objection to the amendments to Article 2 of the

reached Tokio on January 6, it was found that here again, as in the first reply of September last, the recognition by Japan of Manchuria and its coast as beyond her sphere of interest — the word "special" not preceding the last word — was insisted upon, while, as before, no mention was made of the territorial integrity of China in Manchuria. As regards the equal opportunity for the enterprise of other nations, it should be noted that Russia now agreed to insert a clause not to obstruct the enjoyment by Japan and other Powers of the treaty

Russian counter-proposals as proposed by the Imperial Japanese Government, the Russian Government considers it necessary: —

"1. To maintain the original wording of Article 5, which had already been agreed to by the Imperial Japanese Government, that is to say, 'mutual engagement not to use any part of the territory of Korea for strategical purposes, not to undertake on the coasts of Korea any military works capable of menacing the freedom of navigation in the Korean Straits.' [The Japanese Government had, as was pointed out by Baron Komura in the dispatch No. 39, never agreed to the first half of Article 5.]

"2. To maintain Article 6 concerning a neutral zone (this for the very purpose which the Imperial Japanese Government has likewise in view, that is to say, to eliminate everything that might lead to misunderstanding in the future; a similar zone, for example, exists between the Russian and British possessions in Central Asia).

"In case the above conditions are agreed to, the Russian Government would be prepared to include in the projected agreement an article of the following tenor: —

"'Recognition by Japan of Manchuria and her littoral as being outside her sphere of interests, whilst Russia, within the limits of that province, will not impede Japan nor other Powers in the enjoyment of the rights and privileges acquired by them under existing treaties with China, exclusive of the establishment of settlements.'" — *N.-R.*, No. 38.

rights which they had acquired from China in regard to Manchuria, but only on the condition of maintaining the clauses on the neutral zone in Korea and the non-employment by Japan of any part of Korea for strategical purposes. Moreover, the treaty rights of other Powers in Manchuria, which Russia would respect, explicitly excluded those concerning the foreign settlements in the open ports,[1] thus again evincing her exclusive policy. Over and above these considerations, it should be remembered that, as has been pointed out by Baron Komura,[2] the treaty rights which China had accorded to other Powers could not be maintained if her sovereignty in Manchuria, the existence of which Russia declined to assure Japan that she would respect, should cease.[3]

[1] See *British Parliamentary Papers : China, No. 2 (1902)*, Nos. 133, 136, 139, 142.

[2] His statements to the journalists on February 10 and at the Lower House on February 23.

[3] It is interesting to note that the Russian Representatives abroad declared to the Powers about the same time as the third counter-note was delivered at Tokio, that Russia "had no intention whatever of placing any obstacle in the way of the continued enjoyment by foreign Powers of the rights acquired by them [in Manchuria] in virtue of the treaties now in force." The exclusion of foreign settlements was not mentioned, but, judging from the counter-note of January 6, was implied.

When Count Benckendorff, Russian Ambassador at London, handed the memorandum on January 8 to Lord Lansdowne, the latter made characteristically blunt remarks, as will be seen from the following dispatch from him to Sir C. Scott: " . . . I could not help regretting that Russia should have found it impossible to take even a single step in pursuance of the policy which she has thus prescribed for herself [regarding the evacua-

In a few days there took place an important event which made the Russian position untenable. The Chinese-American [1] and Chinese-Japanese [2] commercial treaties which had been concluded on October 8, 1903,[3] the date appointed for the final evacuation of Manchuria, were ratified on January 11, 1904, the former opening to the world's trade Mukden and An-tung, and the latter, Mukden and Tatung-kao, thus not only multiplying the treaty rights, including rights of foreign settlements, of Japan and the United States in Manchuria, but also forcibly reinstating the sovereign rights of the Chinese Empire in the territory, and directly reversing the exclusive claims of Russia therein. It will be recalled that Russia had recently seized Mukden, and had been strengthening her forces upon the Yalu, on which the other two new ports were situated. The United States Government, immediately upon the ratification of the treaty, appointed Consuls for the three new open ports.

To return to the Russo-Japanese negotiations. Thus far notes and replies, exchanged three times

tion of Manchuria]. I trusted that his Excellency would forgive me for telling him frankly that, in this country, people were looking for some concrete evidence of Russia's intention to make good her promises. An announcement, for example, that Niuchwang was to be evacuated at an early date would certainly have a reassuring effect. So far as I was aware, there was no local difficulty in the way."—*China, No. 2 (1904)*, Nos. 162, 163.

[1] The text is found in the *Monthly Summary of the Commerce and Finance of the U. S.* for January, 1904.

[2] In the press and the *Kwampō* of January 20.

[3] See pp. 252–254 and 317–318, above.

within a period of five months, must have made the
position of each negotiating Power perfectly clear
to the other. No further discussion could possibly
bring the two Governments nearer to a reconciliation of wishes so diametrically opposed. In the
mean time, the Japanese people were suffering from
enormous economic losses. A large part of their
raw materials had ceased to come, the shipping and
trade with Korea and Northern China had declined,
the fishing industry had been paralyzed, and, contrary to the tendency at normal times, the banks
had been embarrassed with an over-abundance of
funds.[1] On the other hand, Russia, while circulat-
ing the optimistic views of her Emperor and Foreign Minister, had continued her sharp diplomacy
at Seul and Peking, and pushed on land and sea
her vast warlike preparations in the East.[2]

Even then the Japanese Government would not
terminate its negotiations with Russia, for it was
well aware that upon the conduct of these negotiations the peace of the East depended. If the principles proposed by Japan were not accepted, the
integrity of China would be threatened, and the

---

[1] See the *Kwampō* for February 1 (p. 5), 5 (pp. 110–114), 18
(p. 243), 20 (pp. 280–281); Mr. E. H. Vickers's letter to the New
York *Evening Post*, March 1; Mr. Soyeda's address, in the
*Kokumin*, February 6; *ibid.*, on the fisheries.

[2] According to the estimate of the Japanese Government, Russia increased her forces in the Far East between April 8, 1903,
and the outbreak of the war, by 19 war-vessels aggregating
82,415 tons, and 40,000 soldiers, besides 200,000 more who
were about to be sent. See pp. 352–354, below.

independence of Korea, as well as the vital interest of Japan, would be profoundly endangered; thus the entire future of the Far East would be plunged into unknown perils. Under these circumstances, it seemed that Japan owed to the world as much of patience, as she owed to herself of determination. The situation was gravely discussed by the states-men on the 11th, and before the Throne again on the 12th.[1] On the next day, January 13, now for the fourth time, and against the wishes of the majority of the people, the Government of Tokio reminded Russia of the serious position in which the two Powers found themselves, and begged her to reconsider the situation. Observe the following telegram of the same date from Baron Komura to Mr. Kurino: —

"You are instructed to deliver to Count Lamsdorff the following *note verbale* in order to confirm to him the views I have communicated to Baron Rosen on the 13th Jan-uary: —

"'The Imperial Government, with a view to arriving at a pacific solution of the pending questions, and to firmly establishing for all time the basis of good relations between the two Powers, as well as to protect the rights and interests of Japan, have, from this point of view, given most careful and serious consideration to the reply of the Russian Government which was delivered by his Excellency Baron Rosen on the 26th instant. They have finally come to the conclusion that the following modifi-cations are necessary, i. e.: —

" 1. 'Suppression of the first clause of Article 5 of the

[1] The Japanese dailies.

Russian counter-proposals (presented to the Japanese Government through Baron Rosen on December 11), that is to say, not to use any part of Korean territory for strategical purposes.

"2. 'Suppression of the whole Article (6) concerning establishment of a neutral zone.

"3. 'The Russian proposal concerning Manchuria to be agreed to with the following modifications: —

"a. 'Recognition by Japan of Manchuria and its littoral as being outside her sphere of interest, and an engagement on the part of Russia to respect the territorial integrity of China in Manchuria.

"b. 'Russia, within the limits of Manchuria, will not impede Japan nor other Powers in the enjoyment of rights and privileges acquired by them under the existing treaties with China.

"c. 'Recognition by Russia of Korea and its littoral as being outside her sphere of interest.

"4. 'Addition of an Article to the following effect: Recognition by Japan of Russia's special interests in Manchuria, and of the right of Russia to take measures necessary for the protection of those interests.

"'The grounds for these amendments having been frequently and fully explained on previous occasions, the Imperial Government do not think it necessary to repeat the explanations, beyond expressing their earnest hope for reconsideration by the Russian Government. It is sufficient to say that the suppression of the clause excluding the establishment of settlements in Manchuria is desired because it conflicts with stipulations of the new commercial treaty between Japan and China. In this respect, however, Japan will be satisfied if she receives equal treatment with other Powers which have already acquired similar rights in regard to settlements. . . .

"'Finally, the above-mentioned amendments being

proposed by the Imperial Government entirely in a spirit of conciliation, it is expected that they will be received with the same spirit at the hands of the Russian Government; and the Imperial Government further hope for an early reply from the Russian Government, since further delay in the solution of the question will be extremely disadvantageous to the two countries.' " [1]

An early reply was urged by Mr. Kurino at least four times,[2] but, even so late as February 1, Count Lamsdorff declined even to name the date on which his reply would be given; [3] and, indeed, the reply [4]

[1] *N.-R.*, No. 39.

[2] *Ibid.*, Nos. 40 (January 23), 42 (January 26), 44 (January 28), 46 (January 30). On January 26, Baron Komura again instructed Mr. Kurino to remind Count Lamsdorff that "in the opinion of the Imperial Japanese Government, a further prolongation of the present state of things being calculated to accentuate the gravity of the situation, it was their earnest hope that they would be honored with an early reply, and that they wished to know at what time they might expect to receive the reply." — No. 42. The probable nature of the forthcoming reply was also inquired into, without success, even so late as January 30.

[3] No. 47. It is unnecessary to point out the various excuses Count Lamsdorff presented for the delay. One of them was particularly significant, that is, that the opinions of Viceroy Alexieff and of the Cabinet Ministers at St. Petersburg had to be harmonized. — *Ibid.*

[4] Mr. Kurino telegraphed to Baron Komura at 5.05 A. M., February 5: —

"In compliance with the request of Count Lamsdorff, I went to see him at 8 P. M., February 4. He told me that the substance of the Russian answer had just been telegraphed to Viceroy Alexieff, to be transmitted by him to Minister Rosen. The Viceroy might happen to introduce some changes so as to meet local circumstances ; but in all probability, there would which was being framed was found later to have contained substantially the same points as the three previous replies — points some of which had been repeatedly and unequivocally demonstrated to be entirely irreconcilable with the vital interests of Japan. Just at this time, the activity of the Russian forces in the East seemed to have been accelerated : on January 21, numbers of infantry and artillery left Port Arthur and Dalny for the Korean frontier, soon to be followed by contingents from

be no such changes. The Count then stated, as his own opinion, that : —

" 'Russia desired the principle of the independence and integrity of Korea, and, at the same time, considered the free passage of the Korean Straits necessary. Though Russia was willing to make every possible concession, she did not desire to see Korea utilized for strategic purposes against Russia. He also believed it profitable, for the consolidation of good relations with Japan, to establish by common accord a buffer region between confines of direct influence and action of the two Powers in the Far East.'

"The above was expressed by the Count entirely as his personal opinion, and, though I cannot be positive, I think that the substance of the Russian reply must probably be the same." — N.-R., No. 50. Cf. p. 350, below.

It should be noted that this note from Mr. Kurino reached Tokio at 5.15 P. M., or three hours and a quarter after the Japanese notes severing relations had been sent.

Count Cassini, in the following striking sentence, includes, among the contents of the last Russian reply, a point which was not in the least mentioned in Count Lamsdorff's personal opinion expressed to Mr. Kurino. M. Cassini says: " . . . However, in another effort to bring the negotiations to a peaceful conclusion, my country did all that dignity would permit, and *offered to give assurances again that the sovereignty of the Emperor of China in Manchuria would be recognized.*" — The *North American Review* for May, 1904, p. 686.

Liao-yang ; on the 28th, Viceroy Alexieff ordered
the troops on the Yalu to be placed upon a war
footing ; on February 1, the Governor of Vladivostok warned the Japanese Commercial Agent at the
port to prepare for withdrawing his compatriots to
Habarofsk, as he had received instructions from
his Government and was ready to proclaim martial
law at any time ; and, on the 3d, all the war-vessels located at Port Arthur, excepting one, steamed
out of the harbor.[1]

It was now considered by the Japanese Government that the critical point had been reached.  The

---

[1] From the reply of the Japanese Government to the Russian
charge that Japan had broken peace and taken Russia by surprise.  See pp. 352–353, below.

It should not be forgotten, at the same time, that Japan had
all the while been taking precautionary measures in the most
careful and exhaustive manner, not only in military and naval
affairs, but also in other matters connected therewith.  The difference between the Russian and Japanese attitude may thus
be stated: Russia apparently played the three-fold game of
employing sharp diplomacy at Seul and Peking, of strengthening her control over Manchuria and the Korean frontier, and of
endeavoring at once to intimidate Japan by vast warlike measures, and to evade her overtures till she might be compelled to
acquiesce in the situation to be at length perfected by Russia;
Japan expressed her wishes in straightforward language, and
relied upon her negotiations with Russia, which she, in spite
of extremely trying circumstances, conducted with the utmost
cordiality and patience, but at the same time prepared for any
emergency in which the unconciliating attitude of Russia might
probably result.  It will perhaps be always regretted by many
that the control of Russian diplomacy throughout the negotiations rested in the hands of those who seemed to fail to grasp
the exact state of Japan's mind in this greatest crisis of her
national existence.

Cabinet members and Privy Councilors held a conference on February 3, and again, on the next day,
before the Throne.   On February 5, at 2 P. M.,
two notes were telegraphed to Mr. Kurino, the one
communicating Japan's decision to break off negotiations which had not been met with proper consideration and had become useless, and to reserve to
herself the right to pursue an independent course
of action, in order to safeguard her interests and
rights and to protect her position menaced by Russia ; and the other stating that Japan had been
obliged to sever her now valueless diplomatic relations with the Russian Government.   We subjoin
the entire texts of the telegraphic messages from
Baron Komura to Mr. Kurino inclosing the above-
mentioned notes : —

"Further prolongation of the present situation being
intolerable, the Imperial Government have decided to
terminate the pending negotiations, and to take such independent action as they may deem necessary to defend
our position menaced by Russia, and to protect our rights
and interests. Accordingly you are instructed, immediately upon receipt of this telegram, to address to Count
Lamsdorff the following signed note: —

"'The Undersigned, Envoy Extraordinary and Minister
Plenipotentiary of His Majesty the Emperor of Japan,
has the honor, in pursuance of instructions from his Gov-
ernment, to address to His Excellency the Minister of
Foreign Affairs of His Majesty the Emperor of all the
Russias the following communciations: —

"'The Government of His Majesty the Emperor of
Japan regard the independence and territorial integrity

of Korea as essential to the repose and safety of their own country, and they are consequently unable to view with indifference any action tending to render the position of Korea insecure.

"'The obstinate rejections by the Russian Government, by means of amendments impossible of agreement, of Japan's proposals respecting Korea, the adoption of which the Imperial Government regard as indispensable to assure the existence of the Korean Empire and to safeguard Japan's preponderating interests in the peninsula ; and the obstinate refusals of Russia to enter into an engagement to respect China's territorial integrity in Manchuria, which is seriously menaced by the continued occupation of the province, notwithstanding Russia's treaty engagements with China and her repeated assurances to other Powers possessing interests in those regions — have made it necessary for the Imperial Government seriously to consider what measures of self-defense they are called upon to take.

"'In spite of Russia's repeated delays to reply without intelligible reasons, and of her naval and military activities, irreconcilable with pacific aims, the Imperial Government have exercised during the present negotiations a degree of forbearance which they believe affords sufficient proof of their loyal desire to remove from their relations with the Russian Government every cause for future misunderstanding. But finding in their efforts no prospect of securing from the Russian Government an adhesion either to Japan's moderate and unselfish proposals or to any other proposals likely to establish a firm and enduring peace in the Far East, the Imperial Government have no other alternative than to terminate the present futile negotiations.

"'In adopting this course, the Imperial Government reserve to themselves the right to take such independent

action as they may deem best to consolidate and defend
their menaced position, as well as to protect the acquired
rights and legitimate interests of the Empire.

"'The Undersigned, etc., etc.'" [1]

"You are instructed to address to Count Lamsdorff
a signed note to the following effect, simultaneously with
the note mentioned in my other telegram: —

"'The Undersigned, Envoy Extraordinary and Minister Plenipotentiary of His Majesty the Emperor of Japan,
has the honor, in pursuance of instructions from his Government, to address to His Excellency the Minister of
Foreign Affairs of his Majesty the Emperor of all the
Russias the following communications: —

"'Having exhausted without effect every means of
conciliation with a view to remove from their relations
with the Imperial Russian Government every cause for
future complications, and finding that their just representations and moderate and unselfish proposals made
in the interest of a firm and lasting peace in the Far East
are not receiving due consideration, and that their diplomatic relations with the Russian Government have for
these reasons ceased to possess any value, the Imperial
Government of Japan have resolved to sever those diplomatic relations.

"'In the further fulfillment of the command of his
Government, the Undersigned has also the honor to an-
nounce to his Excellency Count Lamsdorff that it is his
intention to take his departure from St. Petersburg with
the staff of the Imperial Legation on the . . . day.

"'The Undersigned, etc., etc.'" [2]

These notes were transmitted by the Japanese
Minister to Count Lamsdorff on February 6, at

[1] *N.–R.*, No. 48.                    [2] *Ibid.*, No. 49.

4 P. M., Baron Rosen having already been informed by Baron Komura of the severance of the negotiations and general diplomatic relations between the two Powers.[1] The first naval engagement occurred at Chemulpo two days later, followed by the naval battle at Port Arthur on the night of February 8–9, and, on the 10th, war was formally declared by the Emperors of both Powers. The Russian Sovereign's manifesto, which appeared in the *Official Messenger*, said : —

"We proclaim to all our faithful subjects that, in our solicitude for the preservation of that peace so dear to our heart, we have put forth every effort to assure tranquillity in the Far East. To these pacific ends we declared our assent to the revision, proposed by the Japanese Government, of the agreements existing between the two Empires concerning Korean affairs. The negotiations initiated on this subject were, however, not brought to a conclusion, and Japan, not even awaiting the arrival of our last reply and the proposals of our Government, informed us of the rupture of the negotiations and of diplomatic relations with Russia.

"Without previously notifying us that the rupture of such relations implied the beginning of warlike action, the

---

[1] Mr. Kurino left St. Petersburg on the 10th, and the next day saw the departure of Baron Rosen from Tokio. It was generally believed that the former had once sincerely desired that a satisfactory agreement between Russia and Japan should be effected. As for Baron Rosen, every one surmised that the respected gentleman was little responsible for the conduct of Russian diplomacy, of which he was regarded as an unfortunate agent. From a personal point of view, the sudden departure of both from their posts had something tragic about it, and Baron Rosen's situation was deeply sympathized with by the Japanese people.

Japanese Government ordered its torpedo-boats to make a sudden attack on our squadron in the outer roadstead of the fortress of Port Arthur. After receiving the report of our Viceroy on the subject, we at once commanded Japan's challenge to be replied to by arms.

"While proclaiming this our resolve, we, in unshakable confidence in the help of the Almighty, and firmly trusting in the unanimous readiness of all our faithful subjects to defend the Fatherland together with ourselves, invoke God's blessing on our glorious forces of the army and navy." [1]

The Japanese Imperial Rescript, countersigned by all the members of the Cabinet, and declaring war against Russia, read as follows : —

"We, by the Grace of Heaven, the Emperor of Japan, seated on the Throne occupied by the same dynasty from time immemorial, do hereby make proclamation to all our loyal and brave subjects : —

"We hereby declare war against Russia. We command our army and navy to carry on hostilities against her with all their strength, and we also command all our officials to make effort, in pursuance of their duties and in accordance with their powers, to attain the national aim, with all the means within the limits of the law of nations.

"We deem it essential to international relations, and make it our constant aim, to promote the pacific progress of our Empire in civilization, to strengthen our friendly ties with other States, and thereby to establish a state of things which would maintain enduring peace in the East, and assure the future security of our Empire without injury to the rights and interests of other Powers.  Our

[1] From the English translation in the London *Times*, February 11, 1904, p. 3.

BARON DE ROSEN
*Late Russian Minister at Tokio*

officials also perform their duties in obedience to our will, so that our relations with all Powers grow steadily in cordiality.

"It is thus entirely against our wishes that we have unhappily come to open hostilities against Russia.

"The integrity of Korea has long been a matter of the gravest concern to our Empire, not only because of the traditional relations between the two countries, but because the separate existence of Korea is essential to the safety of our Empire. Nevertheless, Russia, despite her explicit treaty pledges to China and her repeated assurances to other Powers, is still in occupation of Manchuria, and has consolidated and strengthened her hold upon it, and is bent upon its final absorption. Since the possession of Manchuria by Russia would render it impossible to maintain the integrity of Korea, and would, in addition, compel the abandonment of all hope for peace in the Far East, we expected, in these circumstances, to settle the question by negotiations and secure thereby a permanent peace. With this object in view, our officials by our order made proposals to Russia, and frequent conferences were held during the last half year. Russia, however, never met such proposals in a spirit of conciliation, but by her prolonged delays put off the settlement of the pending question, and, by ostensibly advocating peace on the one hand, and on the other secretly extending her naval and military preparations, sought to bring about our acquiescence. It is not possible in the least to admit that Russia had from the first a sincere desire for peace. She has rejected the proposals of our Empire; the safety of Korea is in danger; the interests of our Empire are menaced. At this crisis, the guarantees for the future which the Empire has sought to secure by peaceful negotiations can now only be sought by an appeal to arms.

" It is our earnest wishes that, by the loyalty and valor of our faithful subjects, peace may soon be permanently restored and the glory of our Empire preserved." [1]

## SUPPLEMENTARY NOTE TO CHAPTER XIX

IN view of the singular circumstances under which the war broke out, it would be a matter of permanent interest to the student of international law to observe the difference of opinion which arose between the contending Powers respecting the legality of opening hostilities before war was formally declared, and also respecting the so-called neutrality of Korea. We reproduce below, without comment, the charges of Russia and replies of Japan regarding these subjects.

On February 18, the Russian Government issued the following official *communiqué:* —

" Eight days have now elapsed since all Russia was shaken with profound indignation against an enemy who suddenly broke off negotiations, and, by a treacherous attack, endeavored to obtain an easy success in a war long desired. The Russian nation, with natural impatience, desires prompt vengeance, and feverishly awaits news from the Far East. The unity and strength of the Russian people leave no room for doubt that Japan will receive the chastisement she deserves for her treachery and her provocation of war at a time when our beloved Sovereign desired to maintain peace among all nations.

" The conditions under which hostilities are being carried on compel us to wait with patience for news of the

[1] The rescript appeared in the *Kwampō*, February 10, 1904. extra. An authoritative English translation, which has been slightly altered in our text in order to bring it nearer to the original language, was published in the London *Times*, February 12, 1904, p. 3.

success of our troops, which cannot occur before decisive actions have been fought by the Russian army. The distance of the territory now attacked and the desire of the Czar to maintain peace were causes of the impossibility of preparations for war being made a long time in advance. Much time is now necessary in order to strike at Japan blows worthy of the dignity and might of Russia, and, while sparing as much as possible the shedding of blood of her children, to inflict just chastisement on the nation which has provoked the struggle.

"Russia must await the event in patience, being sure that our army will avenge that provocation a hundred-fold. Operations on land must not be expected for some time yet, and we cannot obtain early news from the theatre of war. The useless shedding of blood is unworthy of the greatness and power of Russia. Our country displays such unity and desire for self-sacrifice on behalf of the national cause that all true news from the scene of hostilities will be immediately due to the entire nation." [1]

On February 20, the *Official Messenger* published the following account of the termination of the diplomatic relations between the two Powers: —

"On January 16, after receipt of the last Japanese proposals, the Russian Imperial Government at once proceeded to examine them. On January 25 Mr. Kurino, the Japanese Minister at St. Petersburg, in reply to his inquiry, was informed that the Czar had intrusted the consideration of these proposals to a special conference, which was to meet on January 28, and that his Majesty's decision would probably not be given before February 2.[2]

[1] The London *Times*, February 19, 1904, p. 3.
[2] The reports from Mr. Kurino do not agree with this statement of Russia. According to the former, it was on January 26, not the 25th, that Count Lamsdorff referred to the conference to be held on the 28th. The date February 2 in this connection does

On the last-named date the Czar gave orders to prepare
a draft of definite instructions for the Russian Minister
at Tokio on the basis of the deliberations of the special
conference.  On the day following, three telegrams were
dispatched to Viceroy Alexieff, containing the full text of
a draft statement, the reasons which prompted the Russian Government in making some modifications in the
Japanese proposals, and the general instructions for the
Russian Minister at Tokio concerning the presentation of
the reply to the Japanese Government.  In order to save
time, identical telegrams were sent direct to Baron Rosen.

"On February 4, forty-eight hours before the receipt
of the news of the rupture of diplomatic relations by
Japan, Count Lamsdorff notified the Japanese Minister of
the dispatch to Baron Rosen of the Russian proposals in
reply to the Japanese note.[1]   On February 5, a message
arrived from the Viceroy stating that he had heard from
the Baron that the latter had received  the Russian reply.
On the 6th, at four o'clock in the afternoon, the Japanese
Minister, quite unexpectedly, handed to the Russian Minister of Foreign Affairs two notes, the first of which notified the rupture of negotiations on the pretext that Russia
was evading a reply[2] to the Japanese proposals, while the

not appear till we  reach Mr. Kurino's dispatch of January 28.
Moreover, on January 30, the Count told him that he could not
tell him the exact date when the Russian reply would be sent.
See *N.-R.*, Nos. 43, 45, 47.

[1]  This is evidently an error.  The Count spoke to Mr. Kurino,
at 8 P. M., February 4, about the probable contents of the reply
purely as the former's personal opinion.  It was not an official
statement of the exact contents of the reply. — *N.-R.*, No. 50.
See p. 340, above.

[2]  This statement is incorrect and misleading.  Referring to the
text of the Japanese note (pp. 342–344, above), it will be seen that
it did not say that the Japanese Government would break off the
negotiations because Russia had been evading a reply to the

second announced the breaking off of diplomatic relations, and added that the Japanese Minister, with the
staff of the Legation, would leave St. Petersburg on the
10th. These notes were accompanied by a private letter
from the Japanese Minister to Count Lamsdorff, in which
the hope was expressed that the rupture of diplomatic
relations would be confined to as short a time as possible.

" On the same day, Admiral Alexieff, Baron Rosen, and
all the Russian Representatives in Peking, Tokio, and the
capitals of the great Powers were informed by urgent
telegrams of the rupture of diplomatic relations with
Japan and the issue of our Imperial order for the withdrawal of the Russian Legation from Tokio. The said
circular dispatch laid the responsibility of all consequences that might ensue on the Japanese Government.[1]

"Although the breaking off of diplomatic relations by
no means implies the opening of hostilities, the Japanese
Government, as early as the night of the 8th, and in the
course of the 9th and 10th, committed a whole series of
revolting attacks on Russian warships and merchantmen,
attended by a violation of international law. The decree
of the Emperor of Japan on the subject of the declaration
of war against Russia was not issued until the 11th instant." [2]

The substance of the reply of the Japanese Government
to these notes, of which the following is a free translation, was made public through the press on March 3: —

Japanese proposals. A reference was made to the prolonged
delays of Russia before giving replies, but the note did not state
that the delays were the only reason, still less that the delay of
"a" reply — i. e., the last reply — was the ground, for the rupture of negotiations.

[1] See a vigorous statement of this charge made by Count Cassini in the *North American Review* for May, 1904, pp. 681–682.

[2] The London *Times*, February 22, 1904, p. 5.

"The Russian Government, by their notes published on February 18 and 20, charged Japan with unexpectedly attacking, and gaining a treacherous victory over, the forces of Russia, a Power anxious to maintain peace, and stated that the severance of diplomatic relations by no means implied the opening of hostilities, and that, although Japan declared war only on February 11, she had since the 8th made revolting attacks upon Russian war-vessels and merchantmen and conducted herself in violation of principles of international law.

"That, however, Russia did not sincerely desire peace may be readily seen from the fact that she never in any manner met the negotiations of Japan in a conciliatory spirit, but put off the solution of the pending question by prolonged delays, and, at the same time, diligently extended her naval and military preparations. Since Russia failed in April, 1903, to carry out her pledge respecting the second part of her evacuation of Manchuria, the facts concerning the increase of Russian forces in the Far East have been as follows: —

"The following war-vessels were added: —

|  |  |  |
|---|---:|---|
| 3 battleships | 38,488 | tons |
| 1 armored cruiser | 7,726 | |
| 5 cruisers | 26,417 | |
| 7 torpedo-destroyers | 2,450 | |
| 1 gunboat | 1,334 | |
| 2 torpedo-tenders | 6,000 | |
| Total, 19 vessels | 82,415 | tons |

"Besides these, Russia sent by rail to Port Arthur material for framing torpedo-destroyers, of which seven had already been made, and armed two volunteer fleet steamboats at Vladivostok and hoisted the naval flag upon them.

"Moreover, Russia dispatched one battleship, three cruisers, seven torpedo-destroyers, and four torpedo-boats, aggregating about 37,040 tons, which were on their way to the East. The total of all these vessels would therefore reach the tonnage of about 113,000 tons.

"As regards the increased land forces, Russia, beginning with the two brigades of infantry, two battalions of artillery, and certain numbers of cavalry and of the commissariat, which she sent to China on June 29, 1903, under the pretext of making experiment of the carrying capacity of the Siberian Railway, continually dispatched troops to the Far East, until there were already, at the beginning of February of this year, more than 40,000 soldiers. Russia was further preparing to send, in case of necessity, over 200,000 more soldiers.

"Simultaneously, Russia hastened her work through day and night in building new forts at the naval harbors of Port Arthur and Vladivostok; repaired fortifications at Kun-chun, Liao-yang, and other strategic points; sent to the Far East by the volunteer fleet and the Siberian Railway large quantities of arms and ammunition; and, so early as the middle of October, 1903, fourteen trains carrying field-hospital equipment left Russia in great haste. From these data, one may conclude that Russia had not the least desire for conciliation, but sought to coerce Japan by force of arms.

"The military activity of Russia was further accelerated from the end of January. On the 21st of January, about two battalions of the infantry and some of the artillery were sent from Port Arthur and Talien to the northern frontier of Korea; on the 28th, Viceroy Alexieff ordered the Russian troops near the Yalu to be placed on a war footing; on February 1, the Governor of Vladivostok asked the Japanese Commercial Agent at the port to prepare to withdraw to Habarofsk the Japanese subjects residing there, as the Governor was, under instructions from his Government, ready at any time to pro-

claim martial law; all the capable warships at Port
Arthur, except one battleship under repair, steamed out
to sea; and army forces were continually leaving Liao-
yang toward the Yalu. Who can say that Russia had
neither desire nor preparation for war? Under these
critical circumstances, rendering another day's delay inadmissible, Japan was compelled to break off the useless
negotiations and take necessary measures of self-protec-
tion. The responsibility of provoking war does not rest
upon Japan, but, on the contrary, entirely upon Russia.

"Moreover, Japan notified Russia, on February 6,
that she would terminate her negotiations with Russia,
and take such independent action as she deemed best in
order to defend her position menaced by Russia and protect her interests, as well as that the diplomatic relations
with Russia were severed and the Japanese Legation
would withdraw from St. Petersburg. An independent
action implies all, including, as a matter of course, the
opening of hostile acts. Even if Russia were unable to
understand it, Japan had no reason to hold herself responsible for the misunderstandings of Russia. The
students of the international law all agree that a declaration of war is not a necessary condition for beginning
hostilities, and it has been customary in modern warfare
for the declaration to follow the opening of the war. The
action of Japan had, therefore, no ground for censure in
international law. It is singular that the censure should
come, as it did, from Russia, for historical instances are
not few in which she opened hostile acts without declaring
war. In 1808, she moved troops to Finland even before
diplomatic relations were severed." [1]

.    .    .    .    .    .    .    .    .    .    .

[1] Translated from the statement published in the Japanese
press on March 3, 1904.
Professor Sakuye Takahashi enumerated in the *Kokumin*

By far the most important document containing Russian charges against Japan was the following circular addressed by Count Lamsdorff, on February 11, to the Russian Representatives abroad : —

"Since the rupture of the negotiations between Russia and Japan, the attitude of the Tokio Cabinet has constituted an open violation of all customary laws governing the mutual relations of civilized nations.

"Without specifying each particular violation of these laws on the part of Japan, the Imperial Government considers it necessary to draw the most serious attention of the Powers to the acts of violence committed by the Japanese Government with respect to Korea.

"The independence and integrity of Korea, as a fully independent Empire, have been fully recognized by all the Powers, and the inviolability of this fundamental principle was confirmed by Article 1 of the Shimonoseki treaty, and by the agreement especially concluded for this purpose between Japan and Great Britain on January 30, 1902, as well as by the Franco-Russian declaration of March 16, 1902.

"The Emperor of Korea, foreseeing the danger of a possible conflict between Russia and Japan, addressed, early in January, 1904, a note to all the Powers, declaring his determination to preserve the strictest neutrality. This declaration was received with satisfaction by the Powers, and it was ratified by Russia. According to the Russian Minister to Korea, the British Government,

(February 27–29, 1904) some of the modern European wars in which declarations of war did not precede the opening of hostilities. He mentioned twelve such cases between 1715 and 1863, besides ten cases between 1700 and 1853 in which Russia was on the offensive. For these latter instances, he refers to Colonel J. P. Maurice's *Hostilities without Declaration of War*, pp. 12, 16, 22, 34, 38, 49, 50, 55, 64.

which had signed the above-mentioned treaty with Japan on January 30, 1902, charged the British diplomatic Representative at Seul to present an official note to the Emperor of Korea, thanking him for his declaration of neutrality.[1]                                              '

"In disregard of all these facts, in spite of all treaties, in spite of its obligations, and in violation of the fundamental rules of international law, it has been proved by exact and fully confirmed facts that the Japanese Government,

"1. Before the opening of hostilities against Russia, landed its troops in the independent Empire of Korea, which had declared its neutrality.

"2. With a division of its fleet made a sudden attack on February 8 — that is, three days prior to the declaration of war — on two Russian warships in the neutral port of Chemulpo. The commanders of these ships had not been notified of the severance of diplomatic relations, as the Japanese maliciously stopped the delivery of Russian telegrams by the Danish cable and destroyed the telegraphic communication of the Korean Government. The details of this dastardly attack are contained and published in an official telegram from the Russian Minister at Seul.

"3. In spite of the international laws above mentioned, and shortly before the opening of hostilities, the Japanese captured as prizes of war certain Russian merchant ships in the neutral ports of Korea.

"4. Japan declared to the Emperor of Korea, through the Japanese Minister at Seul, that Korea would henceforth be under Japanese administration, and she warned the Emperor that in case of his non-compliance, Japanese troops would occupy the palace.

"5. Through the French Minister at Seul she sum-

[1] See p. 322, above.

moned the Russian Representative at the Korean Court to leave the country, with the staffs of the Russian Legation and Consulate.

"Recognizing that all of the above facts constitute a flagrant breach of international law, the Imperial Government considers it to be its duty to lodge a protest with all the Powers against this procedure of the Japanese Government, and it is firmly convinced that all the Powers, valuing the principles which guarantee their relations, will agree with the Russian attitude.

"At the same time, the Imperial Government considers it necessary to issue a timely warning that, owing to Japan's illegal assumption of power in Korea, the Government declares all orders and declarations which may be issued on the part of the Korean Government to be invalid.

"I beg you to communicate this document to the Government to which you are accredited.

"LAMSDORFF." [1]

In reply to the above, the Japanese Government issued, on March 9, the following statement: —

"The Russian Government are understood to have recently addressed a note to the Powers, in which the Japanese Government are charged with having committed certain acts in Korea which are considered by Russia to be in violation of international law, and in which Russia further declares all future orders and declarations of the Korean Government to be invalid.

"The Imperial Government do not find it necessary in the present instance to concern themselves in any way with views, opinions, or declarations of the Russian Government, but they believe it to be their right and duty

[1] The London *Times*, February 24, 1904, p. 7, and other papers.

to correct misstatements of facts which, if permitted to remain uncontradicted, might give rise in the opinion of neutral Powers to incorrect inferences and conclusions.

"Accordingly, the Imperial Government desire to make the following statement respecting the five acts which are declared, in the Russian note above referred to, to be fully proved and confirmed facts: —

"1. The Imperial Government admit that a number of Japanese troops landed in Korea before the formal declaration of war was issued by Japan, but they must say that such landing did not take place before a state of war actually existed between Japan and Russia. The maintenance of the independence and territorial integrity of Korea is one of the objects of war, and, therefore, the dispatch of troops to the menaced territory was a matter of right and necessity, which, moreover, had the distinct consent of the Korean Government. The Imperial Government, therefore, drew a sharp distinction between the landing of the Japanese troops in Korea in the actual circumstances of the case and the sending of large bodies of Russian troops to Manchuria without the consent of China while peaceful negotiations were still in progress.

"2. The Imperial Government declare that the Russian allegation that they stopped the delivery of Russian telegrams by the Danish cable and destroyed the Korean Government's telegraphic communication is wholly untrue. No such acts were done by the Imperial Government.

"Regarding the alleged sudden attack, on February 8 last, upon two Russian men-of-war in the port of Chemulpo, it is only necessary to say that a state of war then existed, and that, Korea having consented to the landing of Japanese troops at Chemulpo, that harbor had already ceased to be a neutral port, at least as between the belligerents.

"3. The Imperial Government have established a Prize Court, with full authority to pronounce finally on the question of the legality of seizures of merchant vessels. Accordingly, they deem it manifestly out of place to make any statement on their part regarding the Russian assertion that they unlawfully captured as prizes of war the Russian merchantmen which were in the ports of Korea.

"4. The Russian Government allege that the Japanese Government declared to the Emperor of Korea through their Minister at Seul that Korea would henceforth be under Japanese administration, and warned the Emperor that, in case of non-compliance, Japanese troops would occupy the palace. The Imperial Government declare this charge to be absolutely and wholly without foundation.

"5. No demand, either direct or indirect, was addressed by the Japanese Government to the Russian Minister at Seul to retire from Korea. The fact is as follows : —

"On February 10 last, the French *Chargé d'Affaires* at Seul called on the Japanese Minister there and informed him, as it was confirmed afterwards in writing, that it was the desire of the Russian Minister to leave Korea, and asked the opinion of the Japanese Minister on the subject. The Japanese Minister replied that, if the Russian Minister would withdraw in a peaceful manner, taking with him his staff and the Legation guard, he would be fully protected by Japanese troops. So he withdrew of his own free will on the 12th of the same month, and an escort of Japanese soldiers was furnished for him as far as Chemulpo.[1]

---

[1] The diplomatic correspondence in connection with this affair has been published, in the *Kwampō*, February 15, 1904,

"The Russian allegation that the Japanese Government forwarded a summons through the French Representative in Korea to the Russian Minister to leave Korea is, therefore, not true. In this connection it may be remarked that the Russian Consul at Fusan remained at his post as late as until February 28 last. It is reported that he was compelled to stay so long owing to the absence of instructions which the Russian Minister apparently did not think of giving to the Consul before his own departure from Seul. When it was known that necessary instructions had at last reached the Russian Consul, and that he desired to leave Fusan as soon as possible, the Japanese Consul at the same port offered him every facility for the departure, and his passage to Shanghai *via* Japan was arranged by the Japanese Consul." [1]

In reply to the above, the Russian Government issued another statement justifying its position, the purport of which may be gathered from the following press dispatch: —

"St. Petersburg, March 12 — 2: 50 p. m. The following reply, inspired by the Foreign Office, to Japan's rejoinder to the Russian protest against the violation of Korean neutrality may be accepted as official: —

"Japan's argument that she was justified in landing troops in Korea before the declaration of war because she had Korea's permission, and also that these troops arrived in Korea after 'the existence of a state of war,' is without value, as Korea in January promulgated her neutrality to the Powers, which received it warmly, Great Britain even

pp. 275–276, which supports the literal truth of the statement contained in this paragraph.

[1] The *Kokumin* (March 9). The above has been taken from an authoritative English translation, which was published in the London *Times* (March 9), p. 5.

officially conveying expressions of gratitude to the Korean Government. Therefore, no state of war gave the Japanese the right to violate her neutrality by landing troops in her territory. Even the consent of Korea, though extorted by the Japanese, is without force, from the fact that the dispatch of troops was not only before the war, but before the breaking off of diplomatic relations, as clearly established and indeed acknowledged by the Japanese themselves.

"Japan's contention in defense of the attack on the Russian ships at Chemulpo, that the port was not neutral on February 9, is false, again because Korea had proclaimed her neutrality.

"Japan's denial of malicious interference with the transmission of Russian telegrams over the Danish cable cannot be sustained. A telegram to Baron Rosen (then Russian Minister to Japan), at Tokio, sent from St. Petersburg February 4, was not delivered till the morning of February 7. That delay did not occur on the Siberian line, as was shown by the fact that a reply to a telegram from Viceroy Alexieff sent at the same time was received the same day. Therefore, it is conclusive that the Rosen telegram was held by the Japanese and not delivered for two days.

"Communication with M. Pavloff (then Russian Minister to Korea) by the Korean telegraph ceased in the middle of January. As the Koreans were enjoying friendly relations with Russia, there is good ground for believing that the interruption was due to the Japanese. Thereafter M. Pavloff used a mail steamer or a special warship to communicate with Port Arthur. The Minister of Russia at Seul February 8, therefore, knew nothing of the diplomatic rupture.

"Japan pleads that the charge against her seizure of Russian merchantmen before the declaration of war cannot lie after the establishment of prize courts. Their seizure before the declaration of war being piracy is not defensible by the establishment of prize courts, which cannot exist before a declaration of war. The steamer ' Russia' was seized in the waters of Southern Korea even before M. Kurino had presented his note here.

"The reply concludes: 'Our information regarding Japan's announcement that in future Korea would be under her administration came from M. Pavloff and also from the Representative of a friendly Power at Seul. Japan's denial, consequently, is fruitless, as also is the attempt to refute our statement that the Russian Minister and Consul at Seul were told to leave. We had conclusive proof in St. Petersburg on February 10 that the French Minister at Seul had officially notified our Representatives that the Japanese Government had intimated that they should leave, and that the Japanese had occupied territory in Korea. M. Pavloff was unable to notify our Consul at Fusan, his telegram being refused at the telegraph office.' "

# CHAPTER XX

CHINESE NEUTRALITY AND KOREAN INTEGRITY

No sooner had the war broken out than the Japanese Government notified other Powers, on February 9, that it had advised the Chinese Government to observe a strict neutrality during hostilities. Below is a translation of the identical note addressed on that day by the Minister of Foreign Affairs to the Japanese Representatives at London, Washington, Paris, Vienna, and Rome : —

"The Imperial Government have carefully considered the question as to what attitude China should assume to the best advantage, in case Japan and Russia should go to war. The conflict between Japan and Russia would affect the interests of China at least to the same extent that it would those of Japan, and the Imperial Government also fully recognize the advantage of utilizing for their aims the resources of China, so immense in population and material. But, on the other hand, they cannot overlook what effects would ensue should China assume a hostile attitude [in favor of Japan]. Such an attitude would probably plunge the finances of China into a still greater confusion [than at present], and, if it did not incapacitate her, it would render it difficult for her to meet her obligations. Her foreign trade would also suffer unfortunate results. There, however, exists an even greater apprehension, namely, that it is not unlikely that thereby an anti-foreign feeling might again be aroused in China, and the Powers of the world might be obliged to encounter troubles similar to those of 1900. For these reasons, the Imperial Government have advised the Chinese Government that, in case Japan and Russia should go to war, they should observe neutrality, and should take all possible measures to maintain order and peace within their Empire.

"You are instructed to address a signed communication to this effect to the Minister of Foreign Affairs of the Government to which you are accredited, and also assure him that, if China maintains her neutrality, and so long as Russia respects it, the Imperial Government will likewise respect it." [1]

Three days after this note was issued, the United States Minister at Tokio, Mr. Griscom, delivered the circular note of Secretary Hay urging on the belligerent Powers the advisability of respecting the neutrality and maintaining the administrative entity of China, and of limiting the zone of hostilities in the Chinese territory. The note, arriving as it did, after the Japanese attitude had been clearly defined, Baron Komura at once replied, on the 13th, that the Japanese Government were in perfect accord with the United States Government in the desires expressed by the latter, and would, so long as Russia made the same pledge and faithfully observed it, promise to respect the neutrality and the administrative entity of the Chinese Empire beyond regions actually in Russian occupation. The result of the correspondence between the United States and other

[1] The *Kwampō*, February 19 (1904), p. 387.

Powers regarding Mr. Hay's circular further confirmed the views expressed in Japan's reply, for the
neutral rights of China could hardly be enforced
in Manchuria, or, in other words, the zone of war
would be best limited to that territory. These points
were agreed to by the Powers, including Germany,
whose Emperor had appealed[1] to the Government
of Washington to take the initiative in this general
agreement.

The Japanese note of February 9 and the general agreement of the Powers secured by the United
States thus confirmed each other, the former establishing the principle of neutrality and the latter
defining the geographical limit of its application.
The latter point, however, involved a debatable
problem, the solution of which was left to China
herself. It will be remembered that Japan, in her
reply of February 13 to the United States, mentioned, as the field for hostile action, not all Manchuria, but only the territory actually occupied by
Russian forces. This territory naturally excluded
that portion of Manchuria lying west of the Liao
River which Russian troops evacuated before October 8, 1902. The Chinese Government, in declaring
the neutrality of the Empire on the 13th, practically confirmed the construction of the Japanese
Foreign Office, for, in her declaration, China announced her intention, which has since been carried
out by Viceroy Yuan and General Ma, of dispatch-

---

[1] Ex-Secretary of War Elihu Root's speech at the Republican
Convention at Chicago, June 21, 1904.

ing forces to the west of the Liao River from which
the Russian forces had withdrawn, in order to defend it against the incursion of troops of either
belligerent.[1]

All the essential points regarding China's neutrality having been settled to the satisfaction of
Japan, the Government of the latter was in a position to reply in the following manner, on February 17, to the Chinese declaration of the 13th : —

"It being the desire of the Imperial Government to
prevent disturbance of peaceful conditions within the
Chinese Empire, they will, in all the Chinese dominion
outside the territory under Russian occupation, and so
long as Russia acts likewise, respect the neutrality of the
Empire. . . . Japan's hostilities against Russia having
been actuated, not by a desire for conquest, but solely
by the necessity of defending her just rights and interests,
the Imperial Government have not the slightest intention
of acquiring territory, as a result of the war, at the expense of China. It is also desired that the Chinese Government will clearly understand that the [warlike] measures to be taken [by Japan] in the field of action within
the Chinese territory, arising, as they will, purely from
military necessities, will not be of a nature to infringe
the sovereign rights of the Chinese Empire. . . ." [2]

.    .    .    .    .    .    .    .    .    .    .

Ten days after Japan disavowed aggressive intentions in Manchuria, on February 27, was published
the new Korean-Japanese Protocol,[3] concluded on

[1] The *Kwampō*, February 19 (1904), pp. 387–388.
[2] *Ibid.*, p. 388.
[3] *Ibid.*, February 27 (1904), pp. 586–587.

the 23d, whereby Japan pledged herself to guarantee for all time the independence and the territorial integrity of the Korean Empire. The text of this remarkable document, in its English translation, is as follows: —

" Gonsuke Hayashi, Envoy Extraordinary and Minister Plenipotentiary of His Majesty the Emperor of Japan, and Major General Yi Chi-yong, Minister of State for Foreign Affairs *ad interim* of His Majesty the Emperor of Korea, being, respectively, duly empowered for the purpose, have agreed upon the following Articles: —

" ARTICLE 1. For the purpose of maintaining a permanent and unalterable friendship between Japan and Korea, and of firmly establishing peace in the East, the Imperial Government of Korea shall place full confidence in the Imperial Government of Japan and adopt the advice of the latter regarding improvements in administration.

" ARTICLE 2. The Imperial Government of Japan shall, in a spirit of firm friendship, insure the safety and repose of the Imperial House of Korea.

" ARTICLE 3. The Imperial Government of Japan firmly guarantee the independence and the territorial integrity of the Korean Empire.

" ARTICLE 4. In case the welfare of the Imperial House of Korea, or the territorial integrity of Korea, is endangered by the aggression of a third Power, or internal disturbances, the Imperial Government of Japan shall immediately take such necessary measures as circumstances require, and in such case the Imperial Government of Korea shall give full facilities to promote the action of the Imperial Japanese Government.

" The Imperial Government of Japan may, for the attainment of the above-mentioned object, occupy, when circumstances require it, such places as may be necessary from the strategic point of view.

"ARTICLE 5. The Government of the two countries shall not, in the future, without mutual consent, conclude with a third Power such an arrangement as may be contrary to the principles of the present Protocol.

"ARTICLE 6. Details in connection with the present Protocol shall be arranged as the circumstances may require between the Representative of Japan and the Minister of State for Foreign Affairs of Korea."

It is impossible to imagine in the history of the Russo-Japanese conflict a more striking indication of the new situation it has opened than this Protocol of February 23, 1904. It is at once a culmination of past events and a background for future activities. It sums up the failures of the past experience and calls forth innumerable new problems and difficulties. It will be seen, in the first place, that the agreement is limited by no fixed term ; it exists for all time. Then the fundamental problem of the Japanese-Korean relations is revealed here in this Protocol in a clear outline, and is solved in the most logical manner. The problem may be stated thus : Japan's interest and conviction demand that Korea should be independent, prosperous, and powerful ; but Korea neither could nor would be so. One remembers how Japan had struggled to solve this problem, ever since she overthrew the feudal régime of her own Government in 1868 and entered upon a new career as a nation. At first, in 1876, she declared Korea independent, and opened a few of her ports to the world's trade. Korea did not desire and China could not tolerate the independence. The result was the war of 1894–5, which succeeded in forcing the independence of Korea. The latter, however, proved neither more desirous nor more capable of an independent career than she was under Chinese sovereignty, while at the time China's position was merely replaced by that of a more active Power, Russia. Japan seemed, after her costly war, which, it is not too much to say, alone had earned the sovereign rights of Korea, to acquiesce in the altered situation to such an extent as to admit Russia into a partnership with herself in the non-intervention in Korea.[1] Bitter was Japan's experience in this artificial arrangement. Korea would not strive for a freer life any more than Russia would abstain from incessant interference.[2] Thus the conviction was every year more forcibly and painfully impressed upon Japan's mind that the threatening situation in the East arose from the two fundamental defects of the existing arrangement: first, Korea's independence would be illusory so long as her administrative system remained, as it did, corrupt to the core, but no reform would result from a system of non-interference; second, no joint reform in Korea would be possible so long as one of the contracting parties to the agreements of 1896 and 1898 found in Korea's decay the source of its

[1] See the three Russo-Japanese agreements regarding Korea, concluded in 1896 and 1898, pp. 263 ff., above.
[2] Chapter XVII.

influence over her. In short, in order to guard the common interests of Japan and Korea, the former would be constrained to reform the latter even against her will; and, again, in order to effect a thoroughgoing reform, Japan would be obliged to part ways with Russia in Korea. One half of the Russo-Japanese negotiations in 1903–4 hinged on Japan's desire for a free hand in Korea in the interest of reform. The negotiations having failed, and Russia having withdrawn from Korea, Japan suddenly found herself alone with the latter, and hastened to conclude with her an agreement which seemed to embody the only possible logical solution of the great historic problem of the Japanese-Korean relations.

Let us look this solution more squarely in the face. Japan's ardent desire for the independence and strength of Korea, as a means of insuring the mutual benefit of the two Powers and of establishing a lasting peace in the East, would seem to constitute the guiding principle of the entire document. The historic inability of Korea to be independent and strong is met in three different methods, each one of which will not fail to bring about far-reaching consequences. In the first place, the political influence of a third Power is absolutely excluded (Article 5), for the latter's interest might lie in the direction of the dependence and weakness of Korea. In the second place, Japan alone guarantees, for all time, the security and repose of the reigning house of Korea and the independence and territorial integrity of the Empire (Articles 2 and 3). For the practical execution of this principle, Japan further pledges herself to defend Korea from dangers, and Korea in return allows to Japan necessary strategic facilities (Article 4). Finally, and immediately the most important of all, Japan undertakes to institute reforms in Korea, for which she shall be invested with the full confidence of Korea (Article 1). These three important methods, it is needless to repeat, are subservient to the central principle : the independence and integrity of Korea. This large issue must always prevail over minor incidents.

Coming still nearer to the practical side of the Protocol, it is not difficult to see that, of the three methods already explained, one stands out as the most important and most difficult, — the reform. No greater burden and no more delicate work for a nation can be imagined than that of regenerating another whose nobility has grown powerful under corruption, and whose lower classes do not desire a higher existence. On the other hand, the inertia and resistance of Korea would be tremendous, in which her "full confidence" would give place to hatred and rancor. The proverbial machinations of the peninsular politicians would be set in motion in all their speed and confusion. It would not be surprising if, under the circumstances, even a military control of Korea of a temporary and mild nature should become necessary in order to cure her malady and set her house in order. On the other hand, when the necessary reform should be so deep and

wide as is required in the present instance, the
temptation of the reformer would be great, and the
suspicion of the reformed even greater, where political reformatory enterprises border upon the economic.[1] Here and everywhere, Japan would save
herself from the gravest of errors, in spite of her
best intention in the large issue, only by the severest
self-control and consummate tact. Great is the penalty of Japan that arises from her peculiar position.
She has never encountered in her long history a
greater trial of her moral force as a nation than in
the new situation opened by the Protocol. As to
the world at large, it will look forward to an in-
tensely interesting experiment of human history.

[1] See the virulent opposition of certain reactionaries of Korea
against the railroad, shipping, and other economic enterprises of
the Japanese in the peninsula, as expressed in a circular letter
issued by them in June, 1904, and published in the *Dōbun-kwai*,
No. 56 (July, 1904), pp. 57–62. Here, as everywhere, the student should carefully observe the nature of the opposition, its
agents, and their motives. Cf. the latest issues of the *Korea
Review*, edited by Mr. H. B. Hulbert, Seul.

# INDEX

# INDEX

Agriculture of Japan, 2; production, 3–4; in finance, 4–5; arable land, 5–6 and notes; improvements, 6; domestic animals, 6 n. 4; wages and profits, 6–7; subsidiary occupation, 7; owners and tenants, 7 and n. 2.

Agriculture of Korea, 26–28; forestry, 28; waste land, 27–28 n. 1.

Alexieff, Admiral, and Tsêng-chi, 166–172; at conference at Port Arthur, 301, 312–313; made Viceroy of the Far East, 301; position in the negotiations, 307, 312–313; 323, 332, 339 n. 3, n. 4.

Alexieff, Kir, 269, 278.

American, trade at Niu-chwang, 16 n. 3, 17, 165; kerosene, 40; cotton goods in Manchuria, 41; trade in Manchuria under Chinese and Russian rule, 41–42; Chinese treaty, 317, 335. (Also see the *United States.*)

Amur, the, 144, 145.

Anglo-German Agreement, 157 ff.; leading to the Anglo-Japanese Agreement, 199; differs from the latter, 207–208. (Also see *England* and *Germany.*)

Anglo-Japanese Agreement, 202–208, 315 n. 1, 355; events leading up to, 197–202; includes Manchuria, 207; compared with the Anglo-German Agreement, 207–208. (Also see *England* and *Japan.*)

Antung, 155; in Russian occupation, 239; strengthened, 292, 319; as a timber port, 290; as an open port, 255, 317, 318, 335.

Artillery, of Chinese police in Manchuria, 175, 192.

Austria, 159.

Balance of power in China, 108, 127 and n. 1, 159, 208.

Bank-notes in Korea, 23, 281.

Barley in Japan, 4.

Beans, 4, 9, 13–14, 18.

Benckendorff, 313, 314, 334 n. 3.

Bezobrazoff, 291 n. 3, 313.

Blagovestchensk, 144, 155, 316.

Boxer trouble, the, 139; cost for Russia, 33. (Also see *China, Manchuria.*)

Brown, McLeavy, 269, 278.

Bülow, von, on Kiao-chau, 102, 106; on the Anglo-German Agreement, 161; on the Anglo-Japanese alliance, 199 n. 1. (Also see *Germany.*)

Cable at Chemulpo, 356, 358, 361.

Cannon, in Chinese police in Manchuria, 175, 192.

Cassini, Count, on the development of Manchuria, 43–44; at Peking, 87, 94; the "Cassini Convention," 87–95, 98, 224–225; on Russian soldiers in Manchuria, 237 n. 1; on Lessar's demands, 248 ff.; on new ports, 253; on the contents of the last Russian reply to Japan, 340 n.; on the responsibility of the war, 351 n. 1.

Cazalis, 279.

Chang Chi-tung, 176, 177, 178, 189, 191.

Chemulpo, trade at, 15, 19–20; Seul Railway, 24 and n. 1; kerosene at, 40 and n. 3; Admiral Starck at, 293; cable at, 356, 358, 361; naval war at, 345, 356, 358, 361.

Chili, Province of, 179, 218, 243.

China, merchants of, in Korea, 14 n. 2, 15; ceding Primorsk to Russia, 66; suzerain over Korea, 257; war with Japan, 257, 369; loan guaranteed by Russia, 83–84; alliance with Russia, 85, 93, 94 n. 2; envoy at the Czar's coronation,